The Environmental Advantages of Cities

Urban and Industrial Environments

Series editor: Robert Gottlieb, Henry R. Luce Professor of Urban and Environmental Policy, Occidental College

The Environmental Advantages of Cities

Countering Commonsense Antiurbanism

William B. Meyer

The MIT Press
Cambridge, Massachusetts
London, England

MIT Press books may be purchased at special quantity discounts for business or sales promotional use. For information, please email special_sales@mitpress.mit.edu or write to Special Sales Department, The MIT Press, 55 Hayward Street, Cambridge, MA 02142.

This book was set in Sabon by Toppan Best-set Premedia Limited, Hong Kong. Printed on recycled paper and bound in the United States of America.

Library of Congress Cataloging-in-Publication Data

Meyer, William B.
The environmental advantages of cities : countering commonsense antiurbanism / William B. Meyer.
    p. cm.—(Urban and industrial environments)
Includes bibliographical references and index.
ISBN 978-0-262-01904-0 (hbk. : alk. paper)—ISBN 978-0-262-51846-8 (pbk. : alk. paper)
1. Urban ecology (Sociology) 2. Urbanization—Environmental aspects. 3. Sustainable urban development. 4. Climatic changes—Social aspects. I. Title.
HT241.M49   2013
307.76—dc23
2012037155

10 9 8 7 6 5 4 3 2 1

Contents

Preface

Although this book deals with the relationship between urbanization and the environment, it concentrates on how to think about that relationship through object lessons in how *not* to think about it. It documents and analyzes actual experiences as far as is necessary to assess what many people have thought and written on the subject and more narrowly to identify mistakes they have made in thinking and writing about it. The beliefs that the book critically examines have several points in common. Individually, and still more in combination, they paint a gloomy picture of the environmental significance of cities and of the implications of continued urbanization. These beliefs are widely held not only by the general public but also by many scholars of the topic. They sound quite plausible, even convincing, on a first hearing. And they all fail to stand up to close logical or empirical scrutiny; though disparate in their subject matter, they display many of the same recurrent underlying errors. I call them, collectively, *commonsense environmental antiurbanism,* by which I mean claims that urbanization or urbanism is undesirable because of its necessarily deleterious consequences in the realm of human-environment relations.

Why not write about cities and the environment directly instead of in a secondhand way through what some people have said about their relationship? Because the smaller task is a manageable one, within the powers of a single author. It can do much to clear the ground for a full assessment. It can also justify one by dispelling many of the errors that make the harmfulness of cities seem too obvious to require further study and may save it from repeating errors that have frequently been made in the past.

I challenge various reasons for assuming that urbanization's effects are necessarily bad, which is by no means the same as saying that all of its effects are necessarily good. Not all claims about the environmental disadvantages of cities are erroneous. We will encounter some examples of ones that are not. Why then center a book on those that are and not at the same time dissect errors in the opposite direction? Because errors about cities as environmental threats make up a large and influential share of what people think and say on the subject and errors about cities as environmental saviors or utopias do not.

This book began to take shape in late fall 2004. I had been teaching for a year and a half in the Department of Geography at Colgate University and I was assigned a course on urban environmental issues to teach in the spring semester. I had extensive research experience in environmental issues generally, and particularly in their human dimensions, but had never thought particularly about the role of cities. In preparing the course, I supposed (and subsequent events bore me out) that the students would arrive thinking cities and environmental quality to be fundamentally at odds with each other, that the rationale for the course they had enrolled in would seem to them to lie precisely in the greater magnitude and severity of the damage that cities do. Providing a few counterexamples at the outset, I thought, a few unexpected instances of urbanization as a force for environmental good, might give the course an interest it would otherwise lack. So I looked for some and was surprised myself at how many I was able to find. Many of the most common reasons for the usual antiurban view, it seemed to me, failed to stand up to a searching examination. I thought such an examination worth conducting in a more systematic way, and this book, exploring the often-ignored environmental advantages of cities, is the result.

I have illustrated the errors that I discuss with quotations and citations from the current literature, both scientific and popular, on human-environment relations. I could hardly do otherwise. To show that a mistake has been made, one must identify some people who have made it. Identifying them cannot help looking like finger-pointing but I assert and believe nothing worse of the authors I cite to this effect (and readers of endnotes will see that I appear among them) than that they have briefly stepped into pitfalls that are highly camouflaged and highly seductive. It would be a waste of trouble to refute errors that are made only by the careless or ignorant. I thought that this book was worth writing because I found examples of the errors that it discusses even in the work of particularly intelligent, insightful, and authoritative writers. Errors that are insidious enough to confuse people of this caliber deserve careful refutation. If the errors are mine, I invite correction in turn. Having said all that, I trust that no author I could have cited for criticism, and did not, will feel offended! The literature is vast and examples are many and the space I have for references is small. Of course I also cite many authors who, it seems to me, have gotten important things right, and I am much indebted to their work.

Almost all of the citations are drawn from the English-language literature, which is a significant limitation. Yet it is the principal medium for the present-day discussion of the human dimensions of environmental change, and, because of the antiurban attitudes long prevalent in English culture (see chapter 8 for further discussion), it is one that is especially prone to exaggeration of the environmental harm wrought by cities.

I would like to thank Colgate University for making this book possible by providing me with employment, office space, and research facilities, as well as funding for a research assistant during the 2010–2011 academic year (Santiago Reyes Contreras, coauthor of the appendix). Much of the material in chapter 5 was presented for discussion at a Colgate Social Sciences Division Seminar in November 2011. I have also benefited from comments and suggestions on some of the ideas and readings that went into this book by my students, notably Shannon Sweeney, Jamie Simchik, and the members of my spring 2012 class in urban geography. I am also grateful to my editors at the MIT Press, Clay Morgan and Robert Gottlieb, for valuable advice and support, and to three anonymous reviewers of the book manuscript for much helpful and constructive criticism. None, of course, is responsible for any errors that remain.

1

Introduction

It has recently become commonplace, almost a cliché, to note that human-kind crossed a notable threshold sometime around the year 2008. For the first time in history (according to United Nations statistics), the number of people said to live in cities exceeded the number classified as living in rural areas. As recently as the dawn of the twentieth century, cities housed only about 15 percent of the world's population, itself a substantial increase since a century before.[1] Predictions are as risky here as in any other area of human behavior.[2] Still, there are few reasons to suppose that the urban share will not increase further in years to come, and many reasons to expect that it will. So drastic a change in human society as the shift from a minority- to a majority-urban world is certain to have profound consequences in many realms and not least in society's relations with its biophysical surroundings. Scientists, policy makers, activists, and private citizens who wish to make responsible choices about where to live and work all need to be able to think as accurately as possible about the environmental significance of cities and urbanization.

Unfortunately, cities are not easy things to think about, particularly in their relations to the environment. Even taken by itself, each of the two topics—cities and the environment—is so complex and cuts across so many of the usual boundaries that define fields of knowledge that few people can have the background and the leisure to master it. This is particularly so when *environment* is understood in the full force of the term, as referring to the set of biophysical phenomena and processes (whether "natural" or human altered) by which we are environed and within which we function. Human-environment relations are the whole array of meaningful interactions we have with these surroundings, inter-actions that include but are by no means limited to those usually connoted by the familiar set of "environmental" concerns, ones mainly of adverse human impact: ecological disruption, resource depletion, and pollution.

Of course, these last make up a major part of human-environment relations, but only a part. Others include the effects on people of environmental hazards, whether those of earth processes such as weather, climate, and tectonics, of the "second nature" that technology has fashioned around us, or of the other species (especially pathogens responsible for infectious disease) with which we share the earth's surface; they also include the greater or lesser suitability to our needs of the surroundings, however "natural" or reshaped, within which we live and work.

When the two topics, environment (in this broad sense) and cities come together, and the question becomes one of their relations to each other, the complexity becomes daunting. But when detailed knowledge is lacking, what describes itself as common sense is always ready and willing to step in and fill the gap, representing what is complex as reassuringly simple. When allowed to do so, commonsense thinking tends to portray urbanization and environmental quality as being deeply antithetical for reasons that cover all of the seven major realms into which the latter can be classified. Widely held and seemingly commonsensical beliefs on each score add up to an indictment of cities as necessarily making things worse in each of these areas, as being:

- Intensive hotspots of ecological disruption
- Ravenous consumers of natural resources
- Severely polluted and polluting
- Particularly at risk from natural hazards
- Disproportionately beset by technological hazards
- Inherently prone to the spread of infectious diseases
- Such dysfunctional and unnatural environments that they cannot form a satisfactory setting for human life

Each assertion is widely believed because each on first thought seems quite plausible. If you close your eyes and try to summon up images of the severest ecological disruption, the most profligate use of resources, and the worst pollution, chances are that they will be urban scenes, and so too for images of the worst natural and technological disasters and infectious disease outbreaks. Conversely, if you try to picture ecological harmony, frugality in resource demands, or a clean and healthy and safe environment, you are unlikely to set it spontaneously in a city. Surely the spatial concentration of people and their activities that we call urbanization means the most radical disruption of the natural environment that occurs anywhere on the earth's surface. Surely, at the same time, it creates the most polluted environments found anywhere, concentrating the most harmful waste emissions precisely where people too are most concentrated, and surely it likewise collects the most people in close proximity to most of the other hazards of technology. City dwellers are proverbially more demanding of natural resources of all kinds than rural ones, and who could deny that cities in fact are where resources are consumed (and therefore where wastes are also emitted) in the far-greatest quantities? Who could deny, too, that crowding people together in a single place greatly enhances the magnitude of disaster when the forces of nature strike or that it greatly magnifies the chances for infectious diseases to spread? And finally, could anyone seriously deny that cities, being the most artificial of settings, must fail to meet many of the needs of the natural creatures that human beings, after all, remain?

I call the negative profile formed by these beliefs *commonsense environmental antiurbanism*. Environmental, though not environmentalist: the former denotes a subject matter, the latter a particular point of view regarding a particular portion of it. Everyone, not merely "environmentalists," has beliefs about the environment or the biophysical surroundings of human life; everyone has preferences for some environmental outcomes over others. Nor is it only or today even chiefly committed green activists who are apt to think of urbanization as leading in the wrong direction, as creating unsafe or unhealthy or unattractive settings for human life. It is more often people for whom the superficially plausible tenets of common sense take the place of more exact knowledge.

The various forms that commonsense environmental antiurbanism takes can be generalized into the formula: "It stands to reason that cities must be environmentally bad because ____." Further inquiry, it implies, is unnecessary. But is the profile really an accurate likeness and are the consequences really as inescapable as they seem? If so, of course, continued urbanization, producing such "far-reaching negative consequences for the environment"[3] will only worsen problems that are daunting already. In that case, the sooner it is brought to a halt, and even reversed, the better; the less likely it is that it can be halted, the more reason to despair of the future. Too often, however, the beliefs that make up the antiurban credo have passed into currency without the close scrutiny that they require. Much of their surface plausibility stems from some errors that exaggerate the environmental harm and hide the benefits that urbanization can bring. Weeding out these errors— separating the bad reasons for worry from any good ones that remain—

is a necessary first step toward an accurate assessment of whether cities produce more or less satisfactory environmental outcomes than other forms of settlement.

An attempt to assess so dauntingly complex a topic as city-environment relations must begin simply, even simplistically, to begin at all. This book takes as its framework the commonsense expectations that urbanization must in its various ways be environmentally harmful. The public health literature offers two useful terms for characterizing the difference that cities can make. An *urban penalty* is incurred when conditions or results produced by urbanization or recorded in an urban setting fall below those achieved otherwise or elsewhere. An *urban advantage* arises when the opposite occurs.[4] Common sense, then, appears to expect an urban penalty to be the norm in the various realms of human-environment interaction. How does this expectation fare when analyzed logically and when tested against the evidence? What countervailing environmental advantages do cities offer that the commonsense view ignores?

The first step in answering these questions must be to define some key terms. The business will be a lengthy one and may be tedious in places but it is necessary. The most important terms to define, of course, which will be omnipresent in the pages that follow, are the noun *city* and the adjective *urban*. To what, exactly, do they refer?

The question arises because the terms, though widely used, do not have standardized and consistent meanings across the many contexts in which they occur.[5] Cities are not the principal subject matter of a single field but rather partial topics of many. Political scientists study them (among other things) as units of government and arenas of conflict, economists as sites of exchange and markets for land, urban planners as a certain kind of built and institutional environment, ecologists as special kinds of faunal and floral habitat, and so on, but no full-blown discipline is responsible for studying cities as such. Cities are almost everyone's business but they end up by being no one's purview. There are no experts to whom outsiders can look for a settled terminology and uniform definitions or who can offer reliable information, explain in simple terms what cities are and how they function, or correct basic errors and misconceptions about them. It is not surprising that false or questionable beliefs abound about global urbanization that can only confuse a discussion of what it means for the environment. The development planner David Satterthwaite has identified an array of myths that he has found particularly widespread: that world urban growth is taking place principally in megacities, for example, that rural-to-urban migration in the less-developed countries (LDCs) is driven chiefly by illusions, by erroneous or irrational expectations; that urbanization in the LDCs is "explosive" and "out of control"; that rapidly growing cities are a phenomenon exclusively of the LDCs.[6]

There are, to be sure, widely held popular errors about the subject matter of almost every major academic field, in which common sense tries to substitute for knowledge of the best that has been thought and tested. Most Americans not only seem to misunderstand some of the simplest insights of economics—about, for example, the mutual benefits of international trade, the role of profit, and short- and long-term trends in human well-being—but seem not even to realize that the experts think differently. Comparable misconceptions have been documented in their beliefs about basic physics. Commonsense assumptions about the trajectories of moving bodies turn out to follow a long-discredited model prevalent in medieval times but differing in some quite fundamental ways from what is taught at the introductory high-school level.[7] Of course, given the limits of time, it would be utterly unreasonable to expect everyone, or even anyone, to possess an accurate outline of every major department of knowledge. Yet on most topics there are recognized authorities who can be called on to correct common errors when they become troublesome and whose own work and expert advice will be untainted by them—precisely what is lacking in the study of cities. Professional engineers do not operate on the basis of pre-Newtonian physics; economic advisors to most governments do not think of international trade as a zero-sum game or high tariffs as a way of protecting national prosperity. Citizens discuss and decision makers shape urban policies without similar expert counsel or criticism. Errors that are widely held because they seem simple matters of common sense can reign unchallenged. And they may arise more easily on urban topics than in some other domains because cities, as we shall see, lend themselves to a good many traps in reasoning. They also carry emotional charges that can seriously interfere with an objective understanding. In some cultural traditions, notably the English and through it the Anglo-American, they symbolize evil and corruption: "God made the country, and man made the town."[8]

In the absence of an established core discipline of urban studies, there is not even any standard terminology for the subject. Anyone trying to discuss cities and urban areas, as I am doing, must begin at the beginning and define these terms themselves. In doing so, I will stay as close as possible to what they mean in everyday usage. First and foremost, the terms *city* and *urban* denote a relatively large number of people living in a relatively small area. A high total population by itself is not enough; China and India have large populations but they are not cities and nobody would say that they are, though both contain many cities. Nor is high density alone sufficient. A 1973 study of the !Kung Bushmen, hunter-gatherers of Botswana and Namibia, found that they live at densities equivalent to about thirty persons per room, vastly above the average for any world city. Yet it has probably never occurred to anyone to call them urbanites because they also live in extremely small groups, averaging only thirty to forty in number.[9] Both a high density and a large total are necessary to be considered *urban*. Some populous areas—in rural South and East Asia, for example—seem to meet both tests, with densities higher than those found in many parts of developed-world cities. They still are not urban areas because the test of high population density is a relative and not an absolute one. "What is an urban level of density in one context," as the anthropologist Ulf Hannerz notes, "may not be so defined in a society which is more densely populated as a whole."[10] An area is urban and joins the list of recognized cities if its population size and density are high for the country within which it is located.

Densely populated rural areas might also fail to qualify as urban because they lack some additional characteristics required in ordinary usage. We tend not to refer to areas as cities unless the chief basis of their livelihood is something other than agriculture. (Or, to meet a possible objection, the criterion should be rephrased: unless the percent of their population engaged in agriculture and perhaps also the proportion of their land area devoted to it is low compared to that of the country overall.) Neither is a city a city in the fullest sense without some kind of functional unity, symbolized in a place name but expressed more significantly in a high degree of political identity and institutions of government, ranging from formal municipal structures to informal and grassroots ones. Land cover is an additional criterion: the degree to which a surface is occupied by structures and artifacts of plainly human shaping. As two geographers aptly observe: "Cities are, in essence, a transformation of the physical environment to a built environment."[11] They are other things as well but they certainly are that. Looking at a landscape, we are more likely to call it urban if a built environment seems to predominate. Here and elsewhere, the authority of popular usage is not to be discarded lightly. There would be little point in defining cities in a way that defined away most environmental problems that they might cause or most benefits that they might bring if the definition differed radically from what we mean when we use the word every day. At the same time, the traits chosen help to elaborate the vernacular concept into what it was not before, one suitable for rigorous inquiry.[12]

The characteristics of a nonagricultural base, institutional capacity, and a largely built environment can be readily traced back to those of population size and density. Agriculture is much less common in a country's cities than outside them because it demands a great deal of land and produces relatively meager economic returns per acre. Space in cities is too valuable for other and more lucrative pursuits to allow much of it to be devoted to cultivation, and what is known as *urban agriculture* usually occurs on the urban fringe. (But though agriculture will be of relatively little importance in cities, it will not necessarily be of great importance in any particular rural area.) The size and the concentration of population require and at the same time make possible the existence of institutions of government, which become larger, more elaborate, and more specialized in their capacities as the number and concentration of the people that they serve increase. The more human occupants an area has, the more intensively, all else being equal, they are likely to have altered its land cover.

When statistical agencies take on the task of defining the urban share of a country's population, a simple and quite reasonable way for them to do it systematically is to establish cut-off values for one or more of these variables, classing areas that fall on one side of the threshold as rural and those on the other side as urban. The United States Bureau of the Census bases its classifications on this procedure, emphasizing population size, density, and political incorporation. For the 2000 census, it defined urban populations as those living in an incorporated place with 2,500 or more inhabitants, and it defined urban regions, or metropolitan areas, as ones centered on an urban place with 50,000 or more residents and extending outward to the point where population densities within contiguous block groups fall below 1,000 persons per square mile. *Non-metropolitan* areas and populations lie outside of metropolitan areas; *rural* ones, an overlapping but not synonymous category, do not reach the urban threshold. A few years later, the Census Bureau added a new, intermediate category of *micropolitan* areas centered on a small urban core as metropolitan ones are centered on a large one. For the 2010 census, it replaced block groups with census tracts and dropped the use of central urban places in defining urban and metropolitan areas. Though far from perfect, the census categories do reasonably well distinguish populations living to a greater or lesser degree in conditions that correspond to the everyday meanings of urban and rural. The US Department of Agriculture has developed a series of nine continuum codes to distinguish more- from less-urban counties, covering the range from those lying in metropolitan areas of a million people or more to those outside of any metropolitan area and themselves having no urban (2,500 population or greater) places.[13] These procedures help avoid a pitfall that is particularly dangerous in the US setting, that of mistaking the core political unit for the urbanized area. In the United States, almost all incorporated political cities are what geographers call *underbounded;* that is, they fail to include the non-rural areas of politically independent suburbs on their borders. The political city of New York has a population of about eight million; the metropolitan area as the Census Bureau defines it, about twenty million. (Many cities in some other parts of the world are *overbounded,* taking in largely rural areas and populations that they should not.)[14]

These are only some of the methods used within one country; other countries have their own. The United Nations does not enforce any uniform criteria for defining what should count as an urban place or population; it merely collects the numbers submitted by member states. Each of the five population censuses China took between 1953 and 2000 used different definitions of *urban* and *rural,* not only making trends within the country from one time to the next difficult to discern but also—give the country's size—having a more than negligible effect on the supposed world totals in each category.[15] Yet a review of practices of United Nations member countries has identified as their most commonly used criteria the very ones that we have already discussed. A majority (more than two hundred) use municipal political units, population size, or population density singly or in some combination; twenty-five rely chiefly on the economic characteristic of mostly non-agricultural employment; and eighteen emphasize the presence of a built infrastructure.[16]

Obviously, then, it would be pointless to argue over the exact share of the world's population that is urban today, still more over the exact year in which that share exceeded one-half (if indeed it has done so yet). The data needed to answer either question are not rigorously comparable and the definitions that guide their collection do not precisely and unambiguously capture what *urban* means. Categorizations based on one criterion will never produce results identical to those based on another. But the confusion, mercifully, has its limits because neither are the results likely to differ radically. Each criterion, properly used, is likely to make a fair surrogate for the others and each has some distinct advantages of convenience in doing research. As government statistics are usually amassed on the basis of incorporated local political divisions of known surface area, measures stressing total population or population density are easy to calculate, and as the capacities of local government, all else being equal, are likely to increase with city size, institutional measures are likely to correlate closely with demographic ones. Methods of satellite-based remote sensing, now much more powerful than ever before, are particularly well fitted to distinguishing more urban from less urban areas on the basis of the agricultural and built-environment criteria. Though highly convenient, the procedural shortcut of using one of these measures to infer the rest is valid only if close links indeed exist among them. Recent studies suggest that they do.[17] Given how closely these factors are involved with one another, it is rarely indeed that, at a minimum, the areas and populations that a study or a national statistical bureau defines as urban on the basis of one criterion will not be more urban, in most or all of the key senses of the word, than those it treats as rural.

Yet, as the geographer John R. Weeks and colleagues argue, we would do much better to think about different degrees of a quality they call *urbanness* than to try to identify some places as *urban* and others as *rural*. In their words, "the standard distinctions of urban and rural or urban and nonurban" are inadequate if treated as either-or choices for classification. "The concept of urbanness," however, "implies that the rural/urban distinction is a continuum, rather than a dichotomy."[18] More urban and more rural are opposite directions along a series (more precisely, of several more or less parallel series, corresponding to the different indicators of urbanness). We can say that an area is more urban or rural than another, that one possesses a greater or lesser degree of urbanness than another, but not that one has the quality and the other lacks it. (And *rural* is not even an end point; wild lands or wilderness would denote an area of minimal or zero human population size and density.) And as Weeks and colleagues note, there are considerable contrasts in urbanness within areas that we are apt to think of entirely as cities; the same holds true for rural areas.

This does not require that we discard the term *city*, only that we be careful in using it. A *city* is a convenient shorthand term for an area with a relatively high degree of urbanness overall. For many purposes, it will still make sense to call some places *urban* and others *rural* and to speak of particularly urban places as cities as long as we can readily translate such terms back into statements of degree when necessary. When thought of in this way, the United Nations data, though cast in the terms of an urban-rural dichotomy, nonetheless tell us much of value about world patterns and trends.[19] On the whole, the developed countries are much the most highly urbanized. As of 2009, 78 percent of the population of the more developed counties (MDCs) was classified as urban (including 82 percent of North America and 73 percent of Europe) against 47 percent of the LDCs, and the least developed subset of the latter registered only 29 percent. The least urbanized countries are among the world's poorest: Burundi with 11 percent, Papua New Guinea with 13 percent, Malawi and Uganda with 16 percent, Nepal and Ethiopia with 17 percent. Within the less-developed world, Latin America has a relatively high level of urbanization and sub-Saharan Africa the lowest of any major world region (but also, followed by Asia, the highest rates of growth in the urban share of national population). Asia, though only 45 percent of its people live in cities, has the world's largest urban population in absolute terms. *Megacities* of over ten million inhabitants are a phenomenon of quite recent times. As late as 1950, there was only one in the world (New York City); in 2011, there were twenty-three, the majority in the LDCs. Their size and prominence notwithstanding, they house only 10 percent of the world's urban population and their share is not expected to increase much in the future. Small and medium-sized cities are and are likely to remain the more typical urban environment.

Some writers have raised the question of whether differences between urban and rural areas have now become so blurred that the distinction should be abandoned.[20] Yet areas do vary greatly according to the criteria of urbanness discussed already, which do correspond to the general understanding of what the words *urban* and *rural* denote. If the criteria are valid, differences among people and places associated with differences in their degree of urbanness remain alive and well. The distinction need not imply, nor should it ever have been used to imply, the existence of two separate, self-enclosed, and noninteracting realms to one or the other of which any individual exclusively belongs. More and less urban areas interact vigorously through many forms of economic and social integration: cash remittances to rural households from members who have migrated temporarily or permanently to cities for employment, for example. Much of the force of the objection applies to the use of the terms *urban* and *rural* as a dichotomy and disappears when urbanness is seen as a continuum. Another valid element in the critique, and it is a

large but limited one, is that many of the traditional connotations of the
two words assuredly no longer hold true—if indeed they ever did. Many
characteristics that one might still think of as typically or essentially
urban (or rural) do not always, in fact, differ greatly or consistently along
the scale. In the United States, the typical rural household, as defined by
the Census Bureau, has no direct connection with farming as a livelihood,
which, indeed, provides less than 10 percent of rural employment, though
in the less-developed countries it still accounts for something like half
of rural income.[21] A definition of rural that would make it rest chiefly
on the dominance or pervasiveness of an agricultural way of life is
untenable—though, as we have seen, within any country agriculture will
almost certainly represent a much larger share of employment in rural
than in urban areas, and for good reasons. Cultural influences once
regarded, correctly or not, as impinging chiefly on urbanites now readily
reach beyond them. Stereotypes of the radical individualism of city life
and of rural conservatism and traditionalism have little to do with reality.
Divorce and drug abuse, though stereotypically urban, are now as
common in the rural as in the metropolitan United States.[22] The idea that
city dwellers and rural folk differ fundamentally in personality and ways
of thinking had powerful advocates in some of the US social sciences in
the early and mid-twentieth century. Few would still defend it.[23] Such
traits or characteristics do not form part of the meaning of the term
urban as used in this book.

As urbanness, here defined, is a matter of degree, it also varies, as
Weeks and colleagues emphasize, within areas that for convenience we
may simply label as urban or rural. Common usage acknowledges this
fact with names for intermediate conditions between the two end points
of the scale. English-language terms for such cases include *urban-rural
fringe, periurban,* and, most commonly, *suburban (exurban* suggests
either the outermost range of suburbia or affluent development within
rural areas).[24] They are intermediate between more urban and more rural
in two ways: spatially (as areas separating the one from the other) and
substantively (as areas that generally lie in between urban and rural in
the degree to which they possess the defining characteristics of either).
A suburban or urban fringe area usually possesses an intermediate population density and also smaller and less elaborate units of government,
land cover not so dominated by built structures as a city's, but more
than a rural landscape's, and a greater land area and percentage of the
workforce devoted to agriculture than in a city but less than in the
countryside.[25]

According to our criteria, the inner, core, or central city will generally be the most urban part of a generally urban region. In some places, the urban core is occupied largely by poor and socially marginal groups. In others, much of it is the domain of the well-to-do elite. The former is the rule in the United States, which is better characterized as a suburban- than an urban-majority country. Affluence within US metropolitan areas tends strongly to increase as one moves outward from the urban core through progressively wealthier suburbs until at the exurban fringe it begins to be diluted by predominantly low-income rural populations. The pattern and several others—the political fragmentation of the urbanized area, low residential densities, and a high prevalence of owner-occupied single-family dwellings—make the US city a distinctive type by world standards. Many urban slum or squatter settlements in the developing world, however, are found where affluent US suburbia usually is, on the urban spatial periphery, and, as in western Europe, too, the urban core, the most urban area according to our five criteria, is often a zone of high wealth and status: "some of the world's most desirable (and expensive) residential areas have high densities."[26] In any particular part of the world, it may seem a matter of common sense that wealth or poverty is necessarily a correlate of a high degree of urbanness—but common sense would be wrong.

Recognizing urbanness as a matter of degree suggests, as a way of winding up this excursion into the meanings of words, a precise definition for the verb *to urbanize*. It should mean "to become more urban," as measured by the criteria of urbanness already discussed. A population undergoes urbanization when the share of it living in more than ordinarily urban conditions rises. It deurbanizes when that share falls. A person urbanizes in moving from a less to a more urban setting and deurbanizes in doing the opposite.[27] One of the pitfalls of using urban and rural as a simple dichotomy comes to light here. The share of a country's population living in areas classified as urban may be high and still growing, yet in some important ways the country may be better described as deurbanizing than as urbanizing, if many of the urban residents are relocating to surroundings with a lower degree of urbanness than they occupied in the past: lower in density, outside the central political city, and with less of the land covered by a built environment. The urban-fringe areas thus settled, it is true, become more urban than they were before but their residents and the urban-area population as a whole become less so. The post–World War II United States is arguably such a country, one in which rural-to-urban migration long ago gave way to urban core–to–urban periphery movement as the chief form of settlement change, to what might, to avoid confusion, be called *secondary deurbanization.*

Likewise, a country's degree of urbanization can be, and often is, used to refer to two different things. One is a pattern, the share of its population living in what are defined as urban areas. The other is a process, the rate of increase of that share over some specified time period. What makes for confusion is that the two values usually stand in something like an inverse relationship. The most urbanized countries in the world by the first measure are, by the second, among the least urbanizing. Statistically, this is almost inevitable. The more concentrated the population already is in cities, the smaller will be the percent increase produced by any further number of people moving to them. Conversely, the more rural a country still is, the greater its potential for very high percentage growth in its urban share. A peculiar consequence is that one can, almost at will, demonstrate urbanization to be a good or a bad thing; one can produce either a positive or a negative correlation between it and any indicator of human or environmental well-being. Such correlations, it follows, should be used only with care, and of the two meanings, the one should be chosen that would best help answer the question being asked.

Where has this detour brought us? As we pause and look around, it may seem to have carried us right back to our starting point: a strong presumption of an urban environmental penalty. Commonsense antiurbanism seems vindicated and indeed established on a firmer foundation than before. By replacing a vague term with a more precise one and defining cities chiefly as dense and sizeable concentrations of human population that profoundly transform the land cover, have we not stripped them of any chance of being shown to be environmentally benign? If that is what cities are, how can they possibly be anything but the places where harm to the environment and risk to its human inhabitants are most concentrated and most intense? These have the ring of rhetorical questions whose answers are already taken for granted. In fact, they are real questions with some real answers to which our definition of cities can point us, answers that explain just how cities indeed *can* be better than less concentrated forms of settlement on these and other counts. Many possible advantages lie hidden behind the apparently inexorable urban penalties imposed by size and density. Perhaps you have glimpsed some of them already.

But if you have not, you are in good company because many of them have been fully recognized and articulated only recently. The study of cities in the various disciplines of the social sciences most concerned with them has undergone something of a revolution in the past few decades. Much of the change can be traced to the work of a writer who was not herself an academic social scientist. Jane Jacobs remains best known to general readers for her first book, *The Death and Life of Great American Cities* (1961). It is, among other things, a vigorous challenge to the idea that high-density urban settlements must be or become sinks of social pathologies and it closes with some provocative claims about the mutual dependence rather than the mutual hostility of thriving urban areas and the successful protection of nature.[28] *The Economy of Cities* (1969) opened with the startling suggestion that "cities came first." Agriculture, Jacobs argued, far from representing a necessary precondition of urbanism, may itself have originated in an urban setting and then been farmed out, so to speak, to its hinterland to free up space for newer urban activities—just as many other later-arising tasks in the period of recorded history, including a good deal of industry in today's world, have been. Dense permanent settlements with elaborate arrays of productive activity, supported by hunting-gathering and by trade, seem indeed to have existed before agriculture did. It is in such a setting, Jacobs reasoned, not in one of scattered and isolated small groups, that so novel an activity as plant and animal cultivation is likeliest to have arisen. There it would have represented not an improbably radical break with established ways of doing things but a natural outgrowth of the existing activities of holding and handling the large and varied quantities of seeds and animals collected for the community's subsistence. In that case, cities, far from being the "parasites" on the rural world that they have often been called, at once exploitative and dependent, were themselves the creators of that world and of what has long represented its most characteristic form of livelihood.[29]

The book went on to generalize the argument by linking the potential for innovations of all sorts and the economic growth they generate to the essential traits of urban areas. It did much to inspire later work by economists and other social scientists, who have for the first time made it clear just what cities are for. Their very existence is a puzzle, though it is one that familiarity may hide. What sense does it make to cluster at high densities when there is plenty of room elsewhere? The needs of defense might have explained it in times long past but not today. Cities can be uncomfortably crowded and are expensive to live in. Why, then, do their inhabitants not decentralize into the less congested land all around? The same question applies to the economic activities that cities house. "A city is simply a collection of factors of production—capital, people, and land—and land is always far cheaper outside cities than inside," in the words of the economist Robert Lucas. "Why don't capital and people move outside, combining themselves with cheaper land and thereby increasing profits?" A twentieth-century US president once asked, "Does it really make sense . . . to have more than 70 percent of our people crammed into 1 percent of our land?"[30]

Density's very advantages provide the basis of any possible answer. The ones that Jacobs herself stressed are those that foster innovation. The profusion in close proximity of different activities, between which fruitful connections can occur, and the concentration of innovative minds make urban areas the incubators of new and better ways of doing things. Innovation, an essential driver of economic progress, has been found to occur more frequently where population density is higher, all else being equal—and cities offer advantages for putting into practice the new ideas that they themselves tend to generate. The spillover benefits of any activity are far less likely to be lost to the economy as a whole than if they occur in an isolated setting where there is no one to take them up and put them to use. The geographer Edward Soja sums up Jacobs's central insight as "the stimulus of urban agglomeration," the central benefit of what he calls *cityness*.[31]

Economists have identified additional ways in which the concentration of people and work can be more efficient and productive than dispersion.[32] Large and clustered populations make specialization and its benefits feasible to a degree impossible in a smaller and lower-volume market. Buyer and seller, being closer together, come more easily into contact than where population is more dispersed. The matching of demand to supply is likelier to be smoother, with fewer troughs of idleness. Because their size allows them to support multiple providers of the same good or service, cities enjoy the benefits of competition in lowering prices. Many collective goods—such as the networked services of electricity, water supply, sewerage, and transportation infrastructure—with their high fixed costs are feasible without massive subsidy only above an urban threshold of a concentrated population. In sum, higher costs of living and working can be more than repaid by higher returns because work in cities is more productive. The economist Edward Glaeser has gone as far as to call cities humankind's greatest invention and to suggest that where Jacobs's work most needs revision is in her aversion to the most urban settings, ones exhibiting very high population densities.[33]

The line of work that Jacobs pioneered before long began to include some discussions of what some specifically environmental benefits of cities might be. In 1975, the social psychologist Jonathan L. Freedman not only challenged the supposed deleterious effects of high residential densities on human behavior, but also capped his point with an essay "In Praise of Cities" arguing that urbanization made many social and environmental problems, notably pollution and the resource consumption that fueled it, less severe and more manageable than they would be otherwise. In 1985, the California architect Peter Calthorpe called cities "the most environmentally benign form of human settlement," one in which the average resident "consumes less land, less energy, less water, and produces less pollution than his counterpart in settlements of lower densities." A few years later, the Australian community activist David Engwicht likewise underlined the linked social and environmental advantages of urban clustering, particularly in the way it could "minimise the need for travel or movement." The work of both helped give rise to the "Eco-City" movement in urban design.[34] In 1989, the political scientist Robert Paehlke devoted a section of his book *Environmentalism and the Future of Progressive Politics* to challenging the belief that the dispersion of people outward from urban centers represented an unqualified good. On the contrary, Paehlke asserted, decentralism was "environmentally unsound." Citing Jacobs and others, he pointed to a remarkable degree of congruence between city life and the imperatives of environmental protection. Rising resource demands, habitat destruction by development, increasing automobile dependence, population growth, wasteful discarding of refuse, greenhouse gas emissions—all of these threats to sustainability, Paehlke argued, would only be intensified by dispersion or deurbanization.[35] In 1990, the economist Ira Lowry wondered why "urbanization is often represented as a vicious trend in human society, by both students of economic development and students of the environment." Many then-prevalent green objections to cities, Lowry argued, were sincere but misdirected. When the independent effect of urbanization was established, he predicted, it would very often turn out to be a positive one because cities afford far better opportunities for reducing resource consumption and controlling pollution than less concentrated patterns of settlement can. For environmentalists, Lowry concluded, "I suspect that cities are, on balance, allies rather than adversaries."[36] In 1992, the geographer Martin Lewis likewise pointed, with ample evidence, to the damage done by diffusing population and to the benefits of concentration for lessening per capita demands on land and energy resources. He called attention as well to the tendency for US urban areas to vote more heavily than suburban and rural ones for ballot measures and candidates favoring environmental protection. "An environmentally sound society," Lewis wrote, "should *encourage* the growth of high-density urban centers, cities in which residential, commercial, and industrial functions are closely configured."[37]

These authors wrote with developed-world environmental issues mostly in mind. The revised second edition, published in 2001, of an important pioneering book on environment and urbanization in the Third World enriched the first (1992) version by adding a section entitled "The Environmental Opportunities Provided by Cities." "Before describing cities' many environmental problems," the authors wrote, "it is worth noting the environmental opportunities that the concentration of production and population in any city provides." It made possible, they observed, economies of scale in the use and recycling of natural resources (land, water, energy, and materials), thereby reducing per capita emissions of greenhouse gases and other wastes. It facilitated the control and management of pollution and of occupational hazards. It might very well help to protect people from natural hazards by lowering the cost of protective and anticipatory measures and by speeding post-disaster relief. And it might do much to promote effective action on environmental problems because urban institutions have an exceptional capacity to respond to challenges in general and to involve the public in the process: "The concentration of people in cities can facilitate their full involvement in the election of governments at local and city levels and their active participation in decisions and actions within their own district or neighbourhood."[38]

Discussions along the same lines, addressed to scholarly and popular audiences alike, have proliferated in the last few years.[39] The 2007 annual report of the United Nations Population Fund (UNFPA) offers some evidence of how far a more favorable view of cities has—and has not—established itself. The report, subtitled "Unleashing the Potential of Urban Growth," notes that an attitude of—to coin a term—*urbanophobia* (a combination of dislike and fear) remains strong among analysts and policy makers, inspiring measures meant to slow or even reverse the concentration of people in cities. The vast majority of the world's national governments maintain policies meant to discourage urbanization. But those measures, the UNFPA argues, are not only futile in most cases but also counterproductive in the very degree that they achieve their intended goals. At best they are an irrelevant distraction from the chief task ahead, which is that of capitalizing on the opportunities that cities offer for improving the state of people and of the environment: "The potential benefits of urbanization far outweigh the disadvantages," the report maintains, going on to say,

proximity and concentration give cities an advantage in the production of goods and services by reducing costs, supporting innovation and fostering synergies among different economic sectors. But proximity and concentration also have the potential to improve peoples' lives directly and at lower cost than rural areas. For instance, cities can provide much cheaper access to basic infrastructure and services to their entire populations. . . . People intuitively perceive the advantages of urban life. This explains why millions flock to the cities every year. Yet many planners and policymakers in rapidly urbanizing nations want to prevent urban growth. Such attitudes are not founded on evidence.

The two chapters that the report devotes to environmental issues emphasize the positive net contributions that urbanization can make. A couple of sentences sum up their message: "Urban localities actually offer better chances for long-term sustainability, starting with the fact that they concentrate half the Earth's population on less than 3 percent of its land area . . . the dispersion of population and economic activities would likely make the problems worse rather than better."[40] Such an analysis, coming from such a mainstream source, suggests how shaky the assumptions of commonsense antiurbanism have become. Yet an urbanophobic bias persists, as do many specific errors about urban effects, and few of the book-length overviews now beginning to appear on the general topic of cities and the environment avoid them entirely.

This bias and these errors are the subject of the chapters that follow. I examine arguments (explicit or implied) that something about cities necessarily or most likely means an urban penalty in each of the various spheres of human-environment relations. Such arguments, when wrong, can be refuted on the ground either of a logical flaw in the argument or its demonstrated failure to correspond to reality—in some cases, both. Is the claim based on faulty or inadequate reasoning or does the reasoning, though impeccable in its own terms, predict something that turns out not to occur? Both forms of error crop up too frequently in the discourse of commonsense environmental antiurbanism not to pose a serious obstacle to understanding, and too frequently also not to present a puzzle themselves. That even many intelligent and knowledgeable authors make such mistakes about cities and the environment suggests that misunderstanding originates in something other than mere carelessness. At its roots, we may uncover profound antiurban biases but more often and more likely we may simply find and bring to light some things about cities that make them difficult to think clearly about, even with the best intentions.

Some kinds of errors will recur so often from one chapter to another that they are worth bringing up at the outset. One is the sloppy use of words in ways that obscure or even reverse their real significance. The journalist David Owen points to a particularly common example, "the technical term that is widely used for sprawl, 'urbanization.'" As he notes, the two words, though often used as synonyms in a way that brings discredit on the latter, in fact mean very different things.[41] In the developed world today, rural-to-urban migration is of only modest importance and the predominant form of settlement change is migration from more- to less-dense settings within metropolitan areas. Thus modern US-type sprawl, far from representing urbanization, really involves the deurbanization of populations that previously lived at a higher degree of urbanness, their resettlement at lower densities, in a less built environment, and usually in smaller political municipalities. Its possible harmful effects reflect too little urbanness, not too much. Jargon is undesirable but rigorous, accurate reasoning is impossible if key terms are not used carefully and precisely.

Two more errors are familiar logical fallacies in the ascription of causality, those of affirming the consequent and equating correlation with causation. One form that the first can take is the too-easy ascription of legitimate urban advantages simply to what the economist Michael Lipton dubbed *urban bias*. Lipton's important and influential thesis points to unequal relations of power as an important cause of inequality; within less-developed countries, better-organized urban interests appropriate an excessive share of national resources at the expense of rural populations and of national well-being in the aggregate. There is nothing fallacious about the argument itself; in many cases, what it asserts undoubtedly takes place. But to conclude from the existence of urban advantages, which the theory predicts, that urban bias was their cause, is to commit the fallacy of affirming the consequent; it ignores the possibility that much or even most of the disparity may instead have been the result of genuine urban advantages, only amplified somewhat by biases in policy.[42]

The related error of assuming causation on the basis merely of correlation is one that Ira Lowry particularly warned against. Many environmental problems, he noted, increase at some scales as the degree of urbanness does but that does not make urbanness their cause. Many environmental objections to cities, he observed, arise from a failure to separate urban growth as a process from such correlated but quite distinct processes as population growth, industrialization, and rising standards of living.[43] The term *urbanization* is often loosely employed as a catch-all synonym for such trends or indeed for modernity in general. And because many environmental problems have intensified in modern times, one can easily slip into the fallacious assumption that urbanization is their root cause. Similarly, many forms of environmental impact, such as per capita resource consumption, are greatest in the MDCs, which happen to be the world's most urbanized countries as well. But it would be vastly premature to ascribe them to urbanization simply on that basis, without seeing first how the degree of urbanness within such countries correlates with the degree of impact.

A frequent opportunity for error lies in the neglect of a point that sounds obvious in the abstract but is all too easy to neglect in practice: that the question being asked, that of the environmental effects of urbanization, is an essentially comparative one. It does not suffice to show that some particular environmental problem occurs in highly urban settings or in association with them in order to prove that urbanness is environmentally undesirable. To suppose that it does is to commit what the early nineteenth-century logician Richard Whately called "the fallacy of objections." Whately defined this fallacy as that of "showing that *there are* objections against some plan, theory, or system, and thence inferring that it should be rejected; when that which *ought* to have been proved is, that there are *more*, or *stronger* objections, against the receiving than the rejecting of it."[44] It is committed when environmental problems that arise in or because of cities are not compared and contrasted with those that arise in connection with a less urban settlement pattern. What is necessary is to ask is not merely what problems appear in urban areas but whether they are worse than those—of the same type and of different types—that the process of deurbanization or a less urban pattern would generate. Many of the excellent and useful studies now appearing on the topic of cities and the environment risk committing this error quite inadvertently or at least risk aiding and abetting their readers in committing it. To cover their chosen topic, they must document and discuss the environmental problems associated with urbanization, and yet those problems may not be unique to cities or even most severe there. The urban focus makes it difficult to add this essential comparative dimension as long as one takes cities to be the topic of study. If, however, one thought of it as urbanness—as a variable that some people and places show a high degree of and others a low—it would be natural and indeed scientifically imperative to investigate conditions along the full range of values, from high to low, in order to understand what different degrees of urbanness mean for environmental problems. The importance of doing just that will appear over and over in the pages that follow.

Moreover, in conducting such comparisons of what is more urban with what is less so, the most useful and reliable results will emerge when all else that may affect them is held constant: for example, when the comparison is within a given country or world region and when, say, total national population and standard of living are held constant so that the pluses and minuses of a more versus a less urban settlement pattern *for that population* and *at that society's standard of living* may be compared. Errors and illusions are likely to arise when this principle is ignored. Cities, for example, are often described as rapacious consumers of farmland and wildland as they expand. And of course it is true that if the city's population simply disappeared, much less land would be occupied for residential use. But in supposing so, we have not been holding all else equal because we have simultaneously altered two variables, urbanness and population size. If we held the latter constant, we would notice that if the population in question did not live in cities, it would have to live somewhere else. The appropriate question to ask is how much land a given number of people would need if instead of living in a highly urban pattern, they lived in a less urban (i.e., a more spatially dispersed) one. To take a second example, few things are more common in the study of Third World cities than comparisons between the well-being of urban slum populations on the one hand and rural populations on the other. When the former falls below the latter, an "urban slum penalty" is often asserted; yet the assertion rests on a stacked and fallacious comparison because the urban poor have been compared not, as they should, with the rural poor but with the entire rural population. Finally, as noted previously, in US metropolitan areas, the areas of highest population density, found in the central city, would by our definition be more urban than the suburbs and exurbs as well as the rural areas beyond them. We may well find what looks like a severe urban penalty in such domains as infant mortality, infectious disease, and many others. But the apparent penalty derived from this comparison may at least in part be an illusion because once again we have not been careful to compare like with like. The inner city and the suburbs differ not only in the key dimension (or dimensions) of urbanness but also in that of economic status as well. Consequently, much of what we might incautiously take as evidence of an urban penalty may instead simply be a penalty of poverty. The inhabitants of highly urban areas, as we have already seen, are not always and necessarily poor; outside the United

States, the opposite is often the case. If we wanted to isolate the effect of urban settlement instead of simply comparing populations in more and less urban areas, we would do better to compare outcomes in such areas within otherwise similar subgroups—particular income strata or racial minorities. Conversely, an illusory urban advantage may arise under conditions often found in Third World or western European cities. Here, what looks like greater urban well-being may, at least in part, be merely an artifact of patterns of residential location that concentrate wealth in the most densely settled and most highly urban locales. Controlling as far as possible for these other factors and holding them constant is the best way to identify the effects of urbanness.

Urban problems, measured in absolute terms, may also seem much worse or larger than those that arise in less urban settings without really being so in any meaningful way. All else being equal, the highest death tolls from natural and technological hazard events will be recorded in cities, the largest quantities of resources will be consumed, the largest quantities of pollution will be emitted, and so on. But to conclude that urban areas are therefore worse is to commit the same error as supposing that India is a richer country than Switzerland because it has a larger GDP. The relevant statistic, of course, is GDP per capita. Only when the data have been corrected by the size of the population involved can meaningful conclusions be drawn. Until then, the questions that must be asked in order to clarify the effects of urbanness remain open ones: whether, in the case of hazards, an individual is safer in an urban or a nonurban setting and whether the aggregate toll of loss from a given hazard would be less or greater if the population were less urbanized, and so too for total resource consumption and waste emissions.

And finally, because cities by their nature will be more visible than human settlements that are less urban, the problems that occur in them will also be more visible and more discussed. Similar to the failings of governments in a democracy, similar to the sins of John Winthrop's "city set on a hill," they are difficult to hide, whereas equally bad or worse conditions in other and more remote places may escape observation. Thus an illusion of urban problems as being always bad and getting worse may arise merely as a result of the disproportionate degree of attention that they receive. And if coping and response measures are more numerous and more effective in cities than elsewhere, they will also be more visible, and as a result they may suggest ("where there's smoke there's fire") worse conditions while actually operating to make things better. The result could be an additional urban penalty in appearance—and an additional urban advantage in reality.

2

Ecological Disruption

Human beings are simultaneously one species among many occupying the earth's surface and unique in their power to modify the environment shared by all. Such modifications represent one cause for concern when they disrupt the ecological systems essential to the lives of other species: the assemblages of plant and animal life and the flows of water, the flows of energy, and the local conditions of soil, chemistry, and climate to which they are adjusted. On first thought, it seems obvious that a high degree of urbanness must mean a high degree of disruption, that cities must be more ecologically damaging than any other form of human settlement. Their central defining feature, the dense concentration of people, points almost irresistibly in that direction. The larger the numbers of an animal as active as *Homo sapiens* that establish themselves in a small area, the more of its other species are displaced, the more new ones are introduced, and the more living conditions are transformed for all. Though they assuredly still exist within the natural world, cities are its most obviously and drastically altered parts, its most ecologically disrupted, and its most unnatural if nature is defined in as common a usage of the word as the set of presettlement conditions. It seems necessarily to follow that the greater the degree of urbanness or urbanization, the greater the ecological damage.

It takes only a little thought, though, to see the fallacy in the line of reasoning that derives such a conclusion from these (indeed valid) premises. Given a human population of a certain size, an urban, high-density way of life is more sparing of residential land than a suburban or rural one. Its economies of space mean reduced conversion of wildlands and lessened pressure on the habitat of other species. Precisely by concentrating human impact, cities contain it. They reduce the area within which it occurs, thereby protecting nature elsewhere, whereas a population of a given size living in more dispersed modes of settlement invades and affects larger expanses of territory. When viewed in this light, cities undergo a remarkable metamorphosis. They cease to seem deadly enemies of nature and start to look instead like its essential allies. As Robert Paehlke wrote in 1989, "perhaps the only way to assure wilderness preservation on a planet soon to be populated by ten billion humans is to accept and even welcome increases in both urban density and the proportion of population resident in urban areas."[1]

The error that commonsense antiurbanism here commits is to ignore the net effect of urbanization and look only at the fraction of it registered within the urbanized area. It is an example of what John Stuart Mill dubbed the "fallacy of overlooking," in which "the conclusion would be just, if the portion which is seen of the case were the whole of it; but there is another portion overlooked, which vitiates the result."[2] Observers may easily see the harm (or the good) done by a certain action and condemn (or praise) it solely on that basis, disregarding additional but less readily visible consequences that might tip the scales in the opposite direction if they too were taken into account. Mill thought the fallacy particularly rife in popular discussions of economics—in jeremiads over the jobs lost to labor-saving machinery or to free trade, for example—but city-environment relations are another field in which it seems to thrive. Within a city, ecosystems will indeed have been severely disrupted, the preexisting land cover replaced by a largely built environment, and the more so, all else being equal, the higher the city's population density and the greater the degree of urbanness. But the "portion of the case," to use Mill's words, that is overlooked here is the damage beyond the city's edge that has *not* occurred because people have concentrated their demands for living space within it. This portion easily escapes notice because damage that has not occurred cannot be seen. Yet without considering it, one cannot fairly judge the city's net effect.

What can be seen, and increasingly is, is the ecological damage that occurs when dwellings do deconcentrate. In the words of the historian Patricia Limerick, "Antiurban sentiment . . . has been an enormous force behind the sprawling of American settlement, and the intrusion of houses into open space."[3] The ecological superiority of compact cities that grow vertically more than they do horizontally is now taken for granted in debates over urban sprawl in the developed world. It is perhaps the point in the entire field of human-environment relations where the case for an urban advantage, traceable to the key variable of population density, has taken firmest root in the scientific community and among the general public and done the most to weaken the commonsense environmental

condemnation of urbanization. Today it is not solely academic researchers or knowledgeable green activists who understand, almost intuitively,
that on this score cities are environmentally better the more like cities
they are and that where deurbanization occurs, ecological disruption
worsens. Low-density peripheral development of housing and the roads
and other infrastructure it requires not only directly displace but also,
over wider areas, fragment and degrade plant and animal habitat. They
promote the entry of invasive species and upset the balance between
existing ones that suffer from development and ones that thrive on it.
And as well as introducing new elements of disturbance, finally, through
such processes as fire suppression, flood control, and coastal zone stabi-
lization, they alter the natural regimes of disturbance to which ecosystems have become closely attuned.[4] The disruptive potential for human
settlement makes its concentration in cities more desirable than its spread
far and wide. As the economist Edward Glaeser sums up the matter:
"Residing in a forest might seem to be a good way of showing one's love
of nature, but living in a concrete jungle is actually far more ecologically
friendly. We humans are a destructive species, even when, like Thoreau,
we're trying not to be."[5]

Even the most energetic and intelligent defense of US-type urban
sprawl yet to appear, by the architectural historian Robert Bruegmann,
as good as concedes the point. In his book *Sprawl: A Compact History*
(2005), Bruegmann devotes a single paragraph to the charge that low-
density suburban expansion "has caused a major loss of habitat and, in
the worst cases, species extinctions." It is, he grants, "a significant problem"
but he gives it no further consideration, preferring to respond instead to
other criticisms on the ground that this objection cannot be profitably
discussed until the scientific understanding of the worst-case effect, species
extinctions, has achieved near-mathematical precision. Bruegmann's
reluctance to engage the issue at greater length is especially surprising,
inasmuch as the ecologically disruptive effects of sprawl have for a long
time been prominent among the objections that he wrote his book to
discredit. As the environmental historian Adam Rome has amply documented in *The Bulldozer in the Countryside* (2001), unease about the
consumption of forest, wetlands, and open space by suburban sprawl was
one of the formative concerns of the post–World War II US environmental
movement.[6] Yet the all-too-common misuse of terms such as *urbanization*
or *urban growth* to mean what really represents their opposite, the secondary deurbanization of population, does much to perpetuate the illusion of an antagonism between cities and ecological protection.

Illusions can also arise from the use of the same words, not as precise terms applied to changes in human settlement patterns but as catch-all labels for a complex of other changes that have taken place more or less in conjunction with them. A large collaborative study of right whales in the western north Atlantic issued a volume of its findings under the title *The Urban Whale* and repeatedly referred to the modern ocean as "the urban ocean." But the processes threatening whale survival that the authors lumped together under the term were "shipping, fishing, ocean noise, pollution (including sewage effluent and agricultural and industrial runoff)," none of which bears any necessary causal relation to urbanization and some of which may even be reduced by it, but which the terminology used blames on it.[7]

Another source of confusion about the net ecological effects of cities may be that, because they are literally less "green" than suburbs or rural areas, they may be thought therefore to be less green in the derived sense of the word. A color-blind view of the matter would stand a better chance of avoiding some common illusions. Agriculture, however green in the first sense, often erases the existing system of flora and fauna, substituting a biologically impoverished cover of a single crop. It sustains that monoculture by inputs of chemical fertilizer (and sometimes, in dry climates, of irrigation) and protects it from other and undesired species by heavy doses of pesticides and herbicides. Bruce Babbitt, former US secretary of the Interior, cites Iowa as "an example of rural sprawl, or more accurately, agricultural sprawl—a landscape obliterated by corn and soybeans. . . . By the end of the nineteenth century more than 99 percent of the tallgrass prairie of Iowa and the other midwestern states had vanished, replaced by row crops."[8] Likewise, low-density suburbia does not merely occupy more living space per person than urban areas do. It too creates and actively maintains an artificial— though again a visually quite green—ecosystem, displacing native plant cover with a monoculture of imported grass (most varieties used in the standard suburban lawn are not native to North America) supported by intensive inputs of fertilizers, pesticides, energy, and water. Research by the geographers Paul Robbins and Julie Sharp suggests the confusion that can arise in this realm between what is literally and what is metaphorically green. They found that the same homeowners who described themselves as environmentalists were the ones likeliest to manage their yards intensively, adding higher than average inputs of lawn-maintenance chemicals. As Robbins and Sharp write, companies selling lawn care products play on existing attitudes in their advertising to promote "the sense of lawn management as a bridge to the biotic, nonhuman, natural world," to "the timeless human activity of planting growing things in the soil . . . sowing and nurturing living green plants." Taking care of a lawn may indeed represent a highly valued interaction with "nature" in the eyes of many suburbanites, who seem less aware that it is a kind of interaction involving the aggressive transformation of the predevelopment land cover.[9]

If suburbia is not an altogether hospitable environment for native species, neither is the city itself an altogether hostile one. Yet on the whole it is true that habitat is altered more intensively the more urban a place is, and true too that the proportion of non-native to native species rises as well, being higher in central cities than in suburbs and higher in suburbs than in rural areas. Such key ecological components as soil, water flow, and climate tend to show the same gradient of increased transformation when measures of urbanness increase as do vegetation cover and species composition.[10] Cities, as a number of writers have insisted in recent years, are not by any means artificial systems existing outside of natural ones. It would be pointless to argue over whether they are or are not "natural" because there is no settling the question by an appeal to what *natural* means. In everyday usage, which after all is what the meaning of a word consists of, it means a number of different things. One of them is "falling within the subject matter of the 'natural sciences,'" and in that sense cities are certainly natural. But another meaning of *natural* is "unaltered or little altered by human action," and in that sense it is no error or illusion to describe cities as indeed highly unnatural.

But again, to look only at the area where the effects occur is to overlook some countervailing advantages of highly urban settlement. The question that needs to be posed and settled before a penalty from urbanization is assumed is, to what extent do the benefits of dense urban development in restricting the area that is altered offset its heightened effects within that area? Will a given population have more overall impact if it lives in a concentrated pattern or a dispersed one? It may be the former, if the concentration of impacts exceeds thresholds below which the system would be capable of absorbing stress. Yet it may be the latter if the chief effect of dispersion is to increase the total burden on the ecosystem or the total area of it harmed. A study of the urban heat island in Atlanta illustrates how the process can occur. Parcels developed for low-density suburban residence contributed proportionally more heat to the urban warming than did ones developed for higher densities.[11] The main sources of nighttime light pollution of the environment, to take another example, are street and building lights; its best-documented consequences, apart from hindering astronomical observation, involve disruption of the day-and-night patterns of activity of other species. Light pollution is likely to increase in intensity, all things being equal, with the clustering of population but the problem may be better controlled by containing it, by concentrating population in an urban settlement pattern in a well-lighted but small area rather than dispersing it and expanding the area affected.[12]

Inadvertent urban-induced disruption is not confined to the urban area itself. The heat island can impinge on wider areas downwind through more numerous and frequent convective rain showers; concentrated urban waste emissions pollute waters downstream and offshore; the replacement of natural with paved land modifies downstream river flows, increasing the extremes of high and low water. But these and similar impacts are not exclusively urban. Rural activities and populations can also incidentally and adversely affect weather, climate, streamflow, and water quality, and over much more extensive areas even if less intensively per unit of land. Urban centers deliberately transform the flow of river systems by decreeing the construction of dams and reservoirs for municipal water supply, thereby altering drastically the conditions of life for species within and around them. Yet dams and impoundments are also built to meet the demands of rural interests, to store and distribute water for irrigated agriculture, much of which, in the western United States and other low-rainfall parts of the developed world, is a highly marginal and subsidized activity at that. Cities in the desert may seem out of place and they make tempting targets for criticism but are they any more unnatural or out of place than farms in the desert? A classic story in the folklore of US environmental history is that of Los Angeles's early twentieth-century "steal" of the waters of the Owens Valley to meet the demands of its present and expected future residents. As befits a Western, it has villains, heroes, and a moral—though as usually told it lacks something else equally desirable: a happy ending. It has the right kind of villain for a US audience—a big city—and the right kind of heroes—the rural folk, the ranchers and farmers of the valley. Some elements rarely emphasized in most tellings of the story complicate its lessons on the environmental side. Los Angeles's opponents were not preservationists; they were rural entrepreneurs. The diversion that they objected to threatened a cherished project of their own, a federally subsidized dam and reservoir on the Owens River to divert its flow in order to irrigate tens of thousands of acres of land they hoped to "reclaim" from a natural state of "useless" desert. If the diversion has adversely affected the valley's ecosystems, and it has, so too would the reclamation project have done, but the double standard by which popular memory has judged them suggests at least an unconscious antiurban bias.[13]

The wider impacts of cities also include funding and political pressure for land-cover conservation. Many of the world's largest urban areas— including Third World cities as large as São Paulo, Rio de Janeiro, Mumbai, and Nairobi—draw their water supplies in part from protected or restored areas of forestland that they guard from development and other forms of human intrusion.[14] The same has happened with considerable areas of land in the northeastern United States that had already been affected by agriculture or logging and would subsequently have been invaded and fragmented by development. Massachusetts's largest block by far of protected forest surrounds the Quabbin Reservoir, constructed in the central-western part of the state in the 1920s and 1930s for the use of the metropolitan Boston area. The forestlands around New York City's reservoirs in the Catskill Mountains serve the same purpose of water supply protection. Pressure from urban interests worried that deforestation might disrupt the flow of water in the state's major rivers and canals led to the creation of New York's largest preserve, the Adirondack Park, in the late nineteenth century. As the park's mission has shifted from hydrological regulation to nature preservation and recreation, an urban constituency has remained a powerful force opposed to measures favored by much of the rural population within and near the preserve for relaxing protection in the interests of economic development.[15] The US environmental historian Samuel P. Hays notes a recurrent pattern of conflict, evident in patterns of legislative and referendum voting, between urban pressures for preservation and rural ones for lenient land-use regulation.[16] The urbanward shift of population in Third World countries is likely to ease conflicts between nature protection in the form of national parks and rural livelihoods and is as likely as in the First World to strengthen political support for conservation.[17]

To the areas deliberately protected or restored must be added those that have incidentally reverted to wildland as populations and livelihoods have urbanized. The British geographer Alexander S. Mather's model of the "forest transition" sums up the process. Mather observed that the early stages of economic development have tended, historically and today, to be associated with a large net loss of forest cover. But as a country continues to develop, it reaches a turning point after which regrowth takes the place of deforestation and forest cover begins to expand. The reversal occurs because agriculture has become more productive, freeing rural labor to shift sectorally into other occupations and spatially to cities where new jobs and means of livelihood most readily arise. As a result, large areas of land once occupied by farming and rural residence are abandoned and return to forest or other natural land cover. And indeed the present-day world map of land-cover change shows regrowth dominant in most of the developed countries, which are predominantly urban, even as forest cover declines in much of the still majority-rural Third World.[18] A graph of forest cover in the New England states over the past two centuries is Mather's model in visual form, modified only at the end by the deurbanization of previously more concentrated metropolitan populations through suburban sprawl (figure 2.1). The story has been repeated in innumerable other locales in the developed world.

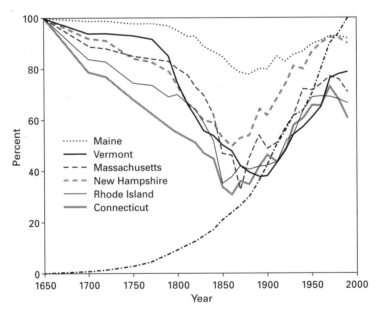

Figure 2.1
Change in forest area and population, New England, 1650–2000. *Source:* David R. Foster et al., "New England's Forest Landscape: Ecological Legacies and Conservation Patterns Shaped by Agrarian History," Chap. 2 in Charles L. Redman and David R. Foster, eds., *Agrarian Landscapes in Transition* (New York: Oxford University Press, 2008), fig. 2.4, 64. By permission of Oxford University Press, Inc.

The case for an overall urban advantage in lessening ecological disruption is an equally compelling one in the less-developed countries. They are of particular importance, being located by and large in the world's lower latitudes, which hold a disproportionate share of the world's biodiversity. Past actions or policies aimed to disperse population more widely have compiled a record of much harm done and little good. A number of the LDCs in the postwar decades, fearing the effects of rising densities in their thickly settled core regions, adopted resettlement programs to move people more or less voluntarily to sparsely occupied rural fringes. Indonesia, for example, sent "transmigrants" to its outer islands and Brazil sent peasant cultivators to its Amazon Basin frontiers. The usual result was deforestation and accelerated environmental disruption in the receiving areas, with rarely any significant benefits in the sending ones to justify the costs incurred.[19]

Left to its own devices, Third World population has tended to urbanize rather than to disperse, even in defiance of government policies aimed at stemming the trend. A number of analysts, notably H. Ricardo Grau and T. Mitchell Aide, have emphasized the beneficial consequences in Latin America of such migration in reducing human pressures on rural land cover and promoting ecological recovery. Taking Mather's theory of the forest transition as their starting point, Grau, Aide, and others have found the same processes that have largely run their course in the First World beginning to operate noticeably in the Third through the shift of employment from agriculture to other occupations. Each rural-to-urban migrant or urban resident, Grau and Aide emphasize, is a person subtracted or withheld from those pressing on rural lands as well as one added to the total pressure on urban ones. Those who leave, they add, tend to be the youngest and most active, those who would have the greatest ecological impact if they stayed, and the agricultural acreage abandoned with the shift is likely to be land that is at once of marginal value for cultivation and more than ordinarily fragile, such as steep hillsides sensitive to soil erosion when they are cleared of forest.[20]

Along these lines, Sandra R. Baptista has examined trends in part of coastal southern Brazil belonging to the now highly fragmented Atlantic Forest, an internationally recognized "biodiversity hotspot." She focused on the state of Santa Catarina and particularly on the hinterland of the state's metropolis and capital city, Florianópolis. In 1940, the state's population was three-quarters rural; by 2000, though it had grown four-and-a-half-fold, it was nearly four-fifths urban, the absolute number of rural dwellers having fallen after 1970. By 2000, Florianópolis held nearly a million people, owing to natural increase, rural-to-urban migration, and migration from cities elsewhere in Brazil. Since 1970, a reversion of cleared land (farm and pasture) to tree cover and an increase in the area of protected forest have accompanied rural population decline, agricultural modernization, and the abandonment of marginal farm and pasture lands, all in accord with the forest transition model and in synchrony with the urban concentration of people. Population grew substantially, but because it grew within an urban center and not across the entire landscape, the forest was able to recover.[21]

Within Latin America, Puerto Rico is of particular interest because of its intermediate character, as a commonwealth of the United States, between more- and less-developed world statuses. Research here too has detected an ongoing forest transition, with regrowth accompanying a shift of population from rural to urban areas. One study evaluated the objection that forest area gained by rural depopulation will merely be lost again to low-density urban-fringe development. The objection is a plausible one, particularly in the Puerto Rican setting. Yet it seems not to be a valid one. Between 1991 and 2000, although the island's population grew by 8.2 percent, forest cover on the island expanded from 28 percent to 40 percent of the land area, whereas developed land went only from 10 percent to 11 percent.[22]

Urbanization in the LDCs is, then, among the most plausible reasons for optimism about the future of their forests and other ecosystems. Grau, Aide, and others have been careful not to claim too much for their findings. Environmentally, the shift of people from rural to urban areas may not, reforestation notwithstanding, be even carbon neutral if an increase in per capita energy consumption accompanies the move. It is unlikely to restore the precise species composition of the preclearance forest—though that is no fault of cities, and in any case, as other researchers note, the degree to which even pre-twentieth century forest can be regarded as "primary" or "virgin" or "undisturbed" is a very questionable one. Environmental costs from intensified cultivation on better lands may offset the benefits stemming from the abandonment of marginal ones. In some cases, when rural depopulation reduces the labor supply available to maintain soil terraces and other land-protective devices, there may for a time be heightened degradation in the form of increased erosion and sediment flow downstream as natural recovery takes its course. Finally, there may be social costs and a decline in the quality of life in rural areas with a shrinking population base, though in the aggregate these may well be balanced or better (see chapter 8) by the higher quality of life obtained by those moving to cities.[23]

This body of research is a recent one, thus far largely focused on Latin America, but the same processes may come to light when detailed examinations are conducted in other parts of the Third World. Statistical studies of the relations of population change with deforestation at the national level in the LDCs already offer it considerable support. They have found, as a rule, that rural population growth is positively associated with deforestation and urban population growth negatively so.[24]

What, though, are the relations of urbanization or urbanness to human population growth itself? Changes in human numbers represent a key element of our own species' ecology as well as a major influence on the other species on which our activities impinge. In weighing the effects that urbanization has on the process, it is easy to conflate the size and growth of cities, as clusters of population, with the size and growth of population itself, as if the two represented only the same phenomenon examined at different scales. We began by defining cities as places with many people in them; therefore the phenomena of population and cities, and hence the processes of population growth and urbanization, can easily come to be associated as if they were closely akin. It is quite common to find terms such as *overpopulation* and *urbanization* lumped together as if they were similar and mutually reinforcing developments. Even if urban areas reduce pressure on land by concentrating settlement, the gain is a dubious one if they also increase the pressure by multiplying human numbers. It makes a plausible ground for the fear and distaste that many observers concerned about population growth express for cities. A former US undersecretary of state, writing in 1976, could warn about the dangers of population growth and at the same time urge policies "to keep people on the land, provide them employment, and prevent the migration to the cities that can only result in disaster."[25] If such writers are correct in thinking population growth the greatest threat to global sustainability, physical and social, they can hardly be blamed for feeling that the growing centers of population are especially problematic.

But what this Pavlovian association disregards is one of the best-established uniformities in human social behavior. To "keep people on the land" and "prevent . . . migration to cities" would promote, much more than it would check, the expansion of human numbers. Population growth does indeed spur the growth of cities but the growth of cities does not in turn accelerate population increase. On the contrary, it has done the opposite under almost all known circumstances in the modern world.[26] And the reason is not that contemporary urban life increases mortality rates, because on the whole it does the opposite; urban life expectancies exceed rural ones across most of the world. Rather, it is that birth or fertility rates for similar socioeconomic groups are markedly lower in urban areas than in rural areas of the same country and world region. In the transition from high to low fertility that usually accompanies a country's economic development, fertility levels have tended in the past and tend today to fall first in urban areas, even as rural ones remain high. The pattern is as apparent in sub-Saharan Africa, the site today of the world's highest fertility, highest population growth rates, and lowest levels of urbanization, as it was in the demographic transition in previous centuries in today's affluent counties—where a rural-urban fertility gap, though much attenuated, is still observable. As a rule, moreover, fertility rates in the LDCs are lowest in the largest (and thus "most urban") cities.[27] The association can be put to a final test by investigating variations in fertility rates within cities. Research, controlling for such other variables as wealth or poverty, suggests that birth rates are indeed lowest in the neighborhoods of cities where the defining features of urbanness are most pronounced: a dense population, a largely built environment, long-term urban residence, a near-absence of agriculture, and the jurisdiction of a large municipal government.[28]

Well-established empirically, the inverse relationship between urbanization and fertility is not something that merely seems to happen but for no known reason. The mechanisms that underlie it are compelling and easy to understand. In rural areas of the LDCs, many households, especially those of smallholder farmers, have strong incentives to increase the family size. The costs of additional children in food, living space, and education are relatively low, and the benefits of additional nonwage labor in farm and household chores and of long-term family security are high. Many postwar family-planning efforts sponsored by national elites and by Western donors fell afoul of the quite rational reluctance of rural families to reduce their number of births.[29] Much changes, though, when the scene shifts to an urban setting. The reasons for lower urban fertility fall into two main categories, which can be seen most clearly in studies of behavioral changes among migrants from rural areas to cities.[30] First, migration is selective; those who move to urban areas are not a representative sample of the rural populations from which they come. They are usually more than ordinarily affluent and well educated and in other ways less likely, all things being equal, to have large families. If this were the only factor, one could hardly ascribe the drop in fertility that follows migration to urbanness as such. Things are different where the second factor, that of adaptation, is concerned. To live in an urban area is to be subject to quite another set of pressures from those that hold sway elsewhere. Additional children in a Third World city bring fewer economic benefits than in a rural area (especially where household-based agriculture is the principal occupation) and the costs, especially of living space, food, and education, are much higher. As infant and child mortality falls, moreover, the felt need to bear many children as insurance against the future weakens. Women in cities have a greater competing set of opportunities for the use of their time; they also have greater access to contraception (and usually a greater freedom to make choices). Consequently, the age of marriage and of first childbearing in urban settings is usually later than in rural ones; average family size decreases and the emphasis in child rearing shifts from quantity to quality. Whoever fears the environmental consequences of further growth in population thus must applaud and encourage the cityward trend of the world's people.

However, anyone who feels threatened by a leveling or a decline in numbers must be equally averse to urbanization, and so must governments that rule by force and that fear riots in cities as a more immediate and less manageable threat than discontent in the countryside. Even many democratic states, as discussed in chapter 8, have adopted policies to restrain city growth. Benito Mussolini's Italian fascist regime, preoccupied with population as a source of national strength, scorned "sterile cities" and celebrated the virtues of the rural folk, fecundity prominent among them; in the same vein, it embarked on large schemes of wetland drainage and rural development with the twin goals of promoting agrarian settlement and demonstrating fascism's capacity to conquer and transform nature.[31] A drastic cautionary tale from more recent years comes from the policies of General Habyarimana, president and dictator of Rwanda from 1973 until his death at the outset of the violence of 1994. His rhetoric and policies in many ways mirrored those of Mussolini's Italy. Glorifying the peasant life, encouraging births, and at the same time fearing the dangers of urban unrest, Habyarimana placed such severe curbs on rural-to-urban migration as to leave late-twentieth-century Rwanda with the smallest percent of its population living in cities of any country in Africa. With the possibilities of urbanization foreclosed, there arose a syndrome of mutually reinforcing stresses: population growth driven by rural poverty, land shortage, deforestation including encroachment into national parks and protected areas, land degradation and soil erosion, rural poverty further entrenched, and further population growth, contributing to the disaster that eventually occurred.[32]

In sum, not only does urbanization reduce the amount of land a person subtracts from nature for living space but it also tends to reduce the number of persons. But commonsense antiurbanism has a ready reply. The urban brake on population growth lessens human impact only if per capita human impact remains equal. And prevalent images of cities as ravenous consumers of resources and witches' cauldrons of pollution suggest that—demand for land area aside—it does not, that when populations urbanize, they begin to consume and pollute much more than their share. Are these images well founded? That is the next question that needs to be addressed.

3

Resource Consumption

Stereotypes have long cast city dwellers as profligate spenders and frugality as a characteristically rural virtue. In an era of global environmental concern, such stereotypes project urbanites as exceptionally rapacious consumers of a finite and dwindling stock of natural resources. A recent book on the environment and urbanization, though it acknowledges that cities have some positive effects, flatly characterizes them as "sites of overconsumption." In 1976, Lester R. Brown predicted that cities could never house a majority of the human population (as in fact they now do) because the world's resource base could not meet what he called "the additional energy costs of urban living." A survey conducted in 2007 asked members of the general public in central New York State whether they would choose to live in an urban, a suburban, or a rural area if they wanted to lessen their resource demands. More than 60 percent of the respondents answered "a rural area," and more than three-quarters thought rural populations the most sparing of the three in their consumption patterns.[1]

Yet when confronted with the evidence, these widely held views fail to hold up, however well-grounded they seem in the wisdom of the ages. The defining features of cities—their high densities above all—can and generally do make their inhabitants more sparing consumers of important natural resources than less urbanized populations who are similar in other respects. As Peter Newman and Jeffrey Kenworthy observe on the basis of evidence from Australia, as a rule, the more urban, the more economical: "as cities get larger they become more efficient." "This is not new in terms of quantitative studies," they assert, "nor should it surprise us in theoretical terms." Yet, they add, it usually does come as a surprise to those who hear of it for the first time.[2] Left to themselves, people tend, apparently, to take the opposite for granted. Why do they do so? Again, some common errors in reasoning distort much of what people think about important relations between cities and the environment.

As already noted, the tendency for urbanization to lower fertility rates and population growth is as well established as almost any other finding in the social sciences. That it also tends to lower per capita demand for land for living space is no less clear. In ecological terms, these economies of space reduce pressure on the habitats of other species. In natural resource terms, they lessen the conversion of productive cropland, pasture, and timber acreage to residential occupation. All would be best preserved by a high-density, that is, an urban settlement pattern. Urbanization is often blamed for the loss of farmland to development but the implication—that there would be more farmland if there were less urbanization—is more than doubtful because it evades the question of where the population concerned would reside and on how much land, if not in cities. "Urbanization does lead to some building-over of agricultural land," as one team of researchers notes, but given the higher land costs and higher population densities of cities, they point out, "similar amounts of land, and possibly even larger amounts, would probably have been lost if the people in question had chosen to live in rural areas instead."[3] The effects of what is often misnamed urbanization but could more accurately be called *secondary deurbanization,* better known as *sprawl,* bear out the point.

With a plausible case for an urban advantage on the score of land use well established, it remains to look at the other major classes of natural resources: those of energy, materials, and water. The relation is particularly worth examining in the developed countries, where the issue is most pressing because per capita resource demands are by far the world's highest. Once some simple optical illusions that support cities' reputation for extravagant consumption are unmasked, it stands up little better than in the domain of land use.

Energy consumption makes a good starting point for several reasons. It is where the adequacy of the resource base at the global scale to future human needs is a particularly urgent question. It is also the main source, through the excessive combustion of fossil fuels, of the world's most pressing environmental issue today: the greenhouse gas emissions that threaten to destabilize the global climate. And it offers some useful lessons about pitfalls in reasoning to avoid when thinking about cities and resource consumption. In particular, it provides some illustrations of the simple error that does more than anything to perpetuate the illusion of an urban penalty in natural resource consumption. The error has

already been criticized by many authors but it remains so easy, at least
in its subtler forms, to commit, that to be inoculated against it is to take
a major step toward a clear understanding of city-environment relationships. In a nutshell, it involves mistaking the places where the greatest
total resource consumption occurs for the places where per capita levels
of demand are highest, the failure to correct the absolute or total resource
consumption that occurs in a place by that place's population.

Begin by looking at two maps generated by the Center for Neighborhood Technology (figure 3.1a and figure 3.1b). Both represent the same
general process—greenhouse gas emissions from a major form of resource
consumption, household automobile use—and both represent it within

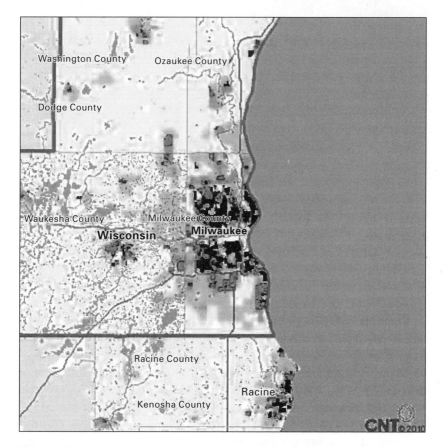

Figure 3.1a
Greenhouse gas emissions per acre from household automobile use by block
group, Milwaukee-Waukesha, WI, metropolitan area. Darker areas represent
higher values. *Source:* Center for Neighborhood Technology.

Figure 3.1b
Greenhouse gas emissions per household from household automobile use by
block group, Milwaukee-Waukesha, WI, metropolitan area. Darker areas represent higher values. *Source:* Center for Neighborhood Technology.

the same spatial unit—the Milwaukee-Waukesha, Wisconsin, metropolitan area, divided into a mosaic of several hundred block groups with
population densities and other urban characteristics highest in the city
center near the lakeshore and shading off through suburbia and exurbia
to rural areas on the fringe. Why, then, do the two maps show such
contrasting patterns, one virtually a photographic negative of the other?
The first map displays the spatial pattern of emissions per acre. It is the
conventional view of cities and resources in cartographic form. Naturally,
the highest values by far occur where people and activities are most
closely packed together, in the Milwaukee city core. The highly urban

neighborhoods indeed look like "sites of overconsumption." But the second map shows emissions per household, and what was a mesa of high values before is a deep crater here. The more urban the block group, the lower the emissions from its average household. The pattern is so far from being unique to Milwaukee that the other 336 US metropolitan areas analyzable at the same site display the same patterns with a monotonous regularity.[4]

They are particularly striking in the United States' largest urban area. "Calculated by the square foot," David Owen writes, "New York City generates more greenhouse gases, uses more energy, and produces more solid waste than any other American region of comparable size. On a map depicting negative environmental impacts in relation to surface area, therefore, Manhattan would look like an intense hot spot, surrounded, at varying distances, by belts of deepening green." But, he notes, the image's apparent lessons are illusory: "if you plotted the same negative impacts by resident or by household the color scheme would be reversed," showing much lower per capita consumption in New York City than in the less densely populated suburban zones surrounding it, with rates rising still higher as exurbia grades into rural areas.[5] When total consumption is used as the measure of impact, cities appear impossibly and intolerably extravagant in their energy use. When the more meaningful measure of consumption per person is examined, the most urban areas and residents usually consume the least.

Why should this be? It is no great puzzle. Settlement density has clear implications for transportation energy use. The longer travel distances and (in developed countries where motor vehicle ownership is most widespread) far greater automobile dependence in suburban and rural areas than in urban ones lead to high gasoline consumption. In Martin Lewis's words: "Public transport . . . is feasible only in and between cities. The denser a city's population becomes, the more efficiently its public transport system can operate. Moreover, in urban core areas, walking is often the most convenient mode of travel. In America's countryside, by contrast, the automobile is generally the sole feasible means of transport," and most destinations are farther away. Vertical movement by elevators, moreover, which is concentrated in the most urban areas, is unusually energy-efficient compared to horizontal travel.[6] A comparative study of large cities around the world by Newman and Kenworthy in 1989 found that per capita gasoline consumption was inversely related to the city's overall population density and was far higher at very low densities—such as those of Houston, Phoenix, Denver, all automobile-age cities of the American West—than at even the moderately low densities found in older cities of the eastern United States and eastern Canada.[7] Urban advantages in energy conservation do not end with transportation. The larger living spaces of rural and suburban areas compare unfavorably to the more compact ones characteristic of cities on the score of energy used per person in heating, cooling, and other domestic activities. Household energy consumption in the urban United States is lower than the national average, whereas the highest values occur variously in affluent suburban zones and rural areas, again suggesting that settlements will be better environmentally the more like cities they are.[8]

Both of these measures have the advantage of offering direct and valid comparisons between otherwise similar populations living in settings of differing degrees of urbanness. They record the levels of consumption registered by individuals or households who can be identified fairly with the ways of life prevalent in those locations. Total greenhouse gas emissions, which in the developed world come chiefly from fossil fuel use, aggregate energy demands in their most environmentally stressful form. The per capita releases in the political unit of New York City (the urban core of the five boroughs, excluding the suburbs and exurbs of the metropolitan area) are less than a third of the average for the United States overall (6.4 metric tons per year versus 19.7) and substantially below national averages for many countries in western Europe.[9]

Thus we now have some revised expectations that line up nicely with the data. But we would be in danger of falling into another easy error, this time in the opposite direction, if we stopped here. The US maps and data we have examined so far may hold another and more subtle illusion. All else being equal, the wealthy will consume more than the poor will. Different socioeconomic classes are not distributed randomly through cities in the United States or for that matter in any other country. In the typical US city—and the New York metropolitan area, despite some localized anomalies, is no exception—the poor cluster in the center, and wealth rises with distance from it. Household income in the political city of New York is lower than in the metropolitan area as a whole and in the United States as a whole. It is true that rural areas beyond the metropolitan area typically have lower incomes still, and the maps show them to have still higher energy consumption, yet the problem remains. The results presented so far are inconclusive because the pattern of reduced energy consumption with increased urbanness may still in large part reflect the social geography of high- and low-consuming households rather than any resource-efficiency advantages of urbanization. Likewise, the international study by Newman and Kenworthy, instead of comparing like with like, mingles cities from very different countries, some of them much more affluent than others, a factor that could have as much to do with their results as the variable of density does.

To get around this obstacle, we can do one of two things. We can compare the energy consumption of more and less urban but socioeconomically similar households within the United States (or other countries) or we can compare central-city with suburban energy consumption in another developed country where the center has remained a zone of high status. Some telling anecdotal evidence offers insight along the lines of the first approach. David Owen describes what happened when he and his wife moved from a Manhattan apartment to a house in rural Connecticut. Here, we are holding socioeconomic status constant, looking at the same household in both locales, and can isolate the effects of urban versus exurban residence from others. On the surface, the move meant leaving an artificial urban setting for a life far closer to nature and presumably more in harmony with it. In fact, Owen writes,

our move was an ecological catastrophe. Our consumption of electricity went from roughly 4,000 kilowatt-hours a year, toward the end of our time in New York, to almost 30,000 kilowatt-hours—and our house doesn't even have central air-conditioning. We bought a car shortly before we moved, and another one soon after we arrived, and a third one ten years later. . . . Almost everything Ann and I do away from our house requires a car trip. The nearest movie theater is twenty minutes away, and so is the nearest large supermarket. Renting a DVD and later returning it consumes almost two gallons of gasoline, because Blockbuster is ten miles away and each complete transaction involves two round trips. . . . Quite often we use a car when taking our dogs for a walk, so that the walk can begin somewhere other than our own front yard. . . . When we lived in New York, heat escaping from our apartment helped to heat the apartment above ours; nowadays, many of the BTUs produced by our very modern, extremely efficient oil-burning furnace leak through our two-hundred-year-old roof and into the dazzling star-filled winter sky above.[10]

More systematically, the economists Edward Glaeser and Matthew Kahn standardized households for size, income, and other determinants of consumption in order to compare the central cities with the suburbs of US metropolitan areas and find out what difference location makes in greenhouse gas emissions. With a handful of exceptions, the emissions of central-city households were lower, and the difference was greatest in New York, the largest city. Restrictions on the density of construction in inner cities, Glaeser and Kahn suggested, may be a reason why an even larger urban advantage has not developed.[11]

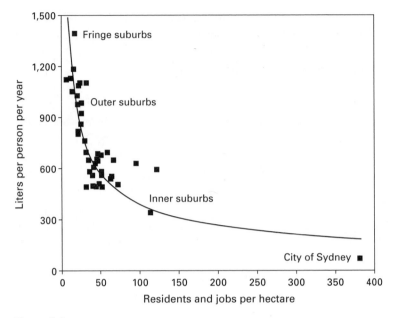

Figure 3.2
Urban density versus liters of gasoline per person per year used for private transportation, Sydney, Australia, 2002. *Source:* Peter Newman and Jeff Kenworthy, "Greening Urban Transportation," in *State of the World 2007: Our Urban Future: A Worldwatch Institute Report on Progress toward a Sustainable Society* (New York: W. W. Norton, 2007), 72. Reprinted by permission of Worldwatch Institute.

We can also circumvent the urban-form problem by looking at cities where the center is not a zone of concentrated poverty and seeing if the same pattern of increasing energy use with decreasing urbanness holds true there, too. In Newman and Kenworthy's study of Sydney, Australia, an important component of total energy use—private transportation energy use—increased drastically with distance from the urban core (figure 3.2). The authors forestalled the objection that arises in the US case in noting that "it is not income that is driving these patterns, because Sydney—like all Australian cities—declines uniformly in wealth from the center outward." The central and more urban areas consume less energy even though their inhabitants are richer, indicating a genuine urban advantage in resource use. A western European city where the center has remained an area of high status presented a similar pattern when studied. Fuel consumption per capita increases steadily from central Paris outward.[12]

Anyone using total or per capita inventories of energy consumed or of greenhouse gases emitted in cities as compared to less urban parts of the same country must navigate past some other methodological hazards. Studies often simply err, as David Satterthwaite and David Dodman note, in supposing that such high-energy sectors as industry or power generation are somehow essentially "urban" activities or that they are always located in urban areas, to whose totals they can be automatically added. We may also exaggerate the urban share if we hold cities responsible for activities indeed occurring within their bounds that are nonetheless undertaken for eventual consumption by nonresidents. It is not clear, for example, where one should locate the consumption of fuel by jets passing through a city airport, many—perhaps most—of whose passengers will not be residents of that city.[13] In any case, when the data used are clearly and directly comparable they strongly bear out Newman and Kenworthy's assertion of an urban advantage. Less urbanization of the same number of people would give us more emissions, not less.

And yet authors like Newman and Kenworthy who report such results often note how much they run counter to conventional wisdom or what seems to be environmental common sense. Satterthwaite has assembled a collage of quotations, many from prominent and respected government or research institutions, that pinpoint cities as the chief culprits in global climate change. The list of such statements would be easy to enlarge greatly, but what is so often taken for granted, even at such high levels, Satterthwaite points out, is very far from being demonstrably or even probably true. As a guide to action, it is likely to be worse than useless: "blaming cities for greenhouse gas emissions," he writes, "misses the point that well-planned and governed cities are central for delinking high living standards/quality of life from high consumption/greenhouse gas emissions."[14] Many of the First World cities that have quite low per capita emissions by the standards of the countries in which they are located also have unusually high levels of residential satisfaction and liveability.[15]

Satterthwaite, Dodman, and others call attention to one additional error that indiscriminate finger-pointing at energy consumption in cities entails.[16] It disregards the very different levels of energy consumption in First and Third World urban areas (as well as between rich and poor in any city) because the latter contribute far less per capita than the former. As mentioned already, resource use patterns in the First World are the most significant to consider because of their much greater per capita magnitude, and they may also offer clues about what will happen when the poorer countries reach developed-world status. All the same, housing as they do five-sixths of the world's population, the LDCs already consume a notable share of the world's resources, even if a small one in per capita terms, and the effect of urban or rural residence in them today is worth a look, too. It is widely assumed that in developing countries, especially rapidly developing ones such as China and India, city dwellers consume much more energy than do people in the countryside. There is some plausibility to the claim but studies of China have repeatedly found per capita energy consumption to be higher among rural than among urban populations—and not because rural China is notably richer than urban China, for the opposite is notoriously the case. The main reason for the difference lies in the very low efficiency with which the cruder devices used for cooking and heating in rural settings extract usable energy from the (mostly biomass) fuel burned. The partial truth confirmed by the results is that LDC city dwellers do consume a substantially greater quantity of nonrenewable and commercial energy, including electricity, and of end-use energy services. The other side of the story is that much less energy is needed to get this quantity to them, just as a leaky bucket must be filled much higher than a watertight one in order to convey the same amount of water to its destination. Urbanites' higher consumption is heavily offset by the more advanced means that they use to obtain it, and rural frugality (or deprivation, rather, because it may be presumed that it is largely involuntary) is heavily offset by highly inefficient technologies.[17]

Urban populations in the less-developed countries have much greater access to electricity than do rural ones, a strong reason to suppose that their energy consumption is higher. But the difference may not always outweigh a greater overall urban efficiency in energy use, as the evidence from China suggests. And it remains an important question what the relationship would be in a country that has reached the stage that is characteristic of most of the developed world, where urban and rural populations enjoy near-complete access to electric power. In these countries, the electrification of rural areas has usually required a substantial public subsidy to overcome the much higher costs of serving dispersed customers, and the same outcome would require subsidy in the LDCs today.[18] The same length of transmission line will serve many more urban households than rural ones, with smaller losses in power through transmission as well. Rural living spaces are likely to remain larger and less energy efficient. As rural electrification proceeds in the Third World, it

may further imbalance the energy efficiency of dispersed versus concentrated settlement.

Electric power is one of many kinds of networked services that cannot
be furnished to dispersed populations nearly as cheaply as to concentrated ones. Others are telephone connections, roads, and water and
sewer systems. They raise an important question: what proportion of
society's total resources, natural and human, must be expended to provide
a certain level of service to an individual, or how does that proportion
differ according to whether the individual lives in an urban or a rural
setting? For services of this sort, the monetary costs diminish as population density increases, perhaps rising again somewhat at very high densities because of the high cost of land. For many of them, the much higher
costs incurred at very low densities have to be paid for by net transfers
of resources from large cities to other parts of the country.[19] There is
little reason to suppose that the per capita cost in embodied energy for
infrastructural networks will do anything but decline steadily as density
increases or that the same will be true for the cost per person in physical
materials.

The last point brings us into the second major realm of resource
demands. Whether the total stock of matter that is extracted from the
earth, processed for use, and eventually released or discarded into some
other part of the system as waste is increasing or decreasing represents
a fair index of the aggregate human impact on the biosphere. Part of it
consists of energy resources such as coal and oil, part consists of food
and water, and another large chunk consists of the earth materials and
timber used for fashioning and constructing things—notably the built
environment in which people live and work. Is there an urban or a rural
advantage in the magnitude of withdrawals in this last category? Once
more, the first image that arises in the mind's eye threatens to settle the
question before it has really been examined. How can a predominantly
built environment, how in particular can the cluster of tall buildings and
their associated infrastructure that make up a downtown skyline be
anything other than the most material-intensive form of human settlement? Early discussions of the topic, Sabine Barles has noted, "do not
go beyond the condemnation of cities as parasites, importing 'fresh'
materials and exporting wastes."[20] And the condemnation seems not
unreasonable at first. Cities, it might truly be said, consume vastly greater
quantities of material from their hinterlands than do sparsely settled
rural areas. Of course, they do, but that is not exactly the question.
Anyone who has read this far should be able to spot and avoid the

looming mistake before committing it. A high-rise landscape can be highly efficient if it more than offsets its large total use of materials by housing more than a proportionately large number of people. The question to ask is, in what setting, urban or rural, are material demands *per person* greater or, put another way, can a given population be accommodated at a lower total expenditure of material in a concentrated or in a dispersed pattern?

Of the three major resource domains this chapter examines, this is the one about which the least is known. Research has only begun to address the question of urban-rural differences quantitatively. One difficulty lies in accounting for the material already embodied in cities. If we calculate only present-day annual flows, we will drastically undercount the past component of their total consumption and ignore the material used to build the urban landscapes that we now possess. All the same, when this pitfall is avoided and the question is posed properly, the seeming obviousness of an urban penalty evaporates, given the smaller living spaces and the more efficient use in cities of elements of physical infrastructure such as roads and power lines. Per person, Barles observes, "construction of a single-family house indisputably requires more infrastructure and public works than the construction of an apartment building."[21] Concentrating human activities in areas already possessing the basic framework of a built infrastructure and the energy and materials that have been embodied in it is likely to be more efficient in material terms than expansion into areas where much of it has to be built and it is likely to be used less intensively.

The third major natural resource to examine is water. Here, too, cities seem often to be thought of as especially demanding: "The city dweller," writes the British geographer I. G. Simmons, "has always been a high consumer of water." Two other authors observe, "The people and commerce of cities are utterly dependent on water," implying that rural people and their livelihoods somehow are not.[22] On what bases are such judgments grounded and what does the evidence indicate about their soundness?

The first point worth mentioning is that total withdrawals of water from surface flow and aquifers worldwide and in most countries are highest in rural areas because most of it is used to irrigate crops. (Second in magnitude is cooling for industry, particularly for electric power generation, which holds first place in western Europe.) Thus the first impression the data offer is that rural areas are the chief locus of consumption. But to the extent that agriculture is engaged in raising crops to feed the entire population, its water withdrawals cannot properly be charged against rural populations, any more than energy expended—or water withdrawn—in cities to meet the needs of a country in general can. Thus it seems that the first impression must be largely discarded. But to the extent (a large one in the United States and other developed countries) that agriculture is subsidized by a variety of government programs (some of which include the supply of water itself at artificially low prices), the matter takes on a somewhat different cast. In that case, much of the rural use of water is indeed for specifically rural benefit.[23]

A look at areas where water supply is under particular stress only weakens further the case against cities. Some of the world's most arid regions offer the most striking instances of rural water waste. In the driest parts of the United States, much of the water withdrawn for agriculture is used to irrigate crops of very little value and is taken chiefly for the purpose of protecting water rights that would lapse as a result of nonuse. Western desert cities such as Phoenix and Las Vegas make easy targets for accusations of profligate urban water waste. Yet at the dawn of the twenty-first century, agriculture still accounted for fully three-quarters of water withdrawals in the western states, and the percentage was no lower in states as arid and as highly urban as Arizona and Nevada. In the year 2005, indeed, a dizzying 77 percent of the water withdrawn in Arizona went to irrigated agriculture, a sector producing less than 2 percent of the state's gross economic product.[24] So, too, in many of the water-stressed countries of the Middle East, government programs of agricultural protection have long kept and still keep unconscionably large volumes of water flowing into economically marginal farming enterprises even as city dwellers suffer from an inadequate and unreliable supply. Anything that could be called an urban bias in the allocation of so vital a resource is conspicuous by its absence. In recent years, irrigation has accounted for 84 percent of the region's water withdrawal, considerably higher even than the global average of 70 percent. Yet the agricultural sector contributed only 6.3 percent of the region's GDP.[25]

We can also look at the question by limiting our scope to what should be directly comparable between urban and rural populations, their domestic water use, and the upshot in the developed world is that urban residents are probably the more sparing in their consumption. The US Geological Survey publishes figures by county for withdrawals for various purposes, with domestic use one of the categories. Ideally, these data would make it possible to compare per capita consumption among highly urban, highly rural, and intermediate areas. In fact they are of no use because the USGS does not base its figures for self-supplied consumers (which would include rural households reliant on their own wells) on actual metering or other direct measures of withdrawal. Instead, it generates estimates from whatever data it can assemble combined with a set of its own assumptions; thus its numbers cannot furnish the basis for a definite comparison with urban withdrawal levels.[26] But one household-level study conducted in central New York State in 2007 found domestic water withdrawals to increase as population density declined.[27] The results suggest an urban advantage and a rural penalty, which are certainly plausible.

Still more strongly do other studies suggest a severe suburban penalty in water conservation vis-à-vis more urban parts of the same metropolitan areas, another way in which the seemingly "greener" landscape of suburbia compares unfavorably to an urban built environment. One set of researchers has traced the rising prevalence of what they call *suburban drought* in the humid climates of the northeastern United States. Rainfall has not declined and yet the physical supply has become increasingly inadequate to the wants of urban-fringe areas because low-density residential expansion has magnified water use, particularly for watering lawns, and it diminishes groundwater and stream recharge by altering the land cover and making the soil less permeable.[28] A handful of studies report similar findings in western Europe as central-city densities decline and low-density peripheral development proceeds.[29] As large developed-world urban areas become less urban, they become more wasteful of water. In the LDCs, domestic water use is indeed higher in urban than in rural areas. As a matter of human well-being, the difference is all in the cities' favor because lack of sufficient water to meet basic needs— which, as a rule, are fully met already in First World countries—is a chronic problem. Residents of cities, even poor ones not connected to piped systems who rely on vendors, enjoy a substantial advantage in water provision.[30] Economies in use, as in the First World, would be better sought in the other areas for which much larger quantities are withdrawn, such as irrigation and industry. And problems traceable to urbanization as such must be distinguished from ones due more fundamentally to population growth. A recent article analyzes the challenges that "global urban growth" will create for water supply but does not take the step that would be necessary to answer that question fully: separate the effects of population increase itself from those of the spatial arrangement of the population or ask the question of whether a given future population would be better supplied with water if it lived in a more or a less urban pattern. Many of the challenges it foresees, and at least implicitly links to urbanization, may well be the result, rather, of sheer increases in human numbers.[31]

Having looked separately at different classes of natural resources, can we pull them together into one measure that we could use, however crudely, to assess and compare total demands on the resources of the environment? In the 1990s, Mathis Wackernagel and William Rees developed such a measure.[32] Their ecological footprint (EF) technique has subsequently come into wide use. It employs a variety of procedures to translate all resource demands—of an individual, a household, or a larger unit such as a city or a country—into a single number, a land area equivalent required to support them. Some demands, such as the land used for living space or to grow foodstuffs directly consumed, are quite easy to quantify. Others require several steps; the EF component for meat consumption, for instance, includes all land used to grow grain or fodder that the livestock were fed. Fossil fuel energy, which is the single largest item in most developed-world EFs, has been dealt with in two major ways: by calculating either the land area of growing forest that would be needed to absorb the carbon emitted or the land area that would be needed to generate the same amount of energy through such renewable means as wind or solar or biomass power. The total EF value, once obtained, can then be compared to the resource capacity of the world (its total area of productive land) to see whether a particular person's or group's level of consumption could sustainably be practiced by the present world population and not exceed the earth's limits. Calculations usually show that developed-world residents have much higher EFs than those of Third World countries and that their level of consumption, if extended to the world's current 7.0 billion residents, would require the resources of several earths over the long term.

Because of their integrative character, EF calculations have become quite popular as a way of gauging the sustainability of different patterns of resource consumption but a number of authors have pointed out that some of the ways in which they are often used may be doing much to tarnish the environmental image of cities, and quite unjustly.[33] Ecological footprint values are often cited to show that cities have footprints startlingly larger than their own areas, which is quite true, especially in developed countries. Leaving the analysis there may suggest what does not at all follow and is probably the reverse of the truth: that city residents are worse in this regard than are people living in less concentrated settlement forms. Thus one book on cities and the environment begins by observing that "cities have sizeable ecological footprints," given "the amounts of energy, materials, water, food, and other impacts essential for supplying urban populations."[34] They certainly do, but why, one wants to ask, just "urban populations" and not human populations in general? The qualifying adjective gives a highly misleading impression. It should be qualified itself by the observation that within developed-world countries, as we have already seen, average suburban or rural residents require even higher amounts of energy and other resources than do their urban counterparts. The United Nations Population Fund in 2007 noted that "the 'urban footprint' concept . . . is now quite familiar. But many people take it to mean that urban concentration itself is the problem, rather than consumption by a large number of more or less affluent people."[35] The finger of blame, in fact, is pointed not at the culprit or at a mere uninvolved bystander, but worse, at one who has actively intervened to set matters right. Singling out cities for invidious mention distorts the facts of the matter in a way that is likely to make things worse, by promoting less urban and more wasteful patterns of settlement. It can only reinforce the delusion still too common among developed-world residents that their lives will be greener and more sustainable the less urban they are. An urbanized population may consume large quantities of resources; the same population, dispersed across the landscape to suburban or exurban densities, would consume even larger ones.

One can best judge the role of urbanness in resource consumption by comparing values within the same country in per capita terms, by calculating and comparing the average or aggregate footprint values that a given number of people would display if they lived in an urban or in a dispersed pattern. The absolute size of a city's footprint is likely to be large and so too is the proportion it bears to the city's own land area. Precisely because they concentrate people in a small area, cities will necessarily have footprint values much more disproportionate to their own size than rural districts will but the calculation furtively transforms what is really a point in their favor into what looks like the opposite. This proportion, the ratio between a settlement's footprint and the land area it occupies itself, may seem commonsensically to be a valid measure of how excessive its resource consumption is, and it is often used as such, generally in a way that reinforces the stereotype of urban overconsumption.[36]

In fact, the ratio of resource base drawn on to land actually occupied is a disastrously misleading measure because a value that seems high may be produced, when all else is equal, either by a high numerator (high resource demands) or by a low denominator (a compact area of urban settlement). A hypothetical tale of two extreme-case US cities—the best of places, the worst of places, respectively—may make the point clearer. Ecolopolis's population, through its institutions of government, has implemented a heroic array of measures, including an urban growth boundary and central-city redevelopment, in order to diminish its demands for land. It has grown in population by 50 percent but has housed the increase by development confined entirely within its previous boundaries. Sprawlton has also grown in numbers by 50 percent and spatially it has doubled in extent because the additional residents have settled mostly on the fringe in an ever-more dispersed suburban pattern, and densities in the center have declined as a result of abandonment and dereliction. Let us suppose, for simplicity's sake, that per capita resource demand in each city has stayed the same. The ratio measure would pinpoint Ecolopolis as a case of alarmingly unsustainable growth because its total resource demands have gone up by 50 percent and its own area has not changed; in other words, its footprint divided by its own land area is now much larger than before. Sprawlton would appear from this measure to be the model city of the two because by doubling the area it covers, and only raising its total consumption to half again as high as before, it has "succeeded" in substantially reducing the ratio of its own area to the area it draws on. It has done so, of course, by growing outward, whereas Ecolopolis has laudably kept its land area constant. In fact, of course, there is another factor that will do something to offset this difference and that is the numerator of the ratio. Ecolopolis's per capita EF will go down because of the many resource economies of higher-density settlement and Sprawlton's will go up for the same reason. So their different ratios will differ only to the extent that the change in the numerator or in the denominator more than cancels out the other. Suppose that they cancel out entirely. Sprawlton's population has become, on the whole, relatively less urban than it was before, increasing its per capita consumption of land and energy; Ecolopolis's has become in every way more urban and per capita consumption has fallen. Ecolopolis has done everything right and Sprawlton has done everything wrong, and according to the EF ratio there is nothing to choose between them. As a measure, it is like a clock whose hands point to twelve alike at noon and at midnight; it lumps the best and the worst cases together as identical. As long as a city expands its land area faster than it does its demands on other resources, this measure will certify it as progressing. In calculations done at the individual or household level, moving to a large living space—say, a detached house on a one-acre lot—would have the same effect in diluting a given EF value and moving to a small space—an urban apartment—would have the same effect in magnifying one.

Divested of the nonsensical footprint-to-area ratio as an index of urban performance, the EF approach still has much to recommend it. It should, in fact, be used much more extensively than it is, among other things as a means of comparing typical footprints of urban consumers to those living in less-urban settings. To date it has been applied disproportionately more often to such conveniently bounded units as cities than to other areas of human population. As one writer sums the matter up, "The concept has been tremendously useful in shaming cities into better environmental behavior, but comparable studies have yet to be made of rural populations, whose environmental impact per person is much higher than city dwellers."[37] If it easily gives rise to distortions and illusions, the fault is not in the method but in the ways it has been misused. What seem to be "real" entities are more likely to have EF values calculated for them than what do not: cities much more than unincorporated rural areas. All developed-world EF values are high but the ones that are likelier to be calculated and published are those of cities, and although they in fact are lower per capita than ones for less urban areas, their ubiquity in the literature gives just the opposite impression and makes cities seem the chief offenders. "The contrast between ecological footprint and area occupied is most apparent in cities."[38] The comparison does indeed make urban demands more apparent, but chiefly in the sense in which appearance is an antonym for reality. Perhaps an unconscious tendency to think of rural life as self-sufficient and of cities, as Barles observes, as parasites sucking their sustenance from elsewhere underlies this set of misconceptions. But it takes more land and resources to be isolated and to appear and feel independent than to live at a similar standard in cities enjoying economies of scale in the provision of goods and services.

A tendency to personify abstract entities may also play a role in forming the image of cities as insatiable and bullying grabbers of resources. But what the population geographer John R. Weeks and colleagues say about human fertility, when they write that "it is people, not cities, who bear children," applies also to other things, such as consuming resources, that people often speak and think of cities as doing.[39] Cities do not consume resources, only the people and activities within them do, as the people and activities in nonurban settings do, too, at levels that can and should be compared.

It is true, of course, that in certain ways cities are more than mere aggregates. One of their defining features, that of political incorporation, allows them sometimes to act as agents or entities or organized wholes. And the ability to do so can be environmentally beneficial because through their institutions of government, whose potential capacity will increase as the size of the city does, they possess far better means of taking positive action and managing problems, environmental ones in particular, than unincorporated or lightly governed rural districts possess. The metropolitan Boston water system in recent decades has accommodated a growing population without the need of adding new physical sources of supply, largely through effective measures for conservation and efficiency in use made possible by the activities and resources of governmental organizations.[40] And even though large cities such as London, Toronto, and New York all display per capita carbon emissions much lower than the average for their countries, conclusive evidence that their people are already doing far more than their share, these cities have been leaders in aggressive campaigns to reduce their annual releases still further in the coming decades. A notable feature of contemporary environmental politics is the rise of transnational city networks addressing carbon emissions and other challenges, including ICLEI-Local Governments for Sustainability and the World Mayors Council on Climate Change. Among their members, large-city governments are disproportionately numerous and active.[41] No comparable initiatives appear to be emerging from the world's rural or suburban populations—not surprisingly, given their paucity of institutions capable of taking on such tasks. The US environmentalist David Orr speaks disparagingly of "the unmanageability of all cities beyond some scale."[42] It is the activities going on in large cities that may in fact be the most manageable. Yet the very capacity of such urban centers to deal effectively with problems may keep those problems in the public eye and lead people to think of them as exclusively or typically urban ones. Then again, rural characteristics such as high energy demands fostered by automobile dependence may indeed make the relative poverty of political capacity a blessing in disguise, given the ends to which it might be devoted. Two political scientists have found a negative correlation between the degree to which rural dwellers are overrepresented in national legislatures, on the one hand, and the level of gasoline taxes and of support for the Kyoto Protocol to combat global climate change, on the other.[43]

The fact that it is generally the world's most urbanized countries that have the highest per capita levels of consumption offers a final possible ground for the widespread belief in an urban penalty in resource use. The correlation at first seems all but conclusive; the two variables seem to stand in the relation of cause and effect, and when they are plotted on a graph against each other they seem even more obviously so.[44] Yet the linkage is largely an optical illusion, an illustration of the classic logical fallacy of cum hoc, ergo propter hoc (with this, therefore because of this). The fact that the two reliably occur in conjunction at the national level is not by itself proof that one is responsible for the other. To gauge the independent effect of urbanism, we would have to hold population and standard of living constant and compare the overall impacts of a dispersed versus a concentrated settlement pattern, which we could do most reliably within a single country. Urbanization will be culpable only if it tends itself to promote either population growth or per capita consumption. As seen already, it does neither and in fact does the opposite. When we examine the correlation of urbanness and consumption at the intranational scale in the highest-consuming countries, the MDCs, it turns from positive to negative. It is the less urbanized parts of the country that bear by far the heaviest responsibility for the United States' high carbon footprint.

Nothing is more commonly said in discussions of global environmental change, and especially climate change, than that the world's cities urgently need to make themselves and their patterns of consumption more sustainable. Assuredly there is something to the claim, not least because that is where most consumers now live. But whether it is highly urban populations who *most* need to take action is far less clear. The evidence suggests that in the developed world, where consumption patterns are least sustainable, it is suburban and rural residents who most need the example that urban ones are setting for them. If city dwellers can legitimately be singled out and urged to do still more than they are doing already, it is for a quite different reason: possessing such advantages as greater size, clustering, and institutional capacity, they are more likely to be able (and perhaps also willing) to do it.

4
Pollution

If images of urban excess and rural restraint in resource consumption are widespread, ones contrasting the polluted city with the clean, fresh countryside are even more so. The accuracy of the former, we have seen, leaves something to be desired. But surely the latter must be essentially correct. Two intertwined arguments for an inevitable urban penalty appear to be matters of mere common sense. The first is that the essential characteristic of cities, the concentration of people and their activities, must necessarily mean the concentration of their waste and pollution emissions and thus higher levels of human exposure. The case for cities as centers of innovation and economic progress, after all, rests on the density of positive spillovers—mostly of ideas—in an urban setting. Are they not also the places where such negative spillovers as pollution must be most prevalent and hardest to escape, all else being equal? The second argument, moreover, is that all else is not in fact equal, that the activities typical of urban areas are dirtier, more productive of pollution, than those carried on in rural areas. If the appeal to common sense has not silenced all doubt, it can be supplemented by an appeal to common knowledge. Where is pollution self-evidently most severe?

No image more classically encapsulates these assumptions than that of the smoky city—of western Europe during the Industrial Revolution, of China, India, and other rapidly developing countries today. The image, as far as it goes, is quite correct. Residents inhale horrific levels of particulate matter into their lungs in cities where coal is the principal fuel, economic development the chief priority, and protection of health and the environment something for the future to worry about. Accurate and overpowering as it is, the picture seems incompatible with anything but an urban penalty on an extremely important point. How could rural people, above all in today's developing world where the worst smoke pollution is found, not breathe far cleaner air than their urban compatriots?

Table 4.1
Average levels of exposure to PM_{10} airborne particulate matter (μ/m^3), urban and rural populations, northern and southern China.

	Urban exposure	Rural exposure
Northern China	441	676
Southern China	336	746

Source: H.E.S. Mestl et al., "Urban and Rural Exposure to Indoor Air Pollution from Domestic Biomass and Coal Burning Across China," *Science of the Total Environment*, 377 (2007): 24.

But they do not. The data comparing smoke pollution exposure in urban and rural areas flatly refuse to cooperate with these expectations. The figures in table 4.1, assembled for northern and southern China by H. E. S. Mestl and colleagues, make it clear that smoke pollution is first and foremost a rural environmental problem.[1] In Third World countries generally, the dose of airborne particulate matter inhaled annually by the average rural resident exceeds that of the average urbanite. Evidently there is something deeply wrong about the assumptions that made the opposite conclusion seem inescapable. Locating the error that lies hidden somewhere among them may prompt us to rethink the necessity of an urban pollution penalty.

Residents of all inhabited places on earth are subject to smoke or small-particulate air pollution, not just those of cities. It is true on the evidence of our eyesight that smoke pollution is worse in urban than in rural areas—or so it seems. In fact, the error we have been looking for lies hidden here. We exaggerate the lower levels of urban exposure because they are, in several ways, much more visible than the higher levels in rural areas. What we chiefly see, of course, when we look at the air of city and countryside is the outdoor air but that is not the only source of exposure to smoke or, as it turns out, the most important one. Indoor smoke pollution—generated and breathed within the enclosed spaces of home and work—which is hidden from view precisely by occurring indoors, is the more important factor. That it should be more important than outdoor exposure is not a difficult point to grasp once it has been made. As Kirk Smith points out, "Most of the breathing is done where the people spend time and most of people's time is spent indoors." Severe air pollution did not await the onset of urbanization to affect people; it became a part of typical human life in prehistory when people began using the tools of shelter and fire in conjunction with each other.[2] The self-evidence of an urban penalty now crumbles away. Certainly indoor smoke pollution will occur in rural as well as urban dwellings and there seems to be no reason automatically to expect an urban penalty.

In a recent book called *Cities and Nature*, two geographers devote a good deal of attention to the hazards of air pollution occurring in Third World urban slums. Quite correctly, they single out "indoor air pollution that comes from indoor smoke, a result of cooking with open wood or dung fires" for especial attention. It deserves it, they emphasize, because it is simultaneously the most important source of airborne particulate exposure and the least visible and recognized.[3] The reader might object impatiently that what happens indoors and through people's own activities is not pollution or an environmental issue in the words' usual senses. But the distinctions are meaningless when both indoor and outdoor settings contribute to the total exposure and when the indoor component in Third World countries cannot realistically be shrugged off as simply a matter of individual or private choice. Smoke is thickest in the confined indoor spaces where much of it is generated and where it has much less chance to be diluted and dispersed before being breathed in. The tiny soot particles of which it is composed, too small to be screened out by the protective devices of the respiratory tract, accumulate in the lungs and impair their functioning; they and the other chemical components of biomass smoke also cause serious eye damage and may contribute to low birth weights, throat and lung cancer, and heart disease. They occur in such damaging concentrations not because a certain private lifestyle choice has been freely made but because the poor in less-developed countries cannot usually afford electricity or clean fuels such as kerosene or liquefied gas. They must rely on "dirty fuels" that generate abundant smoke—coal, wood, cow dung, and crop residues—and burn them in either open fires or crude stoves that consume the fuel so imperfectly that much of it drifts into the air as particles of soot. How serious a problem is the pollution that such fuels and devices cause can be gauged by expert estimates of the health toll they inflict: between one and two million premature deaths per year along with a heavy additional burden of disease and discomfort.[4]

As such, indoor smoke pollution is an essential and often-omitted part of the picture of Third World environmental conditions today. But in discussing it, the authors of *Cities and Nature* err when they describe it as a "particular type of pollutant *unique* to populations living in shanty cities" (emphasis added).[5] A broadening of their focus would have shown that it is no such thing. The error follows from treating cities as a topic, which leads to a discussion of the environmental problems that occur in them, rather than treating the topic as the relation between urbanness and environmental problems, which would direct attention equally to the same problems in the degrees in which they occur in areas of high and low urbanness. Within cities, high levels of indoor air pollution are indeed much more characteristic of slum areas than of nonslum ones but the evidence makes it clear that high exposure to indoor smoke is most of all characteristic of rural areas of the same countries.

The mistake in question is one form of Whately's "fallacy of objections." This, it will be recalled, involves judging a matter in dispute by looking only at the arguments against one side without considering the arguments for it. In the subspecies that now concerns us, the very same objection—high levels of exposure to smoke—can be made against each of the sides being compared but in fact is raised against only one, as if the other were exempt from it. In David Hackett Fischer's words, this fallacy "renders a special judgment upon a group for a quality which is not special to it." The New England Puritans are routinely summed up as witch hunters, Fischer notes, as if they were distinctive in that regard, but they lived in an era when witch hunting was common outside New England and among non-Puritans as well and possibly even more frequent than it was among them. A sentence Fischer quotes elsewhere from the philosopher Arthur C. Danto illustrates the fallacy again: "It is as though a man were to lament that it is a sad thing to be a Frenchman, for all Frenchmen die."[6] For the sake of a convenient label, I will call it *the "mortal Frenchman" fallacy.* What Danto's invented speaker says makes no sense because all human beings are mortal. It would, if that were possible, make even less than no sense if Frenchmen, though mortal like everyone else, actually had a higher-than-average life expectancy by world standards—as they do. The fallacy occurs when authors point to environmental problems of one sort or another that do indeed occur in cities but without adding that the very same problems also occur outside of them, and sometimes more severely. Thus the erroneous impression arises that the problems are distinctively and characteristically urban ones and would not occur if we did not have cities. There will never be any difficulty in showing that cities and their residents face environmental problems but a valid assessment of what urbanization means environmentally can be based only on a comparison of those problems with the problems, and first of all the same problems, that occur in nonurban settings.

Two questions naturally arise. First, why is indoor pollution worse in rural than urban areas? And second, why do indoor smoke pollution and the rural penalty in air quality receive so much less attention than they clearly merit? In answer to the first, rural populations are likelier than urban ones to rely on the smokiest fuels and the least-efficient devices for using them. Cost is one reason. Rural populations are less able to afford cleaner and more expensive ones, especially with the added cost of distribution to dispersed consumers, nor can they as readily afford better stoves that would release less smoke. In discussing natural resources, we have already seen how the crude combustion devices that prevail in rural areas make their users more profligate consumers of energy than urbanites. Another reason is that locally collected biomass fuels, however dirty when burned, are more feasible fuel staples for individuals and households to depend on in rural areas than in cities. With population scantier and the supply more abundant, they are more capable of meeting rural needs than those of a large and dense population living within a largely built environment. It is estimated that 90 percent of the world's rural population uses solid smoky fuels—biomass or coal—to meet their energy needs but only half of the world's population overall do so.[7]

"By far the world's number-one air pollution problem is indoor air pollution—mainly in rural areas," as David Victor notes.[8] Yet rarely does it appear on lists of the world's severest environmental challenges. Its absence becomes understandable (if not justifiable) on reflection. First of all, occurring indoors, it is concealed; it is literally harder for outside observers to see than the open-air pollution that prevails in full public view. But it is also harder to see for some reasons that are sociological rather than physical. For whom does it most affect? The groups that particularly suffer from it make up something like a composite profile of the least powerful members of the world's population. They are among the poorest residents of poor countries; they are women, who spend the most time indoors close to the main sources of smoke, cooking stoves; they are very young children, also more confined, more exposed, and more physically vulnerable; and finally, they are rural people, whom isolation, distance, and dispersion keep less influential than even equally poor urban populations, less able to get the problems that affect them addressed. Descriptions and photos of urban air pollution in India and China abound in the news media; ones of indoor rural air pollution in the same countries do not. If the attention given to problems were proportioned to their objective seriousness, it would be the other way around and such remedies as the design and distribution of improved and cleaner stoves and the supply of cleaner fuels to rural areas would long since have been made priorities for action.[9]

Some analysts might acknowledge the difference without agreeing that it really reflects real and legitimate urban advantages in the determinants of human well-being. But does the disparity in exposure and response to dirty air represent a case of urban bias? To some degree, surely; but when traced to its sources, much of the urban advantage in air quality hidden behind the illusory urban penalty remains a genuine one. It arises, directly and indirectly, from the characteristics of urban and high-density settlement. And here, as elsewhere, even the greater clout that poor urban populations can wield to have their problems addressed might be considered a legitimate advantage of their location because it facilitates political participation. All the same, the costs of overcoming the rural disadvantage are well worth paying; it remains unconscionable, as Smith and others have argued, given the amount of death and suffering caused by indoor smoke, that it should not have earned the same amount of attention and effort given to problems that fall more lightly on better-connected and more articulate constituencies. In another sense, though, the whole story illustrates a form of antiurban bias at the same time that it does an important urban advantage. The failure to recognize the greater prevalence of rural smoke exposure, to question and qualify the taken-for-granted image of the dirty air of cities further blackens their environmental reputation, hiding an important benefit of urban compared to rural life. In this case as in others, moreover, some optical illusions may make problems in cities look worse than they actually are compared to those elsewhere. Because they occur in populous and often-visited areas, they are exceptionally visible—even (or especially) those such as outdoor smoke and smog that make the city itself less so.

It is true that on the whole outdoor air quality in First World cities is lower than in rural areas and total particulate exposure is higher.[10] It does not follow, though, that deurbanization in the MDCs would in every way be beneficial. To the extent that city dwellers consume resources more sparingly than others, as discussed in chapter 3, their waste emissions will be smaller. "Simply by virtue of its energy efficiency," in Martin Lewis's words, "the city pollutes far less on a per capita basis than does the countryside, given the same living standards."[11] The well-documented developed-world urban advantage in consumption of fossil fuels thus means an urban advantage in lessening greenhouse gas emissions. To the degree that urbanization decreases energy consumption and deurbaniza-

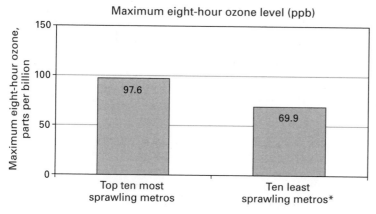

Figure 4.1
Maximum ground-level ozone concentrations in most- and least-sprawling US metropolitan areas. *Note:* *New York City and Jersey City excluded. *Source:* Reid Ewing, Rolf Pendall, and Don Chen, *Measuring Sprawl and Its Impact* (Washington, DC: Smart Growth America, 2002), 21. Reprinted by permission of Smart Growth America.

tion raises it, the former will reduce and the latter will worsen the energy-related emissions that give rise to many other forms of pollution, from localized ozone smog to crossregional movement of acid rain. Models devised by Brian Stone and colleagues indicate that higher densities of settlement in US metropolitan areas would bring lower overall emissions of important atmospheric pollutants by reducing the number of vehicle miles traveled. In US metropolitan areas, the number of days exceeding health standards for ozone pollution increases as the degree of sprawl does (figure 4.1). Deurbanization expands the demand in the northern United States for road pavements kept free of snow and ice in the winter and the harmful application of road salt as the cheapest means of doing so. As in the case of ecological disruption, disadvantages from concentrating harmful activities spatially must be weighed against the advantages of reducing their range and perhaps their total magnitude.[12]

The factor of differential visibility, as illustrated by the neglect of indoor air pollution, can distort the effects of urbanness on environmental quality, keeping a glaring rural penalty all but unnoticed. It is not, though, alone in doing so. Two widely held assumptions also do much to make it seem that cities will necessarily be the most polluted locales anywhere, and the more so the more urban they are. The first is the assumption that manufacturing is essentially an urban activity; the second, that it is a particularly polluting one. Neither assumption is valid.

Habit and usage have coupled the terms *urbanization* and *industrialization* so tightly that it takes a deliberate effort to break them apart but the effort is necessary and worthwhile. The most valid division one can make between the economic sectors characteristic of city and countryside respectively is no longer (if it ever was) between industry in the one and agriculture in the other. All economic activities—agriculture included—would in some ways profit from the easier access to inputs, workers, and customers offered by an urban location. All—industry included—would have to pay more (in land costs, wages, and taxes, for example) for those advantages. The activities that benefit the most by having an urban location or that have to pay the least for it can outbid the rest for space and remain. Those that profit little from being in a city will decentralize to escape its costs. Two examples illustrate some of the trade-offs involved. First, production sectors that are dynamic and rapidly progressing all but require a location within a dense urban network of contacts and activities, whereas ones that are so standardized that they have little to gain from such a location have little to lose from deurbanizing. The latter include routinized forms of manufacturing that are in a late phase of what economists have dubbed the *product cycle*. In the United States, "high tech industries are disproportionately urban, while low-tech industries are disproportionately rural. . . . When high tech industries do locate in rural areas they tend to locate near large cities."[13] Second, activities that can generate large revenues from relatively small workspaces will find the cost of space a negligible consideration, whereas ones that cannot do so will have to pay it close attention. Both points explain why modern agriculture, without being found exclusively in rural areas, is nonetheless usually found there. Though certainly not static, it does not generate most of its own innovations in the place of production; most come to it from outside. Above all, it requires so much land per dollar of output that it cannot compete for space with most other forms of business (and it cannot readily expand upward as others can). As a result, when it does appear in urban areas, it is typically on the periurban fringe. For much the same reasons, natural resource extraction—notably timbering, mining, and quarrying—is a predominantly rural occupation.

These same considerations also make it clear why industry is much less likely to be concentrated in cities than either agriculture or resource extraction is in the countryside. Rural industrialization, and not in the archaic form of cottage crafts either, is now so widespread a phenomenon in the developed and the less-developed worlds that there is no excuse for still thinking of it a contradiction in terms. In the United States today, it covers a wide range of specific activities. They include, of course, the processing of agricultural output (as in the "broiler belt" of rural chicken-packing establishments in the southeastern states). But the United States' other rural industries of fairly long standing, such as textiles, clothing, and furniture, have been joined by many establishments in production lines such as automobile assembly, chemicals, and electrical appliances. More telling than an array of examples is an overall indicator: since the 1990s, manufacturing jobs have represented a larger share of total employment in nonmetropolitan counties in the United States than in metropolitan ones.[14] Though it would be inaccurate today to think of US industry as an essentially rural livelihood, on the evidence, to think of it as an essentially urban one would be even more of a mistake. Nor would either assumption be a safe one to make in other parts of the world. "The growth of rural industry in China," one expert wrote in 2007, "is one of the most dramatic changes that has occurred in the developing world over the past 25 years; rural industrialization has transformed the Chinese countryside."[15]

So even if we suppose that manufacturing is indeed the most polluting of major economic sectors, its economic geography today offers no guarantee that city dwellers will be the only ones exposed to its effects, whether in the workplace or nearby. In cities, a given level of industrial pollution may indeed, all else being equal, impinge on more people than in less densely settled areas. But there, too, and for the same reason, it may confront more insistent and effective opposition. One additional rural advantage that some industries may find is a relative weakness of occupational and environmental regulation. Particularly polluting industries may seek rural safe havens if poverty and a paucity of jobs trump concerns about environmental damage or if the sparseness of population and of effective institutions of government prevents effective interference. A number of Canadian and US researchers have explored the role of rural areas as what they call dumping grounds for noxious facilities, polluting industries included, that are not wanted elsewhere. As Victoria Lawson and colleagues sum the process up, in remote and economically disadvantaged rural areas, "leaders are obliged to loosen environmental, zoning, and labor standards to lure new investments. . . . This economic environment encourages a race to the bottom . . . [and] communities often take whatever investments come along."[16] The same outcome may also arise less because a deliberate relaxation of standards has occurred than because the institutional means to resist such incursions are lacking. What has come to be known as *Cancer Alley* is a patchwork of small towns and countryside stretching for some eighty miles along both banks of the lower Mississippi River south of Baton Rouge and north of New Orleans, an "industrialized rural region," as Barbara Allen describes it, home to a large number of oil refineries and other petrochemical plants. They are, to put it mildly, not popular with their neighbors—many of whom blame the plants for acute and chronic health problems as well as for everyday nuisances of air and water pollution, dead vegetation, unsightly high fences, pipelines, smokestacks, and loud alarms triggered by leaks or accidental releases—yet they have not proved easy to dislodge.[17] Though the exact health impacts of the lower Mississippi chemical corridor industrial cluster are hotly debated, its very existence contradicts the stereotype of cities as the natural habitat of such operations.

In China, too, industrial shifts have greatly deurbanized the burden of pollution. "Rural factories currently emit two-thirds of China's air and water pollution," approximately the same as the rural share of the nation's population. In the eastern-central province of Henan, when other causes are controlled for, rural residence brings a higher burden of industrial pollution exposure than urban residence does.[18] The problem is worsened by lesser institutional capacity, by the lower efficiency of small-scale village enterprises, and by the devolution of responsibility for enforcing national pollution laws, which may clash with higher priorities that officials of small local governments place on economic development and on the tax revenues they gain from polluting firms.[19]

In some other ways, rural areas function as dumping grounds for pollution of urban origin. Such spillover effects can occur by default or by design, although in either case they may, once recognized, be allowed to continue because of the greater power of urban interests. They take many forms: air pollution drifting downwind and sewage and other forms of water pollution carried downstream into rural areas, even weather patterns made stormier when the excess heat developed in urban cores is carried beyond their limits by the prevailing winds.[20] But though such effects are certainly a factor that must be taken into account, it is not clear that they would represent a major subtraction from the urban burden in most places, and it is more than likely that, spatially concentrated and limited as they must be, they cannot represent a major addition to the overall rural one, however heavily they fall on particular localities and populations.

The mental link between industry and pollution and the iconic role of the factory smokestack as a symbol of the latter are almost as established as the association of industry and cities. But manufacturing is highly diverse in its environmental impacts and the implied contrast with equally "typical" rural livelihoods is overblown. Some largely rural forms of resource extraction are as dirty as any form even of heavy industry. Counties in the United States in which coal mining is a major employer display unusually high rates of mortality overall and of deaths from cancer and respiratory diseases. Oil extraction has had devastating effects on the Niger River Delta area of southeastern Nigeria, causing severe contamination of air, water, and land and widespread degradation of the fish and soil resources on which the predominantly rural population depends. As one authority on the region notes, there is more than a chance connection between the severity of the damage that has been allowed to occur and the rural character of the region.[21]

Nor is modern agriculture by any means a clean, pollution-free activity. Their largely nonagricultural economic base, in fact, spares city dwellers close contact with some of the most harmful and most poorly regulated toxic chemicals in the contemporary environment. Farms, like suburban lawns, are only equivocally "green," more so in the literal and visual than in the metaphorical sense. The chemicals now employed in large quantities on lawns and fields include, first and foremost where human health is concerned, pesticides and herbicides. After research in the 1960s unmasked the once-ubiquitous synthetic pesticide DDT as a chemical so long-lived and persistent in the environment that it could bioaccumulate in wildlife species with disastrous results, one of the less fortunate results was a shift to new, more toxic "nonpersistent" pesticides. The much shorter-lived, more reactive compounds that have taken DDT's place are not nearly as medically innocuous for human beings as DDT was. Their adoption satisfied the environmentalist concerns that DDT had raised; the new compounds were far less prone to bioaccumulate in the environment. They were also likelier than their predecessor to break down chemically before reaching fruit and vegetable consumers, an important consideration for developed-world growers and for ones in less-developed countries producing for First World markets. But the cost of avoiding such long-term and wider effects was to intensify the acute ones felt by the farm workers handling pesticides in the field. As Angus Wright observes in a study of toxic exposure among farm workers in Mexico, "The general trends in pesticide use tend to favor nonpersistent chemicals that under proper conditions leave relatively small quantities of residues but that are terribly dangerous to people, animals, and in some cases plants that are exposed to them at or near the time of application." These are the ones "most likely to cause both moderate and severe poisonings within hours after contact. . . . The trend toward the very acutely toxic nonpersistents in Culiacán [Wright's study area] had immediate and tragic consequences for farm workers."[22] As well as acute poisonings, extensive and prolonged contact at lower levels with the post-DDT pesticides has been implicated in an array of human health problems including skin diseases and reproductive and nervous system disorders.[23]

Those most exposed to these effects, farm workers, represent an exceptionally vulnerable and powerless group whose vulnerability has a good deal to do with their rural location. In the United States, pesticide use is particularly intense on the crops worked by migrant seasonal laborers, who are almost entirely lacking in political influence: poor, itinerant, with few roots or connections in their host community, often not fluent in English. The nonurban setting of the work they do, the absence of a dense surrounding population, keeps them and their problems remote from view. "Migrant workers and their flimsy shacks are invisible," in the words of the geographer Yi-Fu Tuan. "One has to drive on side roads and search before one can discern a line of cabins too modest to make a statement on the landscape. The curiosity of an outsider is, in any case, strongly discouraged by 'no trespass' signs and armed guards."[24] Proper procedures for the safe handling of pesticides are difficult to communicate and often ignored by farm owners; regulations to ensure compliance with them are difficult to enforce.[25]

It is not only the farm workers who handle pesticides who feel their effects. Their families are also exposed, as the International Labour Office observes, given the fact that in much of the world "there is no sharp division between living and working conditions in agriculture." Pesticides drift from the fields to nearby workers' dwellings and are carried indoors on workers' clothes.[26] Wind-carried pesticide drift also can impinge on neighbors, a phenomenon that has drawn increasing attention in US states such as California and Florida where intensive agriculture and exurban residential development have been coming into ever-closer contact.[27] In rural areas, the overwhelming political power of large agricultural interests in resisting the enforcement of safety regulations may be impossible to overcome. The land cover of suburbia attracts the same toxic materials. Heavy applications of pesticides and weed killers on lawns create risks of exposure for those applying them and for households into which the substances may be tracked.[28]

The acute exposure of farmworkers to toxic pesticides bears much resemblance to indoor smoke pollution. It, too, though a relatively little recognized problem, is a severe one by world standards and increases in importance as urbanness decreases. Its severity and its geography are more than coincidentally associated. Like indoor smoke pollution, it has a characteristic ecology of its own. First, of course, there is the affinity of agriculture for cheaper rural land. Next, low population density and political powerlessness keep the problem from being as visible as it would be elsewhere. Poverty and the meagerness of economic opportunities can make the trade-off of exposure for employment more appealing than it might be in cities. Weak institutional capacity in largely unincorporated or lightly governed territory reduces the chance that anything effective will be done to address the problem. This bundle of characteristics does much to account for a rural environmental penalty. It is difficult to imagine a recurrent phenomenon such as pesticide drift being accepted as business as usual in more urban, more densely populated, and more institutionally empowered regions of the developed world.

Pesticides are not the only chemicals that modern agriculture releases in large quantities. Runoff of fertilizers, magnified in places by concentrated livestock wastes from large-lot feeding operations, is a major cause of impaired water quality in streams, rivers, lakes, reservoirs, and other surface waters in the United States, along with urban runoff and releases from municipal sewage collection and treatment plants. Of the two, the Environmental Protection Agency identifies agriculture as much the more important source of pollution in inland waters, whereas urban sources contribute a greater share to estuarine and coastal pollution.[29] The point is not that rural areas or agricultural activities are to blame (except perhaps insofar as the latter are maintained by subsidies at a level higher than would otherwise occur) because urban consumers are likewise implicated in the activities used to satisfy their demands. It is, rather, that life—human and nonhuman—in rural agricultural districts is not necessarily freer of serious levels of pollution exposure than life in cities and that efforts to lessen pollution need not be aimed solely cityward, though indeed it is there that they are most likely to be effective because of urban advantages in management.

And indeed urban inputs, which agriculture already surpasses in the aggregate as a pollution source, offer much easier possibilities for improved waste treatment to lower the total pollutant load. Such concentrated point sources as municipal sewage stations can be regulated with much greater ease than the nonpoint sources typical of rural and suburban land uses, those of heavily fertilized cropland, lawns, and household plumbing in particular. Researchers in the Baltimore area have found levels of nitrate inputs to surface streams, flowing eventually into Chesapeake Bay, to be lower in urban than in suburban and rural areas. They judged the finding "counterintuitive," as indeed commonsense environmental antiurbanism would find it, but they offered two reasons to account for it: the higher applications of fertilizer in the less urban areas and human waste inputs from suburban and rural septic tanks, unconnected to main sanitation systems equipped with treatment plants.[30] The example illustrates how cities can turn the spatial concentration of pollution sources that results from urban clustering to the advantage of people and nature, and bears out an observation by Ira Lowry: "It should be much easier to monitor, regulate, and detoxify effluent emissions in an urban than in a rural setting."[31]

Lowry's point is confirmed in another case. Water pollution will impinge most directly on human health through impure drinking water. Contamination by disease-causing microorganisms is one of the most important causes of infectious disease globally and will be discussed in chapter 7 in that connection. But even where other pollutants are concerned, a greater availability of water from protected sources and of improved sanitation operates to the benefit of city dwellers. Large centralized city water systems, whether in the First or Third World, have the means to guard their sources of supply and to monitor them for contaminants more effectively and more cheaply than can small-town and rural dwellers dependent on small supply systems, on wells, or on poorly protected ponds or streams. The point may at first appear a minor one compared to what, it seems, must be the greater pollution of waters in densely settled cities. After all, which would one drink from with less worry, an urban or a rural river? But rephrase the question: which would one drink from with less worry, a well or a tap? The answer is likely to change or it should because urban supplies are usually not drawn directly, immediately, and indiscriminately from wherever water is available. There are many reasons for concern about typical rural sources of supply that must be weighed against ones affecting urban sources and that, on the whole, make their safety the more rather than the less suspect of the two.[32] One is the application of agricultural chemicals, which can be serious pollutants at the local scale when nitrates and pesticides contaminate groundwater used for drinking. Well water at rural study sites in the United States has shown increasing nitrate levels in recent years in association with increased levels of agricultural fertilizer application.[33]

There is no better way of managing the waste products of any human activity than finding a way in which they can become valuable inputs into some other activity. Doing so abolishes the problem of disposal, reduces the waste stream, and profitably expands the stock of resources at the same time. The process is easiest in a highly urban setting. Collecting waste products from widely scattered producers exacts a heavy cost in time and effort. Recycling—the most straightforward form of reuse—is, all else being equal, less feasible for dispersed than for clustered populations, for reasons that range from the longer distances involved to the smaller and less marketable quantities of material to the lack of specialized expertise in small local governments.[34] Jane Jacobs long ago pointed out how the urban characteristics of size and concentration make it easier and cheaper to assemble refuse for processing once a use has been found for it. As the technology of reclaiming and recycling wastes developed, she predicted, cities would become "huge, rich and diverse mines of raw materials. . . . The largest, most prosperous cities will be the richest, and most easily worked, and the most inexhaustible mines."[35] Tomorrow's—and even today's—urban advantages in resource recovery were prefigured by an array of premodern activities concentrated in cities, including ones as small-scale as ragpicking, garbage winnowing, and scrap collection, and including others as elaborate as nineteenth-century municipal "sewage farms," pig farms, and garbage reduction plants that transformed organic urban wastes into inputs for agriculture.[36]

The scavenging of useful materials from refuse remains an important process in Third World cities today, and it serves as a means of livelihood to millions of people. Though it would be inappropriate to idealize an activity that is dirty and dangerous, as Martin Medina notes in his 2007 book *The World's Scavengers*, observers and governments alike have more often gone to the other extreme, accepting a number of disparaging myths that hide the constructive roles that scavenging can play.[37] Apart from its economic value to both scavenger and seller and to resource buyer, it removes garbage that would otherwise harmfully accumulate because of the inadequacies of public sector collection and disposal. Closing the loop between waste emissions and resource extraction, it forms a model for what Medina calls "sustainable production and consumption."[38] As scavenging's contributions have become more evident, governments have begun to shift from a policy of neglect or even of active repression to one of support and encouragement, and bottom-up organizing has enhanced the efficiency of the process and the well-being of those engaged in it. In one of his case studies, of scavenging in Colombia, Medina notes how the country's high level of urbanization, 72 percent of the population at the time he wrote, "translates into a concentration in the generation of wastes, and opportunities for recovery of materials by scavengers." Key steps in realizing this potential urban advantage have included the organization in 1962 of a pioneering scavenger cooperative, which developed into a full-scale, countrywide movement, and a shift in public policy that began with legalization and went on to various measures to promote safety and effectiveness.[39]

For less productive means of disposal, too, urban size and density bring economies of scale and efficiencies of operation. Large municipal incinerators, even if they do not use the process to generate electricity, can burn trash at high temperatures, using advanced equipment under detailed operating regulations, and reduce large volumes of waste to smaller quantities of ash for disposal. They can also destroy or capture most of the toxic materials liberated by combustion. The backyard burning of household trash in the United States offers a stark contrast. It occurs mostly in rural areas, where distance and dispersion make waste disposal by safer means costlier than it is in cities. Plastics are now a large part of the household solid waste stream. They can be processed much more safely in high-temperature incinerators than by low-temperature, open-air burning, which releases dioxins and other toxic compounds at levels that far exceed national safety standards. The dispersed pattern of backyard burning also makes it much more difficult to monitor and regulate than if it occurred in an urban setting.[40] Low land costs, too, make rural sites attractive for refuse disposal by the most space-demanding and often the most environmentally irresponsible means—landfill—whether the material being disposed of is ordinary trash or toxic waste. Pressures for safe design are likely to be weakest, all else being equal, where surrounding populations are thinnest—that is to say, in rural areas.

That rural processes and rural problems are less visible than urban ones of equal magnitude has been a recurrent theme throughout this chapter. Victoria Lawson and colleagues point to the prevalence of a companion phenomenon to rural "dumping grounds," that of rural "unseen grounds."[41] One more manifestation is worth noting. Our knowledge of the amounts and quantities of pollution released must omit much waste that is surreptitiously and illegally dumped. A thinly populated rural setting can be an especially tempting one for illicit disposal, and population density, far from always intensifying pollution, can thus be an important safeguard against it. A report issued in 2009 by the Center for Rural Pennsylvania found illegal trash dumps disproportionately numerous in rural portions of the state, a pattern suggesting that "those who dump trash illegally target municipalities with lower population densities. . . . The lower the number of persons per square mile, the more likely there is a dumpsite." Both law enforcement and ordinary observation are likely to be weaker in such locales. A further reason for the pattern, the report's authors add, may have been the higher cost and lesser availability of legitimate means of disposal in rural areas. "The majority of rural municipalities (68 percent) in the counties surveyed did not have trash collection or curbside recycling. . . . Urban municipalities were almost the mirror image of rural municipalities as 64 percent had both trash collection and curbside recycling."[42]

This book is a critical examination of commonsense assumptions about the environmental disadvantages of cities, not a comprehensive study of urbanness and the environment. In an inventory of the latter kind, it would be highly misleading to stop here, neglecting to catalog major forms of pollution that do display an urban penalty, as many do. Overall conclusions about the net patterns of exposure must be harder to reach than in the area of resource consumption. Whereas much of the demand for natural resources can be divided into a few major categories—those of land, energy, materials, and water—pollution is a much more heterogeneous phenomenon and one much more resistant to generalization. Even so, of all the topics examined in this book, pollution does seem to offer the most examples of an urban penalty in specific cases and the most promising possibility for finding an urban penalty overall. Outdoor particulate pollution of most sorts is higher in urban than in rural areas in the developed and developing worlds, and particularly so in megacities. Levels of most other air pollutants of concern—such as ozone smog, carbon monoxide, volatile organic compounds, and sulfur and nitrogen oxides—seem to follow the same pattern (though not all might, especially in developing countries, if indoor exposure were factored in).[43] These are important problems but so are the ones that have been emphasized in this chapter where an urban advantage is apparent. They have been emphasized here because instances of an urban penalty fit smoothly and unobtrusively into most people's preexisting expectations and ones of an urban advantage do not.

We began with some widely held reasons for believing that pollution problems must necessarily be worse in cities than in rural areas. They are not altogether mistaken but they do not tell the whole story. The activities that release undesirable wastes into the environment are by no means confined to cities, and the very characteristics of urban density and concentration that supposedly must intensify exposure to harmful emissions can also create the means for more effective management of pollution than nonurban areas can undertake. The greater visibility of urban problems also tends to exaggerate the prevalence of an urban penalty. Patterns of what is, moreover, are not patterns of what necessarily must be, and among the possible might-bes, some are more probable than others. Many of the urban advantages in pollution are potential rather than necessary ones but reflective of real and important possibilities. Though higher today in cities than in the countryside, levels of almost all major developed-world air pollutants were also higher in cities in the past than they are today. They have been reduced and can be reduced further in ways that the distinctive capabilities of cities—whether economic or technological ones involving economies of scale or greater institutional capacity for regulating and reducing pollution output or exposure—can only favor.

5

Natural Hazards

In the preceding chapters, we have looked at the three main categories of human impact and have seen that some of the commonest reasons for concern about urbanization have little basis. But if the environment is something human beings can endanger, it is also something that—even in its natural state—can endanger them. To assess the full environmental consequences of urbanization, one must also ask how it affects the safety of individuals and societies from the hazards of their surroundings. Such was already a concern in the discussion of pollution; we turn next to the hazards people face from the forces of nature.

It may be as difficult to generalize here as it was in the case of pollution because natural (or geophysical) hazards are also a highly diverse lot. They span the classical elements of air, fire, earth, and water; they range in duration from the near instantaneous (lightning strikes, earthquakes) to ones like drought that unfold over periods of months to years; some are as localized as landslides, avalanches, and collapsing sinkholes and others as wide-reaching as ocean-basin tsunamis and volcanic eruptions whose ash clouds circle the planet. Some (drought, cold) are the opposite or the absence of others (flood, heat). Why should hazards so different one from another all be affected in the same way by urbanization? Some might be safest to encounter in a megacity and others in the middle of nowhere. And yet the prevalent opinion seems to be that city growth amplifies their dangers. Discussions by recognized authorities of what the world's urbanward trend means for natural hazard losses typically warn of magnified risk: "The impacts caused by natural hazards are increasing as a result of societal changes such as urbanization," says, for example, a summary issued by the US Global Change Research Program.[1]

The claim has won wide acceptance even among experts in the field. Able and knowledgeable critics, most notably the geographer John Cross, have not succeeded in dislodging it from its status as accepted wisdom.[2] But the skeptics have more good arguments on their side and the believers fewer than has generally been recognized. As with other human impacts on the environment, many of the most prevalent reasons given for pessimism about the consequences of urbanization rely too heavily at crucial points on the substitution of common sense for close reasoning or thorough research; they are either logically fallacious or ill-supported by the facts. Too little attention has been paid to the ways in which the defining features of cities can spell greater safety, not greater danger, for their residents.

Let us begin with a thought experiment involving a simple and well-documented hazard: tornadoes in the United States. Consider two ways, rural and urban, in which the households of a county in a tornado-prone region might be distributed. Either they live evenly dispersed across the county's entire area or they all dwell tightly clustered in a single town. If we suppose that tornadoes are frequent and that their paths are random, which arrangement leaves the county's residents more exposed to harm than the other? The correct answer is neither because over time, the number of people who will encounter a twister at close range will average out to the same total in the two scenarios. There will be many strikes on individual dwellings in the first, whereas in the second, the strike that will endanger many people at once (the only one that will do any harm at all) will, in just the same proportion, be a far rarer occurrence. When population is dispersed, a tornado is likely to strike someone. When population is concentrated, a tornado will usually pass everyone by. Viewed from a distance, though, the second, concentrated settlement pattern will probably be judged the more dangerous because a strike on the town will be far more newsworthy than anything occurring in the first scenario; it has a much better chance of exceeding the threshold of damage that will qualify it for attention by the outside world. Thus people will be more likely to hear about it than about smaller events that add up to the same total of loss. The concentrated pattern may then be said to have foolishly invited disaster by having collected people squarely in harm's way, though it could just as truly be said to have collected them, in the vast (but little noticed) majority of cases, safely out of harm's way. It will seem, erroneously, to have increased the total loss from the hazard. In a situation of equal net exposure, an illusion will develop that a concentrated settlement pattern is more dangerous than a scattered one, and an urban penalty will be supposed where none exists. Urbanness, in the form of population density, will appear to have been a key risk factor even though a mere rearrangement of a given number of people, if the hazard is spatially uniform, does not affect total risk at all.

Referring to tornadoes, an editorialist in the *Wall Street Journal* fell into this error when writing, "The depressing incidence of death from these deadly winds is most likely the result of people moving from open country and bunching up in neighborhoods close to where they work."[3] Expressed in more general terms, the same fallacy is perfectly exemplified in a 1996 publication by the United Nations International Decade for Natural Disaster Reduction: "When people are concentrated in a limited area, a natural hazard will have a greater impact than if people are dispersed."[4] If *hazard* were changed to *disaster,* the assertion might at least be technically, if trivially, true: trivially, because the total impact is no greater, merely assorted into fewer and larger events that are more likely to qualify as disasters rather than into many smaller ones. Thus another author is literally correct in saying that urbanization may raise the likelihood of "natural *disasters* through the concentration of people and assets" (emphasis added).[5] What it would not do is raise the overall loss.

The illusion that danger rises with concentration and that safety lies in dispersal is bolstered by a quirk in reasoning apparently endemic to human psychology. Researchers on risk have found that people will judge the frequency and character of a hazard by the known examples of it that they can call to mind. There is no richer source of illusions about cities and natural hazards than this *availability heuristic,* as it is called.[6] The cases that will do the most to form people's impressions of tornado safety will be the best-publicized ones, the ones they have heard the most about, and among them the large but infrequent strikes on urban centers will be disproportionately represented. The best-known and most available single case will be the one involving the largest absolute loss of life, which statistically is apt to be an urban case. In general, the larger cities become, the more people's mental stock of examples will be dominated by the large "disasters" that dominate media reports, creating a greater impression of urban endangerment and rural safety than the facts warrant.

Over time, moreover, as global population grows and urbanization proceeds, cities grow larger in absolute size. Take the following statement: "The growth of cities means an ever-growing potential for larger and larger disasters." It not only sounds plausible; it may well be true. The largest disaster events, measured in absolute losses incurred, may in fact become larger (though if cities offer additional elements of safety, they may not). It is also, however, a blinkered view that emphasizes one aspect of the hazard at the expense of a more meaningful and comprehensive one. Even larger and larger disasters are perfectly, though paradoxically, compatible with greater and greater safety. To be meaningful, losses must be calculated on the basis of all occurrences of a given hazard, not just the most costly individual ones, and they must be calculated as proportional losses: what fraction of a given population, what fraction of its assets did the hazard harm? As population and wealth grow, does a hazard take a larger or smaller percent toll on each? To assess the effects of urbanization, the questions should be, would the loss experienced, in total or by the average person, have been greater or smaller under a different (more or less urban) settlement pattern? Under which pattern will a given number of people and their possessions be safest, all other things being equal? Only then can a genuine urban penalty or advantage vis-à-vis the hazard in question be identified.

Of course, a single disaster involving many people might in some ways be more disruptive and harmful than the same number of deaths occurring in many smaller events spread over a longer period. It also might not be, though. The single most important social unit, the immediate family or household, would be equally liable to disruption in either case. Larger disasters can bring major networks and institutions to a halt but really calamitous consequences from this effect are easier to imagine than to document from actual cases. And larger disasters are also likelier to bring help; moreover, the concentration of loss within a small area can facilitate the distribution of help. If it sounds crude and unfeeling to say that the victims of a large disaster are only as much victims as the same number killed or injured in many smaller events, it is no more so than saying the opposite or than acting as if the opposite were the case—which often seems to be the implied message of the news coverage and disaster response that large events disproportionately evoke.

Back to tornadoes. So far, the thought experiment merely suggests equal net losses in a dispersed and a concentrated settlement pattern, along with a prevalent illusion of greater safety in the former. We have assumed that the danger of a brush with a tornado is no greater in an urban than in a rural setting. But at least one writer of note has argued otherwise. *Tornadoes of the United States* (1953) by Snowden Flora, for a long time the standard work on the subject, asserted that "in a city the chances of surviving a tornado are much less than in open country." In rural areas, "there are few obstacles to the view and a tornado can be seen for miles as it bears down on a farmstead or small community." In a city, "[b]uildings, and sometimes trees, obscure the whirling cloud and city noises deaden its roar. . . . Most cities have rows of brick buildings that are almost sure to collapse from the force of the wind. . . . Streets in the business section of a city are almost sure to be filled by death-dealing debris as a tornado passes over."[7]

Flora merely reasoned his way to this conclusion. He did not test it by comparing the actual levels of urban and rural loss. Data on deaths from tornado strikes in the United States, collected in the National Weather Service's *Storm Events* database, make such a comparison possible. The actual pattern of settlement in the most tornado-prone US states is a complex mosaic of cities, suburbs, exurbs, large and small towns, rural areas of varying population densities, and nearly empty wildlands, vastly less simple than either of our two hypothetical cases. Nonetheless, expectations derived from the model situation can be tested reasonably well in the real-life one. The *Storm Events* entries are coded by county rather than any finer-grained spatial unit and must be analyzed at that level. If there is neither an urban nor a rural penalty, we should find the same proportion of tornado deaths to population in both the most urban and the most rural counties of a given state as in the state overall. The most urban counties are those that meet the Census Bureau's 2000 criteria for identifying urban core counties, ones containing the incorporated central city or cities, with fifty thousand or more residents, of a state's metropolitan areas. The most rural are those lying outside census-defined metropolitan and micropolitan areas altogether.

Between 1990 and 2010, ten states registered at least fifty tornado fatalities. Even if danger were equal, one would have expected in some of these states to see the urban core counties register a somewhat larger and in others a somewhat smaller share of tornado deaths than their proportion of the total population because chance fluctuations in storm paths would be unlikely to even out entirely over so short a period as twenty years. In some states, it turns out, the urban core counties show much lower death rates than the state overall, and in others, they are close or equal to the statewide norm, which in no case do they exceed. The rural totals, in nine of out of the ten states, are higher, sometimes much higher, than chance would produce, and in only one case lower (table 5.1; see appendix A for further details). There were indeed more deaths in urban counties than in rural ones and the most deadly urban tornado took many more lives than did any single one that did not pass through an urban area. But as a percent of the number of residents, tornado deaths were above the average in rural counties and below it in urban ones. The results do not indicate an equal risk in urban and rural

Table 5.1
Tornado deaths in ten US states, 1990–2010

State	Number of deaths	Urban core county percent of state population	Percent of deaths
Tennessee	135	47	22
Alabama	130	43	36
Florida	114	73	20
Georgia	84	22	1
Arkansas	83	30	13
Missouri	74	43	7
Texas	72	68	11
Oklahoma	72	45	41
Kansas	54	49	17
Illinois	50	60	60

	Most-rural county percent of state population	Percent of deaths
Tennessee	11	27
Alabama	12	23
Florida	2	11
Georgia	10	17
Arkansas	28	43
Missouri	16	36
Texas	7	15
Oklahoma	22	6
Kansas	20	37
Illinois	6	12

Source: See appendix A.

areas, still less the urban penalty that Flora predicted, but a greater rural risk. Apparently, living in an urban area offers extra protection from a tornado.

An explanation can be sought in a concept that natural hazards researchers have developed and elaborated: that of differential vulnerability. The total losses inflicted by a dangerous natural agent are not simply a result of physical exposure to the hazard agent—of residing in the path of a tornado or hurricane, for instance, or on a floodplain or a tectonic fault. Losses are the joint product of exposure and of *vulnerability,* the latter term denoting the particular inability of a person or a group "to anticipate, cope with, resist and recover from the impact of a natural hazard."[8] Two persons or groups equally exposed to a hazard will differ radically in the losses they suffer from it if one is much more vulnerable than the other. If hazards researchers have long felt uncomfortable with such terms as *natural hazards* or *natural disasters,* it is less because some of the hazard agents themselves may now have been affected by human action (hurricanes by global climate change, for example) than because what makes a geophysical event into a disaster for people and society is never merely the natural or physical event itself. What generates losses is the way in which exposure to the event combines with human vulnerability, and the latter can never be fully described in the terms of the natural sciences. The crucial differences between those who are more and less vulnerable, even when equally exposed, are differences created by society, not nature. Though the idea that "there is no such thing as a natural disaster" has only recently become familiar to the US public through the contrasting experiences of different groups in Hurricane Katrina, it has for decades been commonplace among hazards researchers.[9]

In the two tornado scenarios, there are a number of good possible reasons for the greater safety or lower vulnerability of urban populations as compared to rural ones. Cities are likelier than unincorporated rural areas to have enacted and enforced building codes that guarantee the strength of dwellings against high winds (illustrating the themes of anticipation and resistance). They are likelier to maintain offices staffed around the clock whose responsibilities include public safety and to have means by which to warn their conveniently clustered residents to seek shelter as a twister approaches (anticipation and coping). Emergency aid after the storm can reach the injured more quickly if they are less dispersed (coping and recovery). Some combination of these factors most likely accounts for the greater deadliness of tornadoes in rural areas. Taken together, they illustrate the advantages provided directly and indirectly by some of the characteristics that define cities: a large total population, its spatial concentration, and the richer institutional capacity that both make possible. It is true that urban areas in the LDCs do not possess the coping abilities of those in the First World but that is the wrong comparison to make. If we are interested, as we are here, in the difference that urbanness makes, the right question to ask is, are urban areas in the LDCs worse off in this regard than rural areas in the same countries? It is an illusion, as we have seen, though a common one, to suppose that urbanization intensifies the net impact of natural hazards by putting large numbers of people in harm's way. But it is very likely that it reduces impact by putting people, much more effectively than a dispersed settlement pattern would, in help's way.

Tornadoes thus illustrate some key themes but far more important for an assessment of the likely overall consequences of urbanization are the four hazards that dwarf all others in their combined damage to life and property worldwide—earthquakes, droughts, floods, and hurricanes— and more important than US experience is that of the less-developed countries that hold five-sixths of the world's population. Of the four, earthquakes offer the best, most-promising test case for the thesis of a necessary urban penalty. The fact that most earthquake deaths are the result of collapsing buildings (quake-triggered landslides account for many of the others) suggests that, as Flora supposed in the tornado case, cities with their dense populations and largely built environment must be an especially dangerous habitat and rural areas an especially safe one. The idea goes back at least to Jean-Jacques Rousseau, whom the great Lisbon earthquake of 1755 inspired to come up with some pioneering speculations on the social causes of natural disasters; he saw it as a warning not to crowd people into cities and not to build upward to accommodate them.[10] On the Internet, what calls itself "the world's leading Q&A site" answers the question, "Why is it safer to live in a rural area during an earthquake?" (notice that the greater safety of rural areas is simply taken for granted): "There is less chance of buildings collapsing on you and your possessions."[11] The seismologists Susan Elizabeth Hough and Roger G. Bilham have recently articulated the case for an urban penalty in a chapter of their book *After the Earth Quakes* (2006) entitled "Demonic Demographics," asserting the rising potential for catastrophic quakes as population, especially in the developing world, shifts to cities.[12]

Hough and Bilham candidly acknowledge, however, that to date the long-term pattern in actual losses points the other way. Over the past four hundred years, their figures show, as the urban share of the world's population has risen and as the largest cities have grown ever larger, the global earthquake-related death rate has steadily diminished. The chance that a person would die in an earthquake during the nineteenth and twentieth centuries was only a third of what it was in the less urbanized world of the seventeenth and eighteenth centuries. It may be, as Hough and Bilham argue, that the data series is too short to capture an escalating risk of rare but catastrophic events and that in time, an urban penalty now latent will make itself felt. Yet it is also possible, though they dismiss the idea as absurd, that the trend they have discovered is a real and meaningful one. One study directly compares urban and rural risk in a single time period and reaches conclusions supporting the thesis of an urban advantage. Examining data from 1980 to 2001, Eugenio Gutiérrez and colleagues found that among the total population exposed to earthquakes of a given magnitude, the percentage killed declined sharply as the population density increased. In their words, "there is a clear trend that indicates higher mortality in less populated zones" and "a pattern emerges of highly vulnerable rural and semirural areas," especially in poorer countries where hazard mortality is highest.[13] Superior building quality and greater speed and effectiveness of postquake aid in urban areas are among the likeliest reasons for the urban advantage.

Hough and Bilham offer an additional argument for concern about natural disaster in a rapidly urbanizing world. The sites of the world's largest cities, they write, coincide with zones of unusually high seismic instability and earthquake potential.[14] But the argument only holds true if the people living in the cities in question would have been less exposed living elsewhere. The supposed increase in exposure from urbanization can be an optical illusion when one has neglected the departure of a person *from* an unstable rural location and counted only the addition of that same migrant *to* an unstable urban one. Much of the land area of countries such as Japan, Turkey, Armenia, Iran, and Peru is highly prone to earthquakes, and almost all of the shift of population to their earthquake-prone large cities takes place within the country itself, in other words, from areas that may be no less quake-prone. Of the world's two most populous countries, China does not have its largest urban centers located in its most earthquake-prone regions, nor on the whole does India.[15] And even to treat the risk in the two locations as equal on the basis of equal exposure neglects the question of whether a city or a rural area, especially in a developing country, is the more dangerous place to encounter a hazard of a given physical magnitude because again, greater exposure, if it exists, only means greater danger if it is not offset by diminished vulnerability. The one study to control for exposure, that of Gutiérrez et al., suggests that urban populations, all else being equal, are indeed less vulnerable to earthquakes than rural ones. If the results contradict some widespread assumptions, they bear out a more venerable bit of folk wisdom: that there is safety in numbers.

Others, broadening the argument, have claimed that the sites of the world's largest cities are disproportionately exposed to severe natural hazards generally, and particularly to hurricanes and tsunamis, given the coastal location of the majority of megacities.[16] The growth of these centers, then, is supposedly concentrating the world's inhabitants in the path of major hazards. This framing of the argument also fails to treat an essentially comparative question in a comparative way, committing the "mortal Frenchman" fallacy that we have encountered before. ("It is a sad thing to be a Frenchman, for all Frenchmen die.") Coastal areas do house more than their share of the world's urban population but they also house more than their share of its rural population. Disproportionate coastal exposure is therefore no less a characteristic of nonurban than of urban populations, though the most thorough recent study indicates that it is indeed somewhat greater for the latter.[17] But again, the argument only holds if greater exposure is not offset by reduced vulnerability in an urban setting. If urban populations on the whole live closer to water and if simple proximity to water necessarily means greater loss from its hazards, the most direct and everyday hazard of such proximity—accidental drowning—should be more common among urban than among rural populations. Evidence from First and Third World settings shows emphatically that the opposite is the case, the result, no doubt, of the higher vulnerability in many ways of low-density rural populations.[18]

And even if we disregard differences in vulnerability, the argument is only valid if it holds true for net exposure to all hazards combined. But a given location may be highly exposed to one hazard or set of hazards but very little to another, and again the city may be less exposed overall than whatever nonurban location a given city dweller would be occupying instead. Some hazard-prone settings are particularly attractive to agriculture and other rural livelihoods: floodplains and volcanic soils for their fertility and coastal locations for fishing grounds and for their accessibility to outside markets. Coastal cities are highly exposed, of course, to tsunamis and coastal storms but much more in some parts of the world than in others. They are also, on the whole, less exposed than inland locations are to deadly extremes of cold and heat, to drought, and to tornadoes and some are and some are not in more earthquake-prone regions than other parts of their countries. The largest city in the United States, New York, though located on the coast, suffers relatively little from the major hazards affecting other parts of the country: extremes of temperature, floods, hurricanes (October 2012 notwithstanding), drought, or earthquakes. The more heavily urbanized coastline of South America, the Atlantic, which holds all of the continent's megacities, experiences few coastal storms and far fewer earthquakes than the less urbanized Pacific littoral does. The cities of sub-Saharan Africa are exposed to few major natural hazards and their inhabitants, by the mere fact of urban residence, are buffered from the effects of the region's worst geophysical threat, drought.

Nowhere is the role of vulnerability in mediating between a natural event and its human impacts more striking than in the case of drought. A shortfall in precipitation is not the only weather hazard that can trigger a famine—in premodern Europe, indeed, unusually cool and wet weather was a more common precursor of mass hunger—but it is the one most commonly linked to famines today.[19] Deaths ascribed to drought are largely deaths from famine or hunger-related disease following crop failures. Liberally interpreted, they far outnumber those blamed on all other natural hazards put together.[20] But a too-liberal interpretation can greatly exaggerate the effects of the weather as such because the relations between drought and famine, as with any natural hazard and its human consequences, are not ones of a sole and simple cause producing an invariable effect. Not all famines by any means result from severe weather anomalies, nor do such anomalies necessarily cause famine. Even when they occur, they lead to large-scale starvation or to hunger-enhanced death from other causes only in conjunction with poverty and with such political pathologies as government collapse or inaction, dictatorship, or civil war.[21] To say this is only to repeat what applies to all natural hazards: that their impact is the product of exposure and vulnerability rather than of exposure alone. Still, if droughts are no longer (if they ever were) strictly sufficient causes of famines, they often enough represent necessary ones without which a particular famine, for all the vulnerability of the population involved, would not have occurred.

One plausible mental model of their effects is true enough as far as it goes but dangerously apt to mislead. Because city dwellers are sustained only by whatever food rural areas can produce above and beyond their own needs, it seems to follow that they will be the first to suffer when harvests fail. But drought and famine fall as a rule most heavily on rural populations, and on reflection the urban advantage is not difficult to understand. It occurs for the same reason that makes a much less serious weather hazard, frost, almost exclusively a rural one. In the less-developed countries, the ones most vulnerable to drought, rural livelihoods depend in large measure on the harvest.[22] Crop failure means the loss of the portion of a year's cash income it represented, plus whatever part of the crop was grown for a household's own consumption. Even landless laborers who have no crops of their own will have no employment if those of landowners have failed. Smallholders may enter the class of landless laborers if they have to sell their land to stay alive. It is not surprising that in times of famine, rural migration to cities, whether permanently or in search of temporary employment or aid, has been the rule throughout history, flows the other way are the rare exception.[23]

None of this is meant to deny that drought-induced harvest failures can fall quite heavily, even calamitously, on urban populations as well. They impose sharply higher prices for food on people whose meager buying power is already stretched thin. Much hardship will result but it is less likely than in rural areas to endanger bare survival. The very fact of price increases will bring mitigation in the form of imports to urban markets drawn from zones where food is cheaper. Emergency relief is also likely to reach city dwellers more readily, partly because of the inherent advantages of cities (as seen already with tornadoes) for assisting a concentrated rather than a dispersed population and partly also because of the greater political influence they exercise. Some who emphasize the latter factor cite it as an example of urban bias in developing countries. In times of crisis, urban populations may appropriate emergency aid even if the need is greater elsewhere. They can press their demands on the national authorities more effectively than rural ones can. One authority on famine in sub-Saharan Africa speaks of "the fact that city dwellers have been immune from famine" as testimony to their greater influence with national decision makers.[24] Undoubtedly such biases exist. There is a real danger of mistaking their results for genuine urban advantages. Yet the opposite mistake is no less possible. Where famine is concerned, to ascribe the difference between rural and urban impacts entirely to urban bias is to ignore some genuine urban advantages in relief provision and a genuine rural disadvantage of inherently greater vulnerability to drought. Because such bias exists does not mean that all differences in outcomes are its product.

Too much water, of course, can be a hazard just as too little can. Hurricane Katrina of 2005 and the flooding that accompanied it affected urban and rural populations. If Katrina appears at first glance to present a clear illustration of an urban penalty, on closer inspection it offers one more instance of ways in which illusions about urban vulnerability arise. Debra Lyn Bassett observes that in 2005 and thereafter "the focus of media attention was unmistakably New Orleans; the plight of those who lived in the urban area received massive, ongoing media attention, whereas the plight of those who lived in remote rural areas of Mississippi and Louisiana did not—despite the equal devastation experienced by both areas."[25] Disproportionate attention to the larger event has again obscured the key question: in which setting would an individual have been safer? In the city, the answer would have been, if the economies of scale in protecting a concentrated population had been taken advantage of and the levees protecting New Orleans had been properly maintained, as they could have been.[26] No comparable system of protective works could ever have feasibly protected the dispersed populations of low-lying rural districts. "It was not Katrina that caused the flooding," as two geographers observe, "but shoddy engineering, poor design and inadequate funding of vital public works"—works that could only have been built in the first place because of the advantage of urban clustering.[27]

Does Katrina illustrate urban bias? Certainly, as Bassett argues, the unbalanced coverage of the storm and its legacy, heavily weighted toward New Orleans, scanted rural problems and may have channeled aid disproportionately cityward. In another sense, though, the same inequality in attention represented what could better be termed a prevailing antiurban bias. It played up to and reinforced a deep-seated association of cities with disaster. It remains an open question as to what the outcomes would have been if only legitimate advantages of urban and rural areas had come into play. The greater feasible extent and capacity of levees and other protective works certainly gives densely peopled cities an advantage, all else being equal, and an antiurban bias in the United States—arguably best classified as a suburban-biased society—can be held accountable for the failure to maintain and improve them. Cities, especially large cities, also have the potential—sadly underrealized in the New Orleans case but still greater than rural areas possess—for advance emergency planning and for crisis response in the existence of a sizeable municipal government. And New Orleans had urban resources for coping such as large protected shelters (e.g., the Superdome) and the option of vertical evacuation to upper floors of many buildings. Nor, once again, should it be forgotten that poverty—the root cause of much of the devastation in Katrina—tends to be concentrated in the central and most urban areas of US cities but not in many other countries, suggesting that it, and not the quality of urbanness as such, was the reason for much of the loss and suffering in New Orleans.

No one trying to assess the global impact of severe storms and floods, though, can afford to focus on cases from the developed world. Losses of life in hurricanes or tropical cyclones, as in most other natural hazards, are far higher in Third World countries than in First World ones, and the best evidence of urban-rural disparities in safety must be sought there. It is a remarkable and telling fact that none of the world's deadliest coastal storms in the past half-century chiefly affected urban populations—

for all that their larger numbers of people would tend to make them disproportionately prominent on lists of the largest disasters.[28] It may be, of course, as Hough and Bilham argue in regard to earthquakes, that enough time has not yet elapsed to reveal a latent urban penalty. It is at least as consistent with the evidence that such factors as better shelter and better warning and emergency aid systems create a genuine urban advantage. A United Nations report published in 2004 found that proportional losses of life among populations exposed to floods and tropical cyclones alike increased as the population became less dense and less urban. An authority on natural hazards in Bangladesh, the country in the world most exposed to both hazards, observes flatly that "rural areas . . . bear a disproportionate share of flood losses."[29]

Some researchers who do not assert that hazard vulnerability increases with urbanization per se still argue that "rapid urbanization" is likely to have that effect.[30] Yet as David Satterthwaite has noted, some of the fastest-growing cities of the late twentieth century are located in the US South and West, and they cannot be considered notably vulnerable to natural hazards.[31] They are safe because they are rich and well governed. Fast-growing Third World cities are vulnerable less because they are cities or even because they are fast growing than because they are poor in resources and institutional capacity. Their greater vulnerability thus has nothing to do specifically with urbanness. When combined with poverty, either any rapid change of settlement location or rapid growth of population in situ probably does exacerbate vulnerability to hazards. Because cities happen at present to be the most rapidly growing locales (something that in itself suggests that they must possess many genuine advantages), in practice they are where this phenomenon will be most visible and most operative. But a moment's thought suggests that rapid dispersion of population *from* cities, rapid natural growth in rural areas, or rapid resettlement from one rural area to another would be just as likely to be problematic and probably more so given the many advantages in coping that cities possess. Thus, though the point as often made asserts a distinctively urban penalty, on closer examination it boils down to the factors of poverty and rapid settlement change. Everything specifically urban in it has evaporated.

A second argument, a closely related one, is that rapid urban growth in the developing world generates low-income slums located on such dangerously hazard-exposed areas as floodplains and steep, unstable slopes, which are the only sites available to them.[32] The situation is unquestionably a frequent one but any conclusions about urbanization drawn immediately from it are flawed by yet another example of the "mortal Frenchman" fallacy. The additional questions that need to be asked are, do poor urban dwellers occupy unsafe sites proportionately more than poor rural populations do, and if so, is it to a degree not matched by other advantages of an urban setting that reduce vulnerability? To answer the first question, the urban poor must be compared with a comparable group, the rural poor. An unstated premise of the argument is that because population density is (by this book's very definition) higher in cities, rural populations ipso facto have much more room available to them for dwelling space and can choose safer locations. But the image of abundant land and free choice of dwelling space in rural areas that seems to follow from their much lower population density contains a great deal of illusion. Land in most parts of the rural Third World is concentrated in the hands of large owners or the state. Landless laborers and holders of extremely small plots in the agricultural sector of developing countries make up a share of the rural populations of Third World countries of about the same order of magnitude as slum dwellers do of their urban populations. In Bangladesh, about 30 percent of the rural population is classified as entirely landless and another 30 percent as owning only a tiny plot. Mass organizations of the rural landless have become a major political force in Brazil in recent decades.[33] It can hardly be supposed that such populations enjoy abundant freedom to choose where to reside. The only spaces readily available may be as prone to such hazards as flooding and slope failure as those occupied by the poorest urban dwellers living in city slums, with few safe and desirable sites left free for the taking. Studies of hurricanes, floods, and landslides in the rural Third World point to the pressures that force the poor and landless onto precisely the kind of dangerous dwelling sites that their urban counterparts so often have to occupy.[34] The fallacy consists of describing a process that occurs in cities as if it occurs only there.

Finally, it has been argued that an urban penalty is likely because cities alter the land cover more intensively than do other forms of settlement, intensifying natural hazards by disrupting the delicate preexisting balance of nature.[35] If the argument, focusing on the built-environment element in the definition of urbanness, holds for any hazard, it should be for flash floods. They increase in occurrence and strength as intense modification of the land surface by urban cover displaces more permeable surfaces by the impermeable ones of buildings and pavement. For this reason, many scholars point to flash floods as a particularly urban problem and one of increasing menace as cities grow.[36] If the argument is valid, we should expect to find an urban penalty already apparent in data from recent years. Data on flash flood deaths in the United States, again drawn from the *Storm Events* database, can provide a simple but crucial test of the claim and of the larger one that underlies it. In the United States, rural residents are surely much freer in their choice of dwelling sites than are those in the Third World, so that here, if anywhere, the simple contrast in population density should translate into a rural advantage in safety. The concentration of poverty in US central cities should mean greater relative vulnerability than in highly urban settings in other countries. Likewise, the paving of the soil, the substitution of impermeable for permeable land cover, ought to have proceeded further than in the cities of the LDCs. Yet the data again indicate a rural rather than an urban penalty. The share of flash-flood deaths in highly rural counties in the most affected states exceeds their share of the population, whereas the opposite is the case in urban core counties (see appendix A for details). The reasons for the urban advantage could include a greater availability or feasibility of warnings, land-use planning, and emergency assistance; it might stem simply from such features of the built environment as paving, gutters, and storm sewers that rapidly remove excess water.

The argument that cities will be more hazard prone because they disrupt their natural environments more—has enough substance to give it an illusion of validity. It is indeed generally true that when nature is disrupted, harm results. But that is a regularity more of linguistic usage than of environmental science. It is true because we reserve the word *disruption* for cases in which alteration of the environment causes harm. Alterations can also be for the better, though, and when they are, we will speak of them instead as improvements. If nature has its hazards, then making it less "natural" will not necessarily make it more dangerous and may well make it safer. If some of the ways in which cities modify the environment enhance the physical intensity of hazards to which their residents are exposed, others reduce it. To estimate their net effect without taking both processes into account is to commit Mill's "fallacy of over-looking." We have seen already that cities can be protected better from floods and storm surges by levees and floodwalls than rural areas can. When the land surface is parched by drought, who is safer from fire: an urban or a rural resident? It is surely the former *because* the land cover is more altered in the urban setting. Disasters in cities, past and present, draw a disproportionate share of attention and far more people know about the Great Chicago Fire of 1871 than about the Peshtigo Fire that ravaged the forests, farms, and villages of the Green Bay district of

Wisconsin and Michigan during the same week. Yet it was the second, rural blaze that claimed more lives in total and a larger share of the people exposed because their situation made them more vulnerable in many ways than were the residents of Chicago. The Peshtigo fire originated chiefly in rural land-cover patterns and land-use practices (notably the accumulation of dead logging debris). Nonetheless, the subsequent government response focused on the enactment of fire safety measures in the towns of the devastated area, illustrating a natural tendency to exploit the greater governance possibilities offered by incorporated municipalities as a way of doing *something*, however irrelevant.[37] Cities today are much more fireproof than they were in the days of Mrs. O'Leary's cow or the largely wooden San Francisco of 1906. It is population dispersion from urban cores where density has been steadily declining into the exurban fringe, a process not of urbanization but of deurbanization, that has increased wildfire losses in the developed world. Lightning, which sometimes ignites wildfires, is a direct hazard to human life in its own right that diminishes in its dangerousness in the largely built environment of a city. The only recorded death from a lightning strike in Manhattan in the past half-century occurred in Central Park.[38]

It is worth repeating that natural hazards are so varied in character that it would hardly be likely that urbanization would bear the same relations to them all. One process, the effect of city growth in intensifying summer heat, does offer a highly plausible case for an urban penalty. Buildings and pavements trap, hold, and reradiate heat and block the free flow of breezes that could disperse it. As a result, urban temperatures typically exceed those found in the surrounding countryside by a margin that varies with city size, city form, season, and latitude. Extreme heat in summer as magnified in urban areas can increase mortality as well as discomfort. Deaths attributed to the European heat wave of 2003 were heavily concentrated in urban populations. In the United States, rates of heat mortality in cities exceed those found in suburban and rural areas.[39]

The phenomenon of the urban heat island is a real and important one and of particular concern given the rising temperatures expected with global climate change. But it is most unlikely by itself to offset the apparent urban advantage in hazards generally, and it is itself subject to some important qualifications. Deaths officially attributed to extreme cold in the United States are double those from extreme heat.[40] Whether or not the figures capture the full toll from either hazard, the heat island effect must prevent some deaths in winter, when a pronounced difference also exists between urban and surrounding rural temperatures, as well as causing some in the hot season. There are, moreover, many possibilities for mitigating the urban heat island, some of which cities are particularly well-equipped to undertake and which protect against the hazards of natural heat waves as well as the increase due to urbanization. They include air-conditioning, "green roofs," and emergency monitoring and sheltering of vulnerable populations. And the fact that episodes of heat stress have much different effects on different groups shows that the simple occurrence of higher temperatures is anything but the sole determinant of heat deaths. So does the fact that the impact of heat on mortality is much less in lower-latitude US cities than in higher-latitude ones.[41] Vulnerability is a crucial element that the simple temperature difference between urban and rural areas does not encompass.

News coverage of some striking events—Hurricane Katrina in 2005, Hurricane Sandy in 2012, and no doubt many more to come—conveys a powerful impression of an urban penalty in safety from hazards. But because large cities, all else being equal, experience larger absolute losses and the larger share of attention that they bring does not mean that their people and property would be safer if they were more spread out—or even as safe, given the notable urban advantages in protective measures before and during the event and in relief and reconstruction following it. Only systematic analysis can settle the question, and what has been done does not bear out what the images of urban devastation suggest. A pioneering study by Kevin Borden and Suan Cutter of the spatial distribution of recorded hazard mortality in the United States, 1970–2004, found rates to be disproportionately high in rural counties, particularly in the South, whereas urban counties in general and the highly urbanized Northeast showed lower-than-average rates.[42]

These results are suggestive and not conclusive but what they suggest is plain enough and in harmony with most of the other evidence reviewed in this chapter: that commonsense antiurbanism errs in seeing increasing levels of urbanness as increasing the dangers of natural hazards. Cities may in fact be the best, not the worst, places to encounter most of the forces of nature. Calls for making them safer often seem to overlook the degree to which cities may be safer already because of the very characteristics that make them cities. Making them less like cities in order to make them still safer might well have the opposite effect. And trying above all to have fewer and smaller "disasters" by dispersing population might well mean less safety and more loss.

6

Technological Hazards

It does, after all, make sense that because their environments have been largely reshaped by people, cities might often be safer refuges from the dangers of nature than more natural settings can be. But the same argument seems to give away the game where human-made risks are concerned. These would appear inescapably more prevalent to the degree that one's surroundings themselves are human-made, that what Cicero called the "second nature" people have created predominates most plainly over the "first nature" from which they have fashioned it.[1] In other words, the hazards of technology, to give them that name, should be more serious in a built than in a natural environment, in an urban than in a rural setting. That when "things bite back," it is ordinarily a city dweller we would expect to find clamped in their jaws seems as safe an assumption as one could make.[2] Are not cities themselves largely artifacts of engineering? Don't their residents live in close proximity to many more devices and to the risks that they pose, and doesn't any single hazardous technology menace more people in cities than it would elsewhere?

Yet on closer inspection, things are not so simple. One can answer "yes" to each of the questions just posed without thereby granting that the average urbanite suffers more harm from technology than a rural counterpart does, or even as much. In fact, many of the most important technological risks in the world are significantly less dangerous to urban than to rural populations. Though it would take a great deal of research to establish whether an overall urban advantage exists, the commonsense reasons for assuming the contrary do not stand up to scrutiny. Distorted perceptions of risks—above all, the exaggeration of the large and spectacular and the neglect of the everyday—obscure some significant urban advantages behind the illusion of a necessary urban penalty.[3]

Patterns of motor vehicle accidents make a good starting point here as did those of tornadoes for natural hazards—better, indeed, because they are a major risk by world standards in their own right. Judged by the number of lives they claim annually, motor vehicle accidents are today's leading technological hazard in almost every country and globally. Is road traffic safer in an urban or a rural setting? The latter, one might first suppose. Because density is their chief defining feature, cities spell congestion. Where the most drivers are sharing or disputing the roads with one another, surely there is more risk of collisions. "Urban areas are the main locus of traffic accidents," a United Nations report says, "given the concentration there of vehicles, transport infrastructure, and people." To support the claim, it adds, "in Latin America, about half of all traffic accidents take place in the region's cities."[4]

Yet if "the main locus of traffic accidents" means the place where they are most apt to occur, then the statistic cited, which on the face of it testifies to an urban penalty, suggests in fact an urban advantage. Also according to UN data, cities hold about three-quarters of Latin America's population (and likely more than that share of its motor vehicles); it follows that if they account for only half of the region's accidents, they are probably unusually safe and rural areas unusually dangerous. To conclude otherwise is to commit the simple fallacy of conflating total impacts with proportional ones. If the toll of loss is not corrected for the volume of traffic involved, it says nothing about whether an urban or a rural setting is the safer one for a given individual to be in.

Traffic safety statistics from developed countries, where the data are most reliable, indeed turn on its head the easy assumption that cities are more beset with technological risk than rural areas. Calculations per vehicle mile traveled reveal a markedly higher incidence of accidents in rural than in urban areas, plus a higher rate per accident of severe injuries and fatalities (figure 6.1). The death rate on rural roads in the United States per mile traveled is two and a half times the rate in cities. Rural areas, as defined by traffic safety analysts, contain 23 percent of the national population but witness 56 percent of fatal crashes.[5] Studies from other First World countries concur in depicting an urban advantage in road safety.[6]

Anything that seems paradoxical about this result quickly evaporates on a closer look at the reasons for it. The very concentration that is one of the hallmarks of cities, if superficially it seems to enhance the likelihood of accidents, operates more strongly still on the side of greater safety. Driving is better governed in cities than elsewhere precisely because activities there are more crowded; it is most ungoverned and as a result most dangerous in rural areas. Key risk factors weaken as population

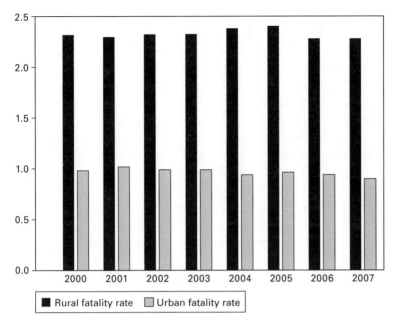

Figure 6.1
Rural and urban traffic fatality rates per 100 million vehicle miles in the United States, 2000–2007. *Source:* Federal Highway Administration, accessed from safety.fhwa.dot.gov/.../fhwasa10012/chap_2.cfm.

density rises and as characteristically urban conditions appear. Driving speeds fall partly because of lower speed limits and better law enforcement and partly because congestion and other obstacles force them to. Road conditions are safer, with fewer dangerous curves and better lighting at night. As well as restraining drivers better, urbanization makes help more promptly available when accidents do occur. On average, it takes emergency personnel in the United States nineteen minutes to reach the scene of a rural crash compared to seven for an urban one; it takes an average injury victim fifty-three minutes to reach a hospital in the former case, thirty-six in the latter.[7] An additional factor widens the urban-rural gap in safety still further. Residents of rural areas in the developed world, where automobile use is almost ubiquitous, are highly dependent on private motor vehicles, and suburbanites more so than urbanites, who, with many of their destinations conveniently close at hand, can perform many errands on foot or by public transportation and have shorter distances to cover when they do drive. Not only is driving riskier per mile traveled on rural roads but residents of rural areas also drive more miles.

In the United States, as William H. Lucy of the University of Virginia has established, the net urban advantage is so large that it reverses the taken-for-granted contrast between dangerous cities and safe suburbs and rural areas. What Lucy defined as "the risk of leaving home," which consists mainly of motor vehicle fatalities and homicide by strangers, is higher overall in the suburban and exurban zones of US metropolitan areas than in the high-density urban core, and it is highest of all in rural areas because the death toll is dominated by traffic accidents. Yet, as Lucy notes, the perceptions have yet to catch up with the reality. He cites a poll taken by the *Atlanta Journal-Constitution* in 2002. Asked which location they thought the safest to live in, 46 percent of the respondents answered "rural," 33 percent "suburbs," and 21 percent "city."[8] Deurbanization in the form of suburban and exurban sprawl, motivated in part by such perceptions, raises the death and injury toll from accidents.[9]

Misunderstandings of travel risk persist when the focus shifts from those of horizontal to those of vertical movement. The elevator is the most distinctively urban of all transportation technologies because the needs it meets arise from the benefits of concentration and a corresponding high value of land that induces upward movement rather than outward expansion. Elevators, especially in the tallest buildings, doubtless play their part in shaping the image of the city as a jungle of mechanical dangers. They probably cause more anxiety among their users than driving does. How many people feel a twinge of anxiety when setting out in a car and how many when entering an elevator? Many more in the latter case, surely, and yet the elevator is by far the safer of the two technologies. Fatal accidents involving passengers are all but unknown.[10]

Why is fear so much greater where danger is so much less? Research on risk by Paul Slovic and others has arrived at a number of generalizations that help to answer the question.[11] One of them is that people will underestimate risks in situations in which they believe (justifiably or not) that events are under their own control and exaggerate them where they do not. Elevator accidents envisioned in the mind's eye are a prime case of the latter, traffic accidents of the former. Situations of the latter kind will probably be more common in cities than in rural areas. To the extent that they are, people will systematically understate the advantages of the urban environment.

Another powerful force for erroneous judgments of safety, one we encountered in the previous chapter, is the way in which people often conflate hazards with disasters, using the incidence of the latter to gauge the magnitude of the former. The classic fallacies of equivocation arise from the careless use of a word that has several different meanings as if it had only one (*green* is an example already discussed); in this case two distinct terms that should be kept separate (as with *urbanization* and *industrialization*) are used as if they were interchangeable. Cities probably *are* more prone to technological disasters than rural areas but that is because the chances are greater in a city—where more people and property are clustered—that the statistical threshold of absolute loss from a single event—whether of deaths, injuries, or damage—can be reached. It by no means follows that a person or a population will be safer from the hazard in a rural setting but we may erroneously suppose that a pattern of losses occurring in disasters holds true for the pattern of loss overall. In the terminology used by Slovic and colleagues, "chronic" risks that add up to a large toll are apt to receive less attention than do "catastrophic" ones that may take fewer lives but do so in a few eye-catching large events.[12] As a result, hazards more typical of cities will be feared, all else being equal, more than ones less characteristically urban, and hazards that are ubiquitous or common in both urban and rural settings will likewise seem more dangerous in the former. Events occurring in cities will, for example, be overrepresented in top-ten lists of disasters, whether based on deaths or on the dollar value of damage done, that are staples of news reports, almanacs, encyclopedias, websites, and other sources of general information from which people will form judgments of risk and safety. Even avowedly fictional sources can strengthen this source of an illusory urban penalty by way of the availability heuristic. "Disaster films," a student of the genre has written, "have had a long-standing fascination with cities."[13] Spectacle for its own sake is the goal, and urban characteristics—size, crowding, and a densely built environment—contribute greatly to achieving it.

Most people worry more about the hazards of air travel than about those of road traffic (greater, whether measured by deaths per mile traveled or per hour spent traveling). The difference surely has something to do with their respectively catastrophic and chronic character just as it also has something to do with people's very different sense of personal control in the two cases. There are very few traffic "disasters," measured by the number of people killed in a single event, whereas such "disasters" do occur in air travel. That does not prevent road traffic from being more dangerous but it does do much to obscure its dangers. The safest form of air travel itself is in large commercial airliners, with fatal accidents occurring disproportionately in small aircraft, but again "disasters," or single hazard events with a large toll of lives, are likelier to occur and to receive wide publicity with larger aircraft. The point incidentally suggests, as far as it goes, an urban and especially a large-city advantage in safety and disadvantage in perception. The larger a city, the larger, on average, will be the aircraft that serve its inhabitants and the larger will be such accidents that occur on takeoff or landing within its territory—which, again, will contribute to the illusion of a penalty because the largest disasters will be the ones involving the largest and safest craft.[14]

Thus even with equal degrees of safety, a misperception of an urban penalty is apt to arise. There are also reasons to suppose that in many cases urban areas will be genuinely safer. Like those from natural hazards, losses from technological hazards are the result not merely of exposure but of exposure combined with vulnerability. One assumption underpinning the expectation of an urban penalty in technological hazards is that exposure to technology, and therefore to its dangers, will be greater in cities. That assumption we will examine in due course. But once the mediating role of vulnerability is recognized, it becomes clear that greater exposure would not necessarily mean greater loss. It is as likely here as it is in the case of natural hazards that vulnerability will be lower and resilience and coping ability greater in urban areas than in rural ones. John Cross, who has made the most compelling case against the expectation of an urban (and especially a megacity) penalty for natural hazards, extended his argument to technological hazards as well, and on many of the same grounds. He pointed out that disparities in such key variables as protective works and services, emergency medical care, the speed and effectiveness of postdisaster assistance, and the degree and effectiveness of regulatory oversight are all likely to operate on the side of greater urban safety. The case of traffic accidents has already illustrated some of the workings of these factors.[15]

In situations of equal exposure to any kind of hazard, then, urban vulnerability will probably be lower than rural. The objection remains that exposure to technological hazards will not be equal but is likely to be much greater in cities. Take noise, for example, a hazard that contributes to hearing loss and to all appearances is more prevalent in cities than in rural areas. Yet statistics from the United States show a higher rate of hearing loss among rural than urban populations in all age groups.[16] Though average noise levels across urban space surely are higher than across rural, human exposure does not follow these averages; damagingly high levels at close range are more typically rural, especially at work (e.g., with agricultural machinery) and perhaps also in recreation. Noise is particularly intense in rural areas where people are, even if much empty acreage is quieter than the average urban area, and the restraints likely to be imposed on the highest-decibel activities in higher-density settings are less likely to be imposed in lower-density ones. Assumptions about density and hazard exposure can easily go wrong by neglecting such considerations as these.

We have not yet defined some key terms—*technology* and *technological hazards* in particular—and doing so may clear up some important misconceptions. The cases with which we began, the hazards of movement, for all their importance, are probably not the first that come to most people's minds at the mention of the phrase *technological hazards*. Many may consciously or unwittingly equate technology with new and advanced technology and its hazards with the realms of the unusual and the unknown, excluding established and everyday risks whose very familiarity hides them from notice. People might never consciously deny that the automobile, for example, is a technology and that accidents resulting from its use are examples of technological hazards. Yet just as they might object that by urban and rural safety they mean safety from street crime, not from traffic accidents, here too they might protest that some kind of verbal trick is being played when the latter are presented as characteristic of technological risks. Doesn't the phrase mainly refer to, say, toxic chemical releases, a nuclear meltdown, or the failure of an electric power system—which would, if used as handy mental stereotypes, incline one to expect an urban penalty?

Anyone who likes may choose to understand *technological* as referring only to novel and advanced technologies. (Yet it hardly seems inevitable that the more "advanced" and less primitive a technology is, the more dangerous it is; its very degree of advancement should be measured at least in part by how safe it has been made. We have already seen how much greater are the dangers to health of primitive cooking and heating devices through indoor smoke pollution than of more modern ones but both, surely, are technologies.) It is even possible to insist that *technological* should refer chiefly or exclusively to the kinds of technologies that are found mainly in cities. In that case, it would be no trouble, to put it mildly, to prove that people who live in cities are more exposed to technological hazards than those who do not. It would also be of no use because one would still then have to find another term to cover the kinds of risks posed by people's physical surroundings, urban or rural, and investigate how they differ from place to place. It makes more sense to recognize that the kinds of devices and know-how that make up what we call *technology* come in many forms and that the ones that receive the most attention are not necessarily the most dangerous. Is an elevator a technology in some way that a flight of stairs is not? A municipal sewage treatment plant but not a bathtub? An electric light but not a candle or a kerosene lamp? And is the first member of each pair really certain or even likely to be more harmful than the second? Anyone who still objects is invited to think instead of *accidents* as the topic of this chapter, to substitute mentally that term for *technological hazards* wherever it occurs and to join in considering how the occurrence of all of the harmful events we call by either name varies between urban and rural areas.

So defined, of course, such a subject matter presents an embarrassment of riches. Technologies so broadly conceived, accident-prone activities of one sort or another, are omnipresent in human life. The challenge is to devise some sort of classification that will cover all of the major forms that they take. The discussion so far has dealt with the hazards of movement; we should end up with a fairly complete overview of the rest if we divide them into those to which people are exposed at home, work, and play.

Home is a shelter from some risks but a theater of others. Among the elements of greater rural vulnerability mentioned by Cross, the greater time it will take emergency help to arrive applies across the board to household accidents, including ones as simple but potentially serious as falls, strains, cuts, accidental poisonings, and electric shocks. Dwelling fires represent the principal hazard of a ubiquitous and ancient technology—that of shelter itself. Similar in this respect to traffic accidents, they are so routine as to be often omitted from inventories or discussions of technological hazards that include much more striking but much rarer and less significant ones. The data on dwelling fires in the United States show a clear rural penalty in safety. The finding may once again seem counterintuitive. Dwelling units within buildings and buildings themselves in cities are more tightly clustered, making it easier for fires to spread from one to another. Tall buildings typical of highly urban settings present challenges in evacuation that single-story ones do not. Arson is notoriously more common in urban than in rural areas—though it might merely be better reported there. But expectations of risk based only on these considerations err by excluding some others that may be more important. In the United States, the chances of death in a house fire are substantially greater in rural areas than in the country as a whole. A search for the reasons makes it clear that population density, though in some ways tending to enhance the hazard, can on the whole tend to mitigate it. "Homes in rural areas," a Federal Emergency Management Administration report observes, "are more likely to be farther from emergency services than homes in non-rural areas." Urban dwelling fires, for instance, are half again as likely as rural ones to be extinguished by firefighters using water sprayed through hose lines from nearby municipal system connections. "Also," the report adds, "lower population densities mean that some fires, especially those that begin while no one is at home, will not be noticed as quickly as they may be in more densely populated areas."[17] Trees and brush, as noted in the previous chapter, may be more hazardous elements of neighboring land cover than streets and buildings.

The urban advantage may hold true in LDCs as well for the same and perhaps additional reasons. In the developed world, government subsidy has helped to make rural electrification virtually complete. In the Third World, the cost of such a networked service among scattered populations has kept it from reaching many rural dwellers. As a result, the latter are more likely to use open fires for household purposes. A study of fire as a hazard to houses in the Indian state of Orissa found a declining trend in loss over time that it attributed to the increased urbanization of the population and the improvements in construction and utilities that accompanied it. The same applies to fire as a direct hazard to people. Rural populations suffer a higher rate of burns in India than urban and even urban slum populations.[18]

Perhaps nowhere do the prevailing stereotypes of urban danger and rural safety obscure more of the truth than in the area of occupational injuries. It might not be too far-fetched to suggest that the real burden of proof lies on anyone who would assert a rural advantage. The high cost of land in cities, all else being equal, will tend to squeeze out businesses that handle heavy and bulky quantities of matter; it will best allow the ones that have most dematerialized their activities to remain. Work in the former class of employment is surely more dangerous than in the latter. And as three Australian researchers observe, "Lower population density is the strongest predictor of trauma death rates in developed countries."[19] The world's most distinctively rural livelihoods, those involving primary production, rank high among its most hazardous ones: fishing, forestry, mining, and agriculture. Among employment sectors in the United States, the highest rates of fatal occupational injuries in 2010 occurred in agriculture, forestry, fishing, and hunting (27.9 per 100,000), mining (19.8 per 100,000), and transportation and warehousing (13.7 per 100,000, chiefly in traffic accidents, especially on rural highways).[20] In Craig Veitch's words, "rural residents, generally, have greater exposure than urban residents to high-physical-risk activities and heavy machinery." Mishaps in agriculture involving farm machinery, ranging from scythes to tractors and harvesters, are particularly significant causes of death and injury around the world.[21] As with motor vehicle accidents, the greater distance to help in rural areas amplifies the effects of a high accident rate, and occupational risks affecting a scantier, more dispersed (and often less politically influential) population may be less effectively monitored and regulated. In the United States, small farms are exempt from many federal occupational safety regulations.[22] The same reasons that magnify farmworker exposure to pesticides may also tend to decrease the effectiveness of safety regulations that exist on the books. They also suggest that the usual data may underestimate agricultural and rural injuries and be more complete for ones occurring in cities.

Chapter 4 noted the widespread occurrence and rising importance today of rural industrialization. Though patterns in the past have made cities and industry seem nearly inseparable, improvements in transportation and communication have liberated many forms of manufacturing from the urban sites they were once compelled to occupy; in the industrialized countries, manufacturing is much more deurbanized than the service sector is. To the extent that industrial jobs are hazardous, their dangers will not be confined to, or even necessarily greatest in, urban areas. Indeed, some differences between the two settings may make a given form of manufacturing more risky in a rural setting than it would be in a city. The geographer David Harvey draws an illuminating comparison between two workplace tragedies, one famous and one little noted: Manhattan's notorious Triangle Shirtwaist Factory fire in 1911 and a blaze that killed twenty-five workers and seriously injured more than twice that number in a chicken-processing plant in the small town of Hamlet, North Carolina, on the day after Labor Day in 1991. The Triangle Fire evoked an outpouring of protest that led to eventual remedial regulations. It is remembered today as a landmark event in the eradication of many of the evils that it highlighted. The Hamlet fire, by contrast, illustrates how many of those evils still exist but in places more hidden from sight than lower Manhattan because, in Harvey's words, it received "hardly any media or political attention." There are many possible reasons for the disparity in the notice taken of the two events but one of them, Harvey observes, was the difference between an urban and a rural location: "the geographical isolation of employees" in rural industry, he notes, creates a workforce that is "far more vulnerable to exploitation than its urban counterpart."[23] Employers who wish to escape the burden of safety costs may find deurbanization the path of least resistance.

There remain the hazards of leisure and recreation. Because the data are better and the share of time they occupy is probably much greater, these two kinds of hazards can best be examined in the developed countries. A precise line separating some of them from natural hazards may not be easy to draw: those encountered in hunting, boating, swimming, skiing, snowmobiling, rock climbing, and hang gliding, to name a few, but the list itself suggests some reasons why rural locales may be disproportionately frequent sites for risky activities and why their rural character, their distance from help, again may worsen their dangers. Comparable leisure activities characteristic of urban settings would almost certainly be safer ones. Ownership of one set of exceptionally hazardous devices—firearms and particularly rifles and shotguns—is distinctly more common in rural parts of the United States than in urban ones for reasons having much to do with different tastes in recreation. Their greater presence and availability are one reason why accidental firearm death and injury are markedly greater in rural than in urban areas, and along with higher firearm suicides sufficiently so to offset the higher toll from deliberate homicide or assault in urban areas. The disparities apply to accidents involving children and adolescents as much as adults.[24] The characteristic land cover of suburbia, the lawn, is also a large though little-recognized source of accidental injury. Lawn mowing accounts for about half as many recorded injuries in the United States as firearms do.[25]

For the Third World, the form of recreational hazard that studies have best documented in detail is drowning by children at play in bodies of water. The example may indeed stretch the concept of technology to or beyond its limits and might strictly speaking be better placed among natural hazards, though few texts on natural hazards bother to mention it. At any rate, it is an activity involving a skill—swimming—that might be classed in a broad sense as a technology. It certainly falls into the class of "accidents" and is a major cause of death and of years of life lost. Its relative prevalence in urban and rural settings offers some evidence of their respective safety. Studies indicate a much higher death rate from drowning in rural than in urban areas, which they attribute to the greater dangers of a sparse population, with help less likely to be immediately at hand and a more natural and unaltered environment, with hazards not clearly marked or placed off limits.[26]

Pulling together these and other sources of hazard, a number of studies have assessed the overall accident rate for specific countries or major portions of them. The results for the developed world and for the two largest and best-studied developing countries, India and China, are unequivocal. Rural accident rates, overall and in most major classes (e.g., occupational, traffic, fires, drowning) are higher than urban ones. Rural accidents are also more severe and more likely to result in death than urban ones.[27] If there is underreporting of accidents, moreover, it is likely to be greater in rural than in urban settings.[28] The results may still be open to discussion and correction on many points. What they assuredly do not do is bear out the commonsense belief that cities are jungles of technological hazard and rural areas safe havens. City dwellers will indeed, be more exposed to any "high-tech" hazards that are more common in cities than outside of them. They may be more vulnerable to the (so far, largely hypothetical) catastrophic collapse of elaborate technological networks from which they draw a net benefit all the rest of the time.[29] But overall, recorded accident rates put such concerns in proper perspective.

The distinction between natural and technological hazards is not a sharp one and many cases—perhaps an increasing number over time—defy easy classification because they include elements of both. Where are dangers from such hybrid hazards likely to be greatest? According to the geographer David Alexander, "it is clear that, by and large, the probability that natural hazards will interact with technological risks is greater in urban than in rural areas."[30] Is it so clear as that? Certainly the dramatic and devastating cases—say, an earthquake and a tsunami overwhelming a nuclear power plant—are likely to appear in the mind's eye surrounded by an urban landscape. Yet when just that happened in real life in Japan in 2011 it was in a rural setting, testimony again to the ruralization of many hazardous activities. In any event, that images and even genuine examples of urban calamity should be interpreted with caution has been a major theme of this and chapter 5. Such large and attention-getting cases are as likely to be rare in reality as they are to be catastrophic if they occur, and it is the ordinary, everyday interacting risks that may do the most harm in the long run and at the same time may be the most apt to be overlooked. Take, for example, the interactions between a quite mundane and recurrent natural event—rain or snow—

and a ubiquitous technology—that of driving. In the northeastern United States, fatal traffic accidents when roads have been made slippery by precipitation increase more in rural than in urban areas, the natural consequence of higher speeds and other risk factors in the former.[31] Or take the way in which another mundane process of nature, a moderately strong breeze, interacts with the spraying of toxic agricultural pesticides to carry them off the farm into populated rural areas—the phenomenon known as pesticide drift.[32] There are counterexamples, to be sure. High winds can spread urban fires from building to building, for instance, and heat waves, intensified in central cities by the heat island effect, can overwhelm electric-generating capacity by leading to excessive power demand for air conditioning. But only a systematic inventory, not simple assumptions or impressions, could settle the question of whether such hazards of nature and technology intertwined endanger urban or rural areas more severely.

Such considerations complicate an already complex topic. Taken individually, technological hazards are at least as varied as those of pollution or of nature, and the ways in which they can combine create more variety still. No more here, then, should we suppose that an urban penalty or an urban advantage will obtain across the board. Yet on general principles and on the evidence of such data as are available, cities may on balance be safer from many important kinds of accidents than rural areas. At the very least, they are probably much safer by comparison than common sense generally represents them. They possess some advantages that flow directly from the defining characteristics of urbanness that too often are thought of as risk factors: the greater availability of regulation and help in a dense and clustered population and the potentially greater safety of a deliberately designed and built environment and of typically urban livelihoods.

7

Infectious Disease

Environmental hazards that affect human beings can come from inanimate forces or objects or from other living creatures. Of these last, it is some of the smallest ones that do the most harm, the microorganisms and parasites responsible for infectious diseases, ones as varied in character and severity as cholera, malaria, tuberculosis, HIV/AIDS, influenza, and the common cold. Of all biological hazards, they seem the most likely on the face of things to display an urban penalty—more likely than attacks by wild animals, surely, or even by domesticated ones. The damage done by locusts, weeds, and blights chiefly falls on crops and the rural livelihoods most directly dependent on them. But it seems obvious that cities, with their densely clustered populations, must offer a much more favorable setting than do rural areas for the spread, epidemic or every day, of infectious or communicable human diseases. By bringing people closer together, do they not unavoidably facilitate transmission, direct or indirect? "The city," writes one authority, "is the bug's dream come true and the human being's greatest weakness." "Whatever else might be said of the impact of cities upon health," writes another, "and much of the impact has been beneficial—it is unarguable that city life entails hugely increased risks of infections." A recent editorial in the *New England Journal of Medicine* describes global urbanization, largely for this reason, as "a humanitarian disaster."[1]

This is perhaps the most deeply entrenched and long-standing of all the presumptions of commonsense environmental antiurbanism. An urban penalty and perhaps a growing one in infectious disease might seem so inescapable that it would be tempting to dispense with the labor of verifying it. Why squander time and trouble in proving the obvious? Wherever else an urban penalty may be in whole or part an illusion, how can it conceivably be one here? It seems not only undeniable, but also a particularly pressing cause for concern in an era of newly emerging or resurgent infectious diseases. Will not an ever-more urban world face unprecedented, perhaps insurmountable, challenges in the area of public health?

Such worries about the future draw strength from the apparent lessons of the past. Of all the supposed urban environmental penalties this book examines, that of radically heightened chances of disease has been feared the longest. The very term *urban penalty* originated in the field of public health and long before anyone conceived of the possibility of an urban advantage. It was coined to denote the apparent tendency throughout most of human history for city dwellers to die sooner than their rural counterparts and chiefly from what are now recognized as infectious maladies.[2] For several centuries, the received wisdom among students of health and population went even farther. It asserted that cities and towns always and everywhere, if left to themselves, would have simply died out by an insufficient number of births to fill the gaps made by deaths; that were their numbers not regularly replenished by migrants born in the healthier (and demographically more fertile) countryside, cities would in fairly short order have ceased to exist. Demographers call the rise or fall of a population due solely to the sum of its own births and deaths—that is, excluding migration in or out—its natural increase or decrease. To several of the seventeenth- and eighteenth-century European writers now remembered as the founders of scientific demography we owe the supposed law of urban natural decrease, also called the *urban graveyard* thesis. In part it rested on a phenomenon already discussed in chapter 2, the characteristically lower fertility of city dwellers, but even more it was thought to reflect a radically higher rate of death in the crowded and filthy city. These early researchers compared the population dynamics of city and countryside by calculating the balance of births and deaths (often using registers of baptisms and burials) recorded in each. When they found that the number of deaths occurring in cities in a given year or span of years typically exceeded their recorded number of births, the urban graveyard thesis was the result, along with the corollary that only a steady flow of rural-to-urban migration allowed cities even to survive, let alone to grow. Thomas Robert Malthus gave the thesis an authoritative statement in the early nineteenth century. Noting the apparently universal pattern of natural decrease in cities and towns, he wrote, "To fill up the void . . . it is evident that a constant supply of recruits from the country is necessary; and this supply appears in fact to be always flowing in from the redundant births of the country."[3]

If correct, of course, the thesis implies one of two things: that people are so irrational that they would continue moving into a setting that would shorten their lives for no good reason long after experience has shown its dangers or, more plausibly, that even premodern cities had such offsetting advantages over rural areas that many people were willing to accept the heightened risk. But the validity of the urban graveyard model as an iron rule of historical demography has itself been brought into serious question. Its own history, in fact, illustrates one error that lies in wait for anyone investigating the subject and into which many of its earliest systematic investigators fell. The data they used, though crude, were probably accurate enough as a reflection of birth and death rates. Yet the conclusion they drew rested in part on a long-overlooked fallacy in reasoning. As the historian Jan de Vries wrote in 1984, the thesis of urban natural decrease as a demonstrated law, the chief finding of the classic literature on the demography of cities, was "based on wholly inadequate foundations."[4] The Italian historian Elio Lo Cascio explains the central problem: "When immigration to an urban center is strong, it is only natural that burials outnumber baptisms because many of the dead were not born there. . . . We tend to underestimate the death rate and therefore to overestimate the natural increase in the area from which the migratory flux comes and, on the contrary, to overestimate the death rate and underestimate the natural increase in the area that receives the migratory flux."[5] To accept the urban graveyard thesis, in other words, because ratios of births and deaths conform to what it predicts, is to commit the fallacy of affirming the consequent. The data as given do not exclude another possible explanation of a mortality surplus: that it was not the result of unhealthiness (combined with lower urban birth rates) but of the inflation of the number of recorded urban deaths by the rural-to-urban migration itself. In that case, cities might indeed have grown, displaying a surplus of births over deaths, if no migration had occurred; it was the migration itself, paradoxically, that made them seem to be experiencing natural decrease. De Vries offers an illustration: "an American retirement community such as St Petersburg, Florida," he writes, would look like a hideously unhealthy urban graveyard for the same reason if one analyzed its vital statistics in the same fallacious way. "The excess of deaths over births recorded there is not a reflection of the city's unhealthiness . . . . It is the migrants to the city—in this case the old-age pensioners—who create the statistical illusion of a city unable to reproduce itself" because "their own births are, of course, registered elsewhere" but "they do die in St Petersburg." In this case, as de Vries adds, the disparity is widened further by the fact that elderly migrants to such a city do not contribute to its tally of births by having their children there.[6] But something similar, as the demographer Allan Sharlin pointed out in 1978, might have occurred in pre- or early modern cities if, as could often have been the case, a disproportionate share of the in-migrants were too poor to be able to marry in the same proportion as the natives. Likewise, if the newcomers were notably less healthy (perhaps because they are less accustomed to their new conditions of life than the natives), again their higher death rates might mask a background natural increase.[7] For all of these reasons, a valid comparison could be drawn only if it were limited to those spending their lives in the same urban or rural setting from cradle to grave.

The error merely inflates the possibility of an urban graveyard effect, which could still appear once the error is corrected. But the belief that premodern cities always and everywhere experienced a natural decrease offset only by migration has not survived closer and more accurate study, though the limitations of the data make firm conclusions hard to draw. Research has confirmed that urban death rates were ordinarily higher than rural ones. To that extent, an urban penalty seems indeed to have been the rule. It has also established many cases of urban natural decrease in western European cities in particular eras but likewise documented others when urban natural increase occurred.[8] Nor is it clear that the same dynamics obtained in other world regions, notably in East Asia, which for many centuries has been the home of the earth's largest total and largest urban populations. Its cities suffered from many fewer sanitary deficiencies than did those of Europe, and may have been as healthy as their rural hinterlands.[9] Lo Cascio has even questioned whether the most notorious of premodern Western cities, imperial-age Rome, was the urban graveyard and the exceptionally deadly human habitat for its time and place that most writers have depicted. For all the sanitary horrors of crowded and flimsy housing, he points out, its residents, even the lower class, enjoyed some notable offsetting advantages over those in the Empire's rural regions and its smaller cities. They had an abundant and guaranteed supply of food and running water and a municipal sewage disposal system unrivaled in the world. More of the potentially malarial lowlands and areas of standing water within the city were drained than in the surrounding countryside. At the end of the nineteenth century, the Italian malariologist Angelo Celli described modern Rome as "a very healthy city surrounded by a pestilential district," precisely because the urban area benefited, as it would have done to some extent in ancient times, from the drainage provided by the sewer system and from the disruption of *Anopheles* mosquito habitat by paving and construction.[10] Though Lo Cascio does not assert an overall advantage in life expectancy for the Rome of the time of the Caesars, his work offers some warnings against taking an urban penalty for granted either in the past or the present because it suggests some possible urban advantages that at least in part might offset the dangers of clustering. Cities possess capacities for action and response that, when vigorously exploited, might more than make up for the greater opportunities they offer for infections to spread.

That cities, as well as harboring higher everyday levels of death and infection, have always been struck harder by epidemics than other places is equally a part of the common image of the past. When Paul and Anne Ehrlich warn of a rising potential for runaway disease outbreaks as growing populations give rise to ever-larger cities, they cite as evidence two familiar cases from the historical record: the Black Death in medieval Europe and the 1918–1919 global influenza pandemic. Both, they argue, offer hints of what a majority-urban world might have to look forward to.[11] These cases, given their prominence in the way we remember the past and anticipate the future, merit a close look.

On first thought, influenza, as a disease spread from person to person through direct contact or the air, would seem necessarily subject to an urban penalty. Yet one possible urban advantage, albeit a development of quite recent times, is the ability to administer vaccines, when they exist, more effectively to a more concentrated population. There was no vaccine against the influenza pandemic in 1918. But even then, studies have indicated, the degree of risk did not simply rise as the density of population did. In some countries, death rates from the pandemic were higher in urban than in rural areas or in larger than in smaller urban centers; in others, there were equal or lower rates in cities than in smaller towns and the countryside.[12] Globally, moreover, mortality reached its highest levels—far higher than among the world's city dwellers—in the areas of the lowest levels of urbanness: in small remote villages and among isolated rural populations.[13] Residents of urban areas, though more often exposed to contact with the disease, benefited from a kind of inadvertent vaccination. They possessed a greater degree of immunity through past disease exposure that city life had brought them and that the world's hardest-hit groups sorely lacked.

In asking whether epidemic outbreaks are likely to display an urban penalty, we can profit from lessons already learned regarding natural and technological hazards about the danger of focusing too narrowly on "disasters." Statistically, urban losses are likely to loom larger than they really are. Where there are more people, there are likely to be more deaths. But that tells us nothing about where death rates were higher, about where it was safer for an individual to live. When a disease outbreak affected urban and rural areas, a look at the proportional losses in the two settings will provide the most valuable evidence about which suffered the worst. When examined in this way, the Ehrlichs' (and many others') prime case from history of a calamitous urban penalty offers, in fact, a striking counterexample. Ole J. Benedictow's history *The Black Death, 1346–1353* analyzes patterns of mortality in this most infamous of pre-twentieth century pandemics, one that killed probably a quarter of the population of Western Europe in a few years, one that routinely evokes images of cities as vast mortuaries and of rural retreats (as in Boccaccio's *Decameron*) as havens of security.[14] Yet these images turn out to be less than accurate because Benedictow's survey supports some surprising discoveries about the geography of plague death determined in earlier studies. The earliest of these, conducted by the English physician E. H. Hankin and published in 1905, looked at statistics from the city of Bombay in India and the surrounding region ravaged by the outbreak of 1897–1898. The larger the settlement size, it turned out, the lower was the mortality rate (table 7.1). Further studies of plague epi-

Table 7.1
Death rates from plague in settlements of different size, 1897–1898, Bombay Presidency of India

Place	Number of inhabitants	Deaths from plague per thousand inhabitants
Bombay	806,144	20.1
Poona	161,696	31.2
Karachi	97,009	24.1
Sholapur	61,564	35.0
Kale	4,431	104.9
Supne	2,068	102.5
Ibrampur	1,692	360.5

Source: E. H. Hankin, "On the Epidemiology of Plague," *Journal of Hygiene* 5 (1905): 56n1.

sodes in other times and places, ranging from the Indian Punjab to China to premodern Europe, likewise showed higher death rates in rural areas than in towns and cities.[15]

However well-grounded in the evidence, as Benedictow observes, a result seemingly so contrary to common sense and inherited legend alike could hardly be accepted until research could explain why it occurred. The spread of the Black Death, he reasons, depended on two animals. It was transmitted to human beings by the bites of fleas that had picked it up from the rats that they infested. Rats are highly territorial creatures that dislike and resist crowding and do not form dense clusters. As a result, there would be more nearby rats (as sources of infection) per individual human being (as its endpoint), all else being equal, in the countryside than in the cities. Moreover, fleas are not newly infected by biting infected people; the bubonic plague is what human epidemiologists call a dead-end disease, one that doesn't continue transmission once it reaches humans. Therefore, a large and dense population does not in any way enlarge the reservoir from which infection is drawn, one common reason for expecting an urban penalty.

In another sense, too, any finding of a drastic urban penalty in the Black Death would really be counterintuitive. In Benedictow's words, "Only a disease with great powers of spread in the countryside and in thinly populated areas in general could, in fact, have the demographic effects that the Black Death was supposed to have had." "On the eve of the arrival of the Black Death in medieval Europe," he continues, "about 90 per cent of the population lived in the countryside, with at most a couple of per cent in urban centres with more than 10,000 inhabitants."[16] On the traditional understanding, one would have had to acknowledge a difficulty and say that Europe suffered as it did from the Black Death *although* it was only meagerly urbanized. It may rather have suffered as it did *because* it was still largely rural, something that would help to account for the plague's failure to recur in still greater force in later centuries as Europe began to urbanize in earnest. It is not surprising that medieval observers did not notice the greater safety of cities, nor is it discreditable to them. The most obvious signs would have pointed the other way, similar to the way natural and technological disasters typically do. Huge piles of corpses could accumulate only in urban areas but they do not necessarily mean that the death rate was as high there as in more sparsely peopled districts. Boccaccio's characters, though they did not know it, might have been wiser to stay in town.

In addition to the possible sources of urban advantage already discussed, the Black Death case offers us a further set of possibilities to investigate, ones already suggested by the example of Rome. Infectious diseases fall into two kinds, those (such as malaria and the plague) that depend for their spread on intermediate carrier organisms (called *vectors*) and those (such as influenza) that do not. A defining element of urbanness, a largely built environment, can be a much less inviting habitat than a rural setting for the vectors of disease, including some of the world's most important ones, past and present. As with geophysical hazards, an artificial setting may be safer than a natural one when it is nature itself that is dangerous. The cases of malaria and of the Black Death illustrate how this kind of advantage can operate even before it is understood; it can do so still better once it is deliberately exploited.

Armed with these insights from the past, we now have reasons to take a hard look at the presumption, which earlier seemed so unquestionable, of an urban penalty today and in the future for infectious disease—and for human health more generally. The effort no longer seems doomed to be pointless. And if we do invest it, we are abundantly repaid with two results. The first is that globally and in the countries of most concern— the LDCs, where most of the world's people live and where infectious disease remains most prevalent—a net urban advantage exists in the key measures of health and mortality.[17] The second is that the burden specifically of communicable disease tends also to be less, rather than greater, in Third World urban areas than in rural ones.[18] And, at the broadest scale, the process known as the *health transition,* in which life expectancy increases and the causes of death shift away from communicable disease in the process of economic and social development, parallels, and not altogether by chance, the demographic transition of urbanization.[19] Countries more or less simultaneously become wealthier, healthier, and more urban, and the correlation holds true not only among countries but within them. The factors that already can be seen at work in the cases from history go a long way toward accounting for the correlation.

As noted already, the intensity of urban ecological transformation, the built-environment component of urbanness, can be a beneficial one for human health when it disrupts the pathways of disease transmission. This may be especially significant in the cases of vectored diseases: malaria, dengue, and yellow fever, transmitted by mosquitoes; trypanosomiasis or sleeping sickness, transmitted by tsetse flies; and so on. Many such diseases follow a complex chain with several intermediate organisms: the bubonic plague is an example. As discussed previously, in some, such as the bubonic plague, human infection is a dead end; it does not represent a source of further human infections. West Nile virus, which circulates between birds and mosquitoes and reaches human beings through the latter, is another example, and one where the urban trait of high population density is relevant chiefly in so far as it happens to affect, positively or negatively, the density of the vectors. For any vector-borne illness, if a city is less suited than natural land cover to any of the organisms necessary to the chain of infection, to that degree it will be a healthier one for human beings. It is a reasonable presumption that such will be the case more often than not, that the urban built environment, on average, will be a less hospitable vector habitat than rural land cover will be, precisely because it will be a more altered one.

And it turns out that, for this and other reasons, malaria, the most important vectored disease in the world today, is much more prevalent in rural than in urban areas of the most affected countries. A clear inverse association exists between infection and the degree of urbanness. Rates of transmission are far lower in the urban areas of sub-Saharan Africa than in periurban and especially rural areas (figure 7.1).[20] The urban

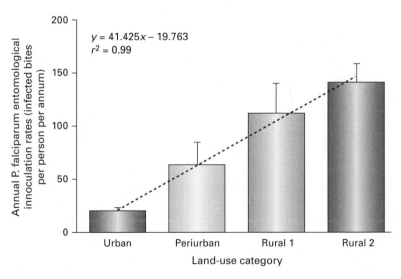

Figure 7.1
Increase in rates of malaria transmission with decreasing urbanness in sub-Saharan Africa ("Rural 1" and "Rural 2" denote relatively high- and low-population density rural settings respectively). *Source:* Simon I. Hay et al., "Urbanization, Malaria Transmission, and Disease Burden in Africa," *Nature Reviews in Microbiology* 3, no. 1 (2005), 84. © 2005; reprinted by permission of Macmillan Publishers Ltd.

built environment does more on the whole to block transmission than to facilitate it. It offers little of the characteristic habitat in which *Anopheles* mosquitoes prefer to breed and deliberate action to reduce mosquito habitat still further is more easily undertaken. Urbanness also facilitates the distribution of protective apparatus against malaria transmission, such as insecticide-treated bed nets. Though "urban malaria" has been a topic of much discussion lately, when not simply a misdiagnosis it largely represents the transient introduction of infection to central cities by migrants from rural or periurban areas.[21] The cityward trend of population, far from intensifying the danger, is, on the whole, a hopeful sign in Africa's struggle with the disease.

Malaria, immensely important in its own right, is also representative of a whole set of infections to which people are likelier for one reason or another to be exposed in a rural setting. Another is Chagas disease, caused by a microscopic parasite that is transmitted to humans by the bites of infected insects, by blood transfusions, or vertically from mother to offspring. Endemic to parts of Latin America, it is distinctly more common in rural than in urban areas, which are less favorable habitats for its carriers.[22] The expansion of irrigated agriculture enhances rural risk for several infectious diseases. It expands aquatic breeding grounds close to human populations for mosquitoes that carry malaria and Japanese encephalitis. Irrigation canals and flooded rice fields harbor the freshwater snails that carry the parasitic worms responsible for schistosomiasis, a chronic and debilitating infection common in much of the rural Third World.[23] These so-called neglected tropical diseases, or NTDs, "are infections that primarily occur in regions of rural poverty in developing countries"; others include trachoma, hookworm, onchocerciasis or river blindness, and leishmaniasis.[24] The expansion of low-density peripheral settlements in the developed world has contributed to the reemergence of infectious disease by encroaching on wildlife habitat and increasing the number of people living amid land cover that is much less modified than that of the urban core and much more enticing to some disease vectors. Classic examples from the United States are two tickborne diseases harbored in wildlife populations: Lyme disease and Rocky Mountain spotted fever, both of which have been strongly promoted by suburban and exurban sprawl.[25]

However, some carrier organisms do find an urban built environment unusually attractive: the crows that harbor West Nile virus, for example, also raccoons and skunks, which carry rabies, aided by interactions with household pets. Dengue fever, like malaria a tropical mosquito-borne infection, is more prevalent in cities than elsewhere largely because urban land cover is more suited to its carrier mosquitoes.[26] The same factor made yellow fever epidemics a particular scourge of cities, especially in warm climates, in the seventeenth, eighteenth, and nineteenth centuries. Yet any resulting greater exposure may be offset by a greater urban capacity for response. Mosquito control and vaccination have relegated massive yellow fever outbreaks to the pages of urban history.[27] Pesticide spraying against insects carrying West Nile and other viruses is more feasible in cities than in rural areas. In the United States, rabies was all but eradicated from urban animal populations in the postwar decades, though a resurgence has since occurred, partly as a consequence of suburban and exurban expansion.[28] In the Third World, where rabies is by far a bigger health problem than in the First, studies have found a rural penalty in exposure to the disease and in vulnerability or ability to cope with infection. Deaths from rabies in Cambodia outnumber those from malaria and they occur disproportionately in rural areas. The pattern reflects a number of factors, notably a higher ratio of dogs to people in rural areas and much lower access to treatment for those bitten and infected.[29]

Infectious diseases that do not depend on vector organisms for their transmission but are spread largely by contacts between people display a different array of potential urban penalties and advantages. The prevalence of one of them, HIV/AIDS, has been and remains highest in urban areas around the world.[30] Yet this one example, however striking, is far from the whole picture. Perhaps more indicative is a much longer-established disease not unlike HIV/AIDS in many ways: hepatitis B, whose present-day patterns may offer some hints of the ones that the newer disease is likely in time to settle into. Hepatitis B is not drastically dissimilar in magnitude; it is blamed for six hundred thousand deaths per year and chronically infects some 350 million people. Its chief modes of transmission are similar to those of HIV: horizontally by exchange of bodily fluids and vertically from infected mothers to newborns. In the Asia-Pacific region, which has the world's highest rates of hepatitis B infection, studies have found it more prevalent in rural populations than in urban ones.[31] Much of the reason seems to lie in the greater access of the latter to vaccination. With its pronounced urban advantage in administration, vaccination was the principal means by which one major infectious disease, smallpox, was eradicated from the world and by which a second, polio, has been eradicated from most of it. If and when an HIV vaccine is developed, the future trajectory of the infection might well lead to a similar spatial pattern. Even as it is, the urban and rural gap in infection has narrowed over time and the greater availability of care in urban areas also plays a role in the net outcome. Two studies in the United States have shown an urban advantage and rural penalty in survival among infected individuals, presumably for this reason.[32] What seemed to hold in the areas of natural and technological hazards seems also to hold for infectious diseases. Though urban populations may suffer greater exposure to some (certainly not all) pathogens, total losses are determined by exposure combined with vulnerability, not by exposure alone. And urban dwellers on the whole are likely to be less vulnerable than rural ones because even when nonvectored infectious diseases are concerned, cities have many advantages to offset the risks that their high densities create. These advantages, particularly pronounced in developing countries, include better access to preventive measures such as vaccinations, health care, clean water from protected sources, and improved sanitation.

The last two identified factors are key safeguards against a third important class of infectious diseases, those that are transmitted from person to person through the medium of contaminated water. Among them, gastrointestinal infections and diarrheal complaints are among the deadliest worldwide because of the role they play in infant and child mortality; cholera holds a large place in the history of disease epidemics and it remains entrenched at an endemic level in many places. On first thought, clean water would seem to be one of the most reliable blessings of rural life at low densities of population. "Urbanization," two authors write in this vein, "promotes the spread of infections through contaminated water supplies, poor sewage systems . . . and crowded living conditions."[33] But the apparent rural advantage dissolves as soon as one takes a close look at the data and the supposed reasons for the advantage and reflects on the underlying processes. The Third World urban advantage in the availability of clean water and sanitation is amply documented. In the most recent statistics collected by the World Health Organization, disparities that exist between urban and rural populations in "improved drinking-water sources" and "improved sanitation" are strongly in favor of the former. In countries of the First World, coverage is close to universal but in most Third World countries urban populations are far better served; the exceptions to the rule are few and mostly quite trivial. In Africa, the statistics show 84 percent of the urban population and 48 percent of the rural enjoying access to protected drinking water, 47 and 26 percent respectively to improved sanitation.[34] Nor, on a moment's reflection, is the difference hard to understand. Such services as clean water provided through pipes or some other means and sewerage systems or other forms of improved waste disposal are greatly facilitated by the economies of scale that stem from dense concentrations of people; they are much costlier and more difficult to provide to thinly scattered populations. Greater access to them has much to do with the strong urban advantage in child survival in the Third World.[35] Cholera likewise has remained entrenched in rural areas of many LDCs at higher levels than in those countries' cities.[36] The outbreaks of the disease that affected portions of Latin America during the 1990s were deadlier in rural areas than in urban ones.[37]

Yet the possibility remains that though urban indicators of well-being may be higher, even much higher, than rural ones, those of urban slums would be lower than any. Does something that can legitimately be called an *urban* slum penalty, as opposed to a mere penalty of poverty, exist where infectious disease is concerned? Chapter 8 will discuss attempts that have been made to define urban slum areas in precise terms; suffice it for now to equate them with the dwelling places of the urban poor. Their residents indeed represent a distinct population from that of wealthier districts in the same cities; they face more threats to their well-being with fewer resources for coping available to them. Treating them, then, as a distinct group for the purpose of assessing urban advantages and penalties therefore makes much sense. It protects researchers and readers from making the erroneous assumption, which might well arise from comparisons of average well-being, that all urban dwellers are better off than all residents of rural areas. It keeps them from conflating access to urban health-care facilities and to clean water and sanitation, measured simply in terms of spatial proximity, with access measured in the only meaningful way, by the right to use such services, from which the slum dweller may well be excluded. High-quality piped water, for example, may reach only the living quarters of the well-to-do and only to them may the doors to high-quality medical care be open. But the comparison in the form in which it is often drawn, between urban slums on the one hand and rural areas on the other, violates the essential principle of comparisons: that they must be made between groups that are comparable. It singles out the lowest-status urban residents on the one side and sets them against all rural residents, the best-off included.[38] A more meaningful result, though certainly much

Table 7.2
Infant mortality estimates per thousand live births for rural, urban poor, and urban nonpoor LDC populations, by world region

	Rural	Urban poor	Urban nonpoor
North Africa	81	60	43
Sub-Saharan Africa	103	89	74
Southeast Asia	59	53	27
South, Central, and West Asia	74	69	49
Latin America	69	62	39

Source: National Research Council, Cities Transformed: Demographic Change and Its Implications in the Developing World (Washington, DC: National Academies Press, 2003), 281.

harder to obtain, would result from a comparison between the urban poor and the rural poor.

Yet the results of comparisons between urban slum and overall rural populations are not entirely meaningless. When the urban slum indicators are worse than the rural ones, not much can be reliably inferred. When the urban slum results are better, though, the very rigor of the comparison eliminates the possibility of an urban penalty. And the absence of an urban penalty is what one can infer, for example, from the figures on Third World infant mortality—a particularly sensitive indicator of the prevalence of infection—assembled by the United States National Research Council in 2003 (table 7.2). Likewise, in a recent study, Daniel R. Feikin and colleagues collected data through household visits on the occurrence of three common symptoms of infection—respiratory illness, diarrhea, and fever—in two areas of Kenya, the urban slum of Kibera in the Nairobi metropolis and a rural district in the west of the country. They found higher rates of all three complaints in the latter; the urban slum was better off than the rural area taken as a whole. By assessing symptoms through household visits, Feikin and colleagues were able to obtain a fuller picture than records of patient visits to clinics provided. Relying only on the latter, they observe, would have led to a serious undercount of rural morbidity, because the greater difficulty of access in rural areas meant that fewer sick people visited clinics there.[39] Thus an important urban advantage, that of greater access to care, would have become an illusory indicator of an urban health penalty if rates of care-seeking had been used as the measure of illness.

One notable attempt to identify an urban slum penalty through carefully designed comparisons found that in more countries than not, infant mortality was still higher in rural than in urban slum settings when other important causes, such as wealth, were controlled for. It found too that most of the initial urban advantage turned out to be attributable to the higher levels of these other causes usually found in cities, one of them being greater access to clean drinking water and sanitation. But this last factor, given its close and by no means coincidental relationship with urbanness, is probably better interpreted as a characteristic component of an urban setting than as an independent determinant that must be removed lest it introduce an illusory urban advantage. It is, in fact, one of the typical forms that an urban advantage takes.[40]

An urban penalty in infectious disease throughout much of human history seems indeed to have been a reality, though today it has become history itself. Yet some cities even in ancient and medieval times made deliberate use of potential urban advantages and some benefited quite unknowingly from advantages that operated without conscious effort. During the twentieth century, the increasing effectiveness with which they have brought both into realization has turned the once taken-for-granted urban penalty into the exception to a new and worldwide rule. But just as some past urban penalties have disappeared along with the overarching one, new circumstances have brought out some new ones. A case in point is the rise in recent years of antibiotic-resistant tuberculosis, which illustrates an urban penalty that can only be understood when the urban advantage that it grows out of is understood. The widespread use of penicillin and later antibiotic drugs has had the result of promoting the survival and rapid spread of mutant strains unaffected by them. It is not surprising that, as studies have shown, such strains of TB are far more prevalent in urban than in rural areas, whether in the developed or in the developing world, where such drugs are more often used.[41] The greater availability of advanced health care turns out to contain the seeds of at least one emerging penalty.

As urbanization has progressed in parallel with the decline of infectious disease and the classic argument for an urban health penalty has eroded, a new argument has begun to take its place. City dwellers, it argues, especially Third World slum dwellers, are subject to a so-called double burden of ill-health. They continue to suffer from many communicable diseases, yet also, and increasingly, from the chronic, noncommunicable, "lifestyle" ailments more typical of the developed world, notably cardiovascular disease, diabetes, and cancer. But the very phrase *double burden* is a hazardous one to employ. It seems to suggest that those midway in the epidemiological transition are worse off than those at the two ends because they experience the ills typical of both. Those in the intermediate group are indeed worse off than one group in infectious disease and worse off than the other in chronic disease burden. But that, of course, is in the very nature of a transition and it is no less true that those in the middle are better off on one count each than those at the ends, having less of each set of problems. Suffering from both is not in any meaningful sense a double burden if each burden has been reduced by at least half. What needs to be shown to establish a genuine double burden and a genuine overall health penalty for those experiencing it is that the aggregate effect of a lingering communicable disease burden combined with a rising noncommunicable disease burden makes urbanites worse off than those who have not yet moved far along in the transition. As seen already, the data on life expectancy, infant mortality, and other indicators do not give the idea much support. A supposed rising burden of accidents with urbanization is sometimes added to the argument but the evidence reviewed in chapter 6 does not give it much support either. In First World countries that have passed through the epidemiological transition, life expectancy and other measures of health do not invariably display an urban advantage but the differences are subdued; in the United States and to a lesser degree in northwestern Europe, they largely reflect the local form of urbanization that concentrates poverty in central cities.

David Leon has noted what indeed must strike anyone who has read it at length: "the pessimistic tone of much of the epidemiological and public health literature on cities and urban life," especially before the last decade or so. More than anything, he notes, the pessimism stemmed from the conviction that "the unprecedented level of population agglomeration may facilitate the spread of epidemic diseases."[42] The preponderance of the facts would seem to be on the other side. That an urban advantage has become more the norm than the exception, whatever it may have been in the past, explains, among other things, the greater attention now being paid by experts to rural health problems and the recent emergence of a field bearing the name *rural and remote health*. The second adjective captures a key component of what makes cities, for their part, safer places to live in on many counts. Clustering brings risks but not, apparently, as many as isolation does. The perception of a natural and necessary urban penalty, that something about cities inevitably means poorer health than elsewhere, is hard to dislodge. Yet much of the case for an urban penalty rests on errors and pitfalls in reasoning endemic to the study of cities. In that sense, at least, the image of dangerous cities, honeycombed with pitfalls, seems to hold some validity after all. Though they may or may not be unusually safe as places to live, they certainly are unusually hazardous as places to think and to write about on no firmer basis than what common sense seems to say.

8

Human Habitat

Commonsense environmental antiurbanism makes its last stand on the ground of overall human well-being. Even if a high degree of urbanness best protects the natural environment and even if it best protects people against environmental hazards, do these benefits justify the other costs? One set of arguments can be classified as sociological: urbanization is undesirable because cities are the places where abject poverty and other forms of human misery are most common and most intense. The second is psychological: city life runs counter to the deepest needs of human nature. In either case, the challenge is a serious one. But in neither case are the arguments and evidence most often advanced compelling ones. The geography of human well-being in its relation to urbanness, in fact, is one more sphere in which a clear understanding is obstructed by some recurrent errors.

The very claim that urbanness is inimical to human well-being is a dubious one on the face of it. The global trend of population over the past two centuries, the massive cityward movement that has now produced an urban-majority world, would be an odd and anomalous fact indeed if people had not had good reasons to expect it to improve their lives. Or rather, it would be unless they made the move under duress. The US environmentalist David Orr claims that they did, speaking of actions taken "to herd people into large cities" in a way implying that few would have settled there of their own accord.[1] But overt efforts to keep people out of cities, and especially large cities, have been much more evident and more strenuous in the modern world than ones to the opposite effect. A study published in 1983 found that of 158 countries surveyed, 121 were seeking to lessen the rate of rural-to-urban migration and 21 were seeking to reverse it altogether: "only three nations," by contrast, "had as policy objectives the acceleration of migration to major urban cities." A couple of decades later, hardly anything had changed.

Of 123 national governments with definite policies regarding the level of migration to cities, 115 sought to reduce it, 2 to maintain it, and only 6 to increase it.[2] The most dramatic modern instance of mass herding along the urban-rural continuum was the abrupt and brutal expulsion of Cambodia's city dwellers *into* the countryside by the Khmer Rouge in 1975, the product of an idée fixe of a small elite cadre who thought modern cities the root of evil. Countries as large as the Stalinist Soviet Union and Maoist China established internal passport systems to prevent a destabilizing rush of rural and small-city populations to the main urban centers. China's is still in effect. Apartheid-era South Africa forcibly discouraged the urbanization of its black majority population.[3] Indirect barriers to urbanization coupled with subsidies for deurbanization remain common in the developed world: height limits and other development restrictions in center cities, for example, that keep out a denser population than the urban core could otherwise have housed and infrastructural and agricultural subsidies and other government programs for rural development.[4] The chief modern examples of coerced densification, the collectivization of agriculture under a number of Marxist regimes and the "villagization" programs of Tanzania and of Soviet-era Romania, involved the transfer of population, eventually by force, not to highly urban settings but from dispersed to more clustered ones still largely rural in character. In Tanzania and Romania, what was undertaken to increase urbanness at a lower level was guided ultimately by the goal of keeping population in rural areas; in the latter, it was fundamentally "a counter-urbanizing strategy, containing the growth of the cities."[5]

Do such urbanophobic government measures tell us that people find cities unattractive and undesirable places to live? Surely they suggest the opposite because if cities offered few attractions, they would not have been necessary. What they do most plausibly suggest is that dictators most intensely, and most other governments more mildly, dislike cities for reasons of their own. It certainly appears that more people have been prevented from urbanizing than have been forced into it, and prevented only for as long as effective barriers existed. As Mario Polèse writes, "The impact of measures to suppress rural-urban migration, in cases where they have been able to do so, has simply been to artificially hold down urbanization for a certain time, leading to even greater rural-urban income disparities and an explosion of urbanization once the measures are lifted."[6] It scarcely would be an adequate answer to say that people, even when nominally free to choose, were in reality forced to move to cities by comparatively unattractive conditions in the rural areas where they would have preferred to stay. The claim simply amounts to saying that people make choices in response to the net balance of actually existing urban and rural advantages, and that the former tend to outweigh the latter.

Perhaps, though, they are consistently wrong; perhaps people have fooled themselves over and over into thinking that life in cities would be better and have never learned from an experience that should have taught them otherwise. But the claim runs headlong into a large body of evidence that, if taken at face value, seems to demonstrate significant advantages in standards of living that urban populations usually enjoy as compared to rural ones. It is clear that the extent of net rural-to-urban migration since the 1950s in developing countries had much to do with urban pull factors, the attractions of greater opportunities thought to be available in the cities, and genuine rather than illusory ones. Chapter 7 has described the urban advantages compared to the rural Third World in health; similar differentials exist in such areas as housing, education, and nutrition as well as economic and cultural opportunity.[7]

Research shows that rates of overall poverty, usually measured by a set cash income per day, are considerably higher in rural than in urban areas of the LDCs. The claim may not be an easy one to accept because urban poverty, similar to many other urban problems already discussed, is much more visible, especially to the casual observer, than its rural equivalent. A potentially more damaging objection is that the measure is an unreliable and misleading one: "poverty lines do not usually take into account the higher cost of most necessities in urban areas, especially in the larger cities."[8] Is not life in cities notoriously more expensive than elsewhere? It is certainly true that land and housing are typically costlier and that food is likelier to be cheapest and most plentiful in farming areas, at least where some of it is grown for a household's own consumption. But to leave the matter there would be to commit once again Mill's "fallacy of overlooking" because not all urban needs or wants are more expensive in real terms. Wages themselves are bound, all else being equal, to reflect any significantly higher costs of living in urban settings and are likely to be higher in real terms because of the higher productivity of work in cities. The cheapening effect of competition lowers prices in cities for many purchased items that in rural areas can only be obtained from one seller who has a spatial monopoly, and city dwellers benefit too from a greater range of useful items readily available for purchase. Many public services that enter into a city household's or individual's total consumption are unavailable in the countryside.[9]

To sidestep the difficulty of controlling accurately for all of these costs and benefits, the economists David Sahn and David Stifel in a study published in 2003 compared outcomes directly rather than the ability to purchase or otherwise achieve them. They looked at measures of urban and rural well-being in the twenty-four countries of sub-Saharan Africa for which detailed household-level data were available. To one monetary (though nonincome) indicator, wealth or assets, they added seven others: education, gender equality in education, infant mortality, availability of neonatal care, availability of contraception, and levels of child and female malnutrition. Their findings, with a few minor and debatable exceptions, were clear and varied little from one indicator to another: "the living standards of those living in rural areas lag far behind those living in urban areas."[10]

Here, as elsewhere, of course, higher levels of urban well-being may reflect not legitimate urban advantages but urban bias reflecting unequal relations of power. In many cases, such bias is undoubtedly an element in the outcome. Yet to conclude from the existence of urban-rural disparities, which urban bias theory indeed predicts will occur, that the theory is correct in identifying their cause would be to commit the fallacy of affirming the consequent. The disparities in outcomes may still in large part be the result of true urban advantages that would remain even if all bias were removed. Many important services are cheaper to provide per capita to concentrated populations than to dispersed ones.[11] Equal spending on their provision would then produce unequal outcomes, better in urban than in rural areas, and producing equal outcomes would require an additional degree of spending per rural recipient that could bear out a charge of rural bias.

The possibility remains of a significant penalty for one important stratum of the urban population in the LDCs—slum dwellers, among whom recent rural-to-urban migrants may be disproportionately numerous. Discussions of the possibility, though, often commit the same error that, as we have already seen, affects many studies of urban health and disease incidence in the LDCs. The error pervades two influential reports issued in 2003 and 2006 by the United Nations Human Settlements Programme (UN-HABITAT). They compared average levels of well-being, measured by an assortment of criteria, among three populations in the less-developed countries: the fraction of the urban population that lives in urban slums, the nonslum urban population, and the entire rural population. In many cases the urban slum figures were no worse or were even better than the rural ones. Yet in enough others they fell sufficiently below the rural figures that UN-HABITAT declared the widespread existence not of an urban penalty, but of an urban slum penalty, one that, given the large absolute and proportional size of the population involved, would cast serious doubt on the benefits of Third World urbanization, as least in its present form, for human well-being.[12]

But the procedure that UN-HABITAT used to arrive at this conclusion is deeply flawed for reasons that have been mentioned already. The simplest way to illustrate its inadequacy is to show how easily it could be used to reach a precisely opposite conclusion, using the same data given in the report. Suppose that one began with the conviction that the Third World rural poor must necessarily be the worst-off segment of the global population. And suppose that, to substantiate the claim, one compared average measures of well-being for three LDC populations: urban, overall rural, and rural poor. The first values, in virtually all countries, are higher than the second, and the obvious disadvantages of poverty when all else is equal mean that the third cannot fail to be substantially lower than the second. Thus a significant penalty for the rural poor exists. If anything, this line of argument is better grounded than the one presented by UN-HABITAT but it shares the same basic failing: it does not compare like with like. To compare the poorest stratum of one zone, urban or rural, with the entire population of the other is to allow two variables to vary at once. The proper question is, who are more disadvantaged, those who are poor in urban areas or those who are equally poor in rural areas? It can be answered only if the two are distinguished from the better-off inhabitants of both urban and rural areas.

In fact, the five criteria that UN-HABITAT use as standard indexes for identifying urban slum conditions could perfectly well be used to locate and number a large rural slum population that could then meaningfully be compared with its urban counterpart in a given country. They are "lack of durable housing," "lack of sufficient living area," "lack of access to improved water," "lack of access to improved sanitation," and "lack of secure tenure." UN-HABITAT in its landmark 2006 report and subsequent publications counted any resident of an urban area meeting at least one of these criteria as a slum dweller. It concluded that slums housed fully a third of the world's urban population and more than half of the Third World's.[13] The criteria it employed are significant and useful. They are not, however, distinctively urban, though UN-HABITAT treated them as if they were. In fact, they are so little confined to cities that if applied uniformly across space, they would not necessarily even be found most prevalent there. The first, third, and fourth are so common in rural areas—often much more so than in urban ones—that if used consistently, they would undoubtedly lead to the conclusion that slum conditions are more of a rural than an urban phenomenon and that a largely overlooked class of rural slum dwellers represents a substantial share of the world's people. Nor is even the fifth count, insecurity of land tenure, a uniquely or even a typically urban phenomenon. Informal and customary land tenure is in many less-developed countries more common in the countryside than in cities, and it carries many insecurities that formal titling can guard against.[14] State tenure, the ultimate right of the government to control and reallocate rights to land, also exists in many countries, and it may well be exercised more widely and heavy-handedly in rural than in urban areas. Although individual and mass evictions from informally occupied lands certainly occur in Third World urban slums, they also occur in the countryside. The latent insecurity of rural tenures has recently been highlighted by a so-called global land grab, a rash of agrarian dispossessions by governments exploiting uncertainties in ownership and eager to rent good-quality acreage to outside farming enterprises in a period of high food prices: "Across Africa and the developing world, a new global land rush is gobbling up large expanses of arable land. . . . stunned villagers are discovering that governments typically own their land and have been leasing it . . . to private investors and foreign governments for decades to come," actions that "destroy villages, uproot tens of thousands of farmers, and create a volatile mass of landless poor."[15]

There is a second argument for a possible partial urban penalty. It has been widely assumed that inequality in urban areas must be greater than in rural ones, with more very rich people offset by more very poor ones. The belief sounds plausible because it chimes in with some cherished stereotypes: of rural communities being more egalitarian, less atomized, and less viciously competitive than cities, with the very paucity of opportunities for advancement limiting the potential for inequalities to widen. If true, this could lead to a distinctive urban penalty for the worst-off, who could fall well below the worst-off in rural areas even in the midst of higher average well-being and represent the single most disadvantaged stratum of a country's entire population. The 2006 UN-HABITAT report asserted just that but without explaining how it had reached its conclusion. Sahn and Stifel, rigorously reporting their data and methods, had already found evidence to the contrary. Their one directly economic measure, household wealth, showed a greater degree of inequality—often much greater—among rural than among urban populations in twenty-two of the twenty-four countries they examined. They likewise found greater rural inequality in education and health.[16] A substantial body of literature on one of their indicators of inequality, male-female differences in access to schooling in LDCs—important in its own right and as a sign of gender equity in other areas—bears out their conclusions.[17] For once in this book, commonsense assumptions turn out to be correct. Most people, surely, would expect women's rights and opportunities to be more equal with men's in urban than in rural areas, and so, on the whole, they appear to be. When the other indicators are concerned, the matter is far from settled, and indeed absolute and relative levels of inequality in the two spheres may rise and fall in different periods or differ in different places. But that urban populations necessarily or even usually show a higher degree of inequality than rural ones cannot be taken for granted.

There is no doubt that an urban slum penalty in well-being exists, *if* by that we mean a disadvantage for inhabitants of slums relative to nonslum city residents. But by the same token, there is no doubt that there is a rural poverty penalty as well: that within rural areas, those who are poor are also worse off than those who are not. Neither penalty says anything about the pluses or minuses of urban or rural life itself. To speak on no firmer basis than this of an urban slum penalty groundlessly and invidiously associates the penalty with cities rather than its only demonstrated cause, poverty. Arguments about the undesirability of urban life based on conditions in slums overlook the many ways in which rural life in the same countries and in the same economic stratum of society can be even less desirable. Given, in any case, that overall urban levels of well-being—again, the most reliable and telling measure—exceed rural ones in the LDCs, if urban slum populations are very large, then any penalty in well-being cannot be large, and if it is, then the slum share of the urban population cannot be.

Commonsense environmental antiurbanism's last-ditch argument invokes some supposed unalterable features of human psychology. People, it asserts, will always find cities unnatural settings to live in, and human nature requires nature around it; similar to any other biological creature, *Homo sapiens* innately needs or prefers a certain kind of habitat, the kind to which the long span of its biological evolution adapted it and which was certainly not an urban one. Even if an urban advantage were admitted on every point this book has so far examined, even if cities are clearly environmentally better than other modes of settlement for a given population, the artificiality of an urban setting will always make it unsatisfying. "At the best, city life is an unnatural life for the human"[18]:

anyone taking a little trouble to go out and look for them can collect assertions like this by the handful.

There can be serious challenges, nonetheless, and they can begin almost anywhere in the argument. How do we know that human beings find city life unsatisfying? To back up the claim, David Orr points to poll results showing that "roughly 50% to 60% of Americans would prefer to live on farms and in small towns, were it economically feasible to do so."[19] But even if we accept these stated preferences at face value and suppose in addition that it is sheer random bad luck that a low degree of urbanness and a low degree of economic opportunity just happen to go together, the results also indicate that at least a substantial minority, whose members are no less human than the supposed majority, does not prefer rural life. There is a good deal of anecdotal evidence that many people find city life more satisfactory than any other kind, even in the United States, which, after all, is where a 1918 song asking "How 'Ya Gonna Keep 'Em Down on the Farm (After They've Seen Paree)?" became a hit. Human wants are more diverse and various than the notion of an innate dislike of cities allows. Or if such a dislike exists, it is clearly only one feeling among many, and it cannot be so strong that it cannot easily be overridden by some of the others. That, at least, is what the actual distribution of the United States' population suggests. Few Americans in fact opt to live on the farms or in the small towns that so many of them say they would like to inhabit. Orr's inferences from the polling data he cites disregard a basic canon of social science: that what people do, or what economists call *revealed preference,* is a more reliable index to their likes and dislikes than their *expressed preference,* or what they say they want to do—and in this case have not been forcibly prevented from doing. Unrealistic idealizations of rural and small-town life, fostered by cultural stereotypes, may have as much to do with the poll results as anything, and people can freely indulge them when not obliged to live up to their words.

And if one does rely on expressed rather than revealed preferences, it is all the more important that they be those of a reasonably representative sample of respondents. When Orr, in a later essay with no additional citations given, rephrases his claim quoted above to speak of the "preferences of a persistent majority of *people* who say that they would rather live in small towns or rural areas were it economically feasible to do so" (emphasis added),[20] he conflates the expressed preferences of the population of the United States with those of the human race in general. The findings of studies that have ranged more widely tell strongly against the belief that city life is somehow at odds with the fundamental promptings of human nature. If it were, one would expect cities to be viewed everywhere with aversion—as perhaps a necessary evil but an evil nonetheless and accepted only when necessary and under protest. If commonsense antiurbanism is correct, people living in cities should express less satisfaction with their lives than ones living in lower-density settlements. But as the sociologist Claude Fischer wrote in 1973, "If any strong relationship is observed, it is that cities across the world contain people more content than those in the countryside. . . . Worldwide, there seems to be more evidence of a rural than of an urban malaise."[21] In certain cultural traditions, notably that of the Anglo-Saxon realm and to a lesser degree in northwestern Europe, at least a moderate degree of urbanophobia does indeed to be a widespread and persistent trait, though it is very far even there from being universal. The geographers Brian Berry and Adam Okulicz-Kozaryn have recently analyzed data from the World Values Survey and found no such global pattern of expressed dissatisfaction with urban life as the "cities are unnatural" thesis would predict. Dissatisfaction was greater in countries of Anglo-Saxon cultural heritage, with its traditional, historically conditioned preference for the country over the city, than elsewhere. The countries of rapidly urbanizing Asia, however, registered an overall preference not just for city but for large-city life.[22] In many developed-world cities, particularly in western Europe, high densities coexist with unusually high levels of residential satisfaction.[23]

And if the dominant cultural tradition of the United States has been an antiurban one, in some minority traditions within it city life has been viewed much more favorably.[24] In 1962, the sociologist Herbert Gans published a study of Boston's West End, a largely Italian American neighborhood before it was designated as a slum and obliterated during the heyday of urban renewal. Its residents, Gans observed, did not see it as a slum, and they preferred its high densities to the landscape of postwar suburbia, which they found "too quiet for their tastes, lonely— that is, without street life." When some children from the neighborhood were taken to Cape Cod for a treat, "the experiment failed, for the young West Enders found no pleasure in the loneliness of natural surroundings and wanted to get back to the West End as quickly as possible. They were incredulous that anyone could live without people around them."[25] Students of Latin American culture within the United States have described it as displaying a set of attitudes toward urbanism quite different from that of mainstream Anglo-Saxon culture, more tolerant and even welcoming of high densities in particular.[26] No less marked than the antiurban strain in Anglo culture is the high value traditionally placed on city life in Mediterranean Europe, where it has often been seen as more essentially suited to human nature than a rural existence is.[27] Within many of the world's urban areas, the past and present spatial patterns of rich and poor often reverse the usual US pattern, with the elite appropriating the most central and most urban districts of the core and lower-status groups relegated to the suburban fringe. Social marginalization in such societies goes hand in hand with spatial marginalization, an unlikely pairing if an aversion to urban settings were a powerful and innate human characteristic. Even if introspection shows you, the reader, that you would prefer living in a setting with a low degree of urbanness to one with a high degree, it cannot show you why you feel that way. Consequently, it cannot show how far the result you obtained can validly be extended to other people: whether you dislike cities because it is in your biological nature, common to all of humankind, or because of cultural influences that operated strongly on you but do not operate at all on some others. History offers a good deal of support for the latter possibility as the more plausible.

Observers who cannot believe that other people could like city life or could ever rationally decide to urbanize often end up decreeing that they are not in their right minds or that they do not know what they really want. Theodore Roszak, for example, chooses the first of these expedients: "people leave the countryside to stream into the cities as if they were hypnotically drawn by the hammering tempo of this new way of life" (he also refers to urbanization as a global disease of "City Pox").[28] But unless we resort to such extreme measures for dealing with unwelcome evidence, we find that the global record of urbanization tells strongly against the hypothesis of a rooted human dislike of cities. A statement such as "How people feel about giant agglomerations is best indicated by their headlong effort to escape them"[29] is reminiscent of the old "Nobody goes to that restaurant any more, it's too crowded." So, too, of course, the shift of population out of metropolitan cores and central cities that has occurred in much of the developed world during the past century would be an anomaly if people always deep down preferred a more to a less urban setting to live in. What urbanization and secondary deurbanization do is place a heavy burden of proof on anyone who would argue that human beings as a species possess a deep-seated preference one way or the other. It is likelier that each trend, when it occurs, is controlled by push-and-pull factors specific to certain eras and regions. Both processes can be observed coexisting at the micro as well as the macro scale. David Orr writes, "Anyone caught in the weekend rush to escape the metropolis knows that urban life does not begin to satisfy all of our deepest needs."[30] But in using the pronoun *our,* he is ignoring what anyone in the New York or Boston metropolitan area, for example, can witness: a rush of other people *into* the city each weekend from outlying areas, presumably to satisfy needs that cannot be met in less urban settings.

We do not, then, simply know empirically that people feel an unconquerable aversion to city life. It remains to examine the arguments that even if the verdict of experience is confusing and unclear, we can securely reason our way to that conclusion. A good one to begin with is the simplest of all. Even a cursory look at "nature" shows conclusively that cities are unnatural and therefore unsuited to a species that is a natural creature itself. Does the argument hold up?

In fact, with at least equal plausibility it can be turned on its head. The environmental historian Martin Melosi writes, "I often begin my courses on the urban environment with the following question: 'What is the difference between an anthill and a city?'"[31] His point in asking is clear. The most common stereotypical images of "nature" bear so little resemblance to ones of city life that they make the latter appear profoundly unnatural. Yet those images, as Melosi's question is meant to suggest, contain a large measure of illusion. No one could deny that ant colonies, honeybee hives, and termite mounds are natural and yet in their own ways they meet all of the criteria that this book uses to identify human cities. They collect the members of the species in question in relatively large numbers and high densities. They transform the natural setting into a largely built environment, in most cases eradicating the natural plant cover, constructing dwelling and work spaces in enclosures connected by passageways, and even controlling the indoor climate to reduce the extremes of temperature and humidity. If the "near-absence of agriculture" is reinterpreted to mean a division of labor in which much of the population spends much or all of its time in activities other than producing food—in construction, in surveillance and defense, in care for the young—the parallel again holds true. Just as human communities do, these collectivities regulate the behavior of their members through systems of control and direction that amount to institutions of government. Even many species that do not have elaborate systems of social behavior or fixed locations nonetheless cluster in large groups—flocks of birds, swarms of locusts, herds of buffalo. And even these nonsocial but clustering animals require at least some rudimentary forms of government, some ways to coordinate the activities of the individual members. For some species, life in isolation or in small dispersed units would be just as unnatural as life in urbanlike assemblages is for others.

On which side does *Homo sapiens* most naturally belong? Is a high degree of urbanness unnatural for human beings, whatever it may be for some other species? In a sense, of course, there is no answer to the question. Where human beings are concerned, the question poses a false dichotomy. They are much freer to choose, much less constrained in their ways of life, than any other animal. At a minimum, though, even some of their basic biological traits make life in a large social unit at least as appropriate for them as a life in scattered tiny groups. One is their relative defenselessness. Unlike many other large animals, they lack elaborate bodily weapons of attack, of armor, and even of unusually agile or rapid escape. A prolonged state of helplessness in early life intensifies their need to seek safety in groups in order to survive. It is no more impossible that a preference for the reassurance of numbers is ingrained in human psychology than an aversion to crowding is. If safety from attack by other animals is no longer, for most of the world's people, the conscious concern that it was in the evolutionary past, it is because the fruits of long association have made the earth a safer place for them than it once was. Lacking somatic tools of offense as well as of defense, early humans could also hunt more effectively in groups than individually. Moreover, the asset that far outweighs in power all others that humans or their competitors possess—intellect—cannot develop to anything like its full potential without abundant and frequent communication and reciprocal learning, both of which require life in close association with others, and the more the better. If we turn from theory to evidence, to the records of human prehistory, "the 'natural' tendency appears to be to live in fairly large groups, in quite high concentrations, under fairly high population density."[32]

In any case, it is sufficient to note that people do build and, increasingly, live in cities to settle the question. In Jane Jacobs's words, "The cities of human beings are as natural, being a product of one form of nature, as are the colonies of prairie dogs or the beds of oysters."[33] Though not specified in human nature, they are logical corollaries of traits that are. In this sense, as John Stuart Mill wrote, "It is natural to man to speak, to reason, to build cities . . . though these are acquired faculties . . . [each] if not a part of our nature, is a natural outgrowth from it."[34] Some classic political theories—whether meant to be taken literally or only as useful fictions—contrasted an isolated state of nature as the original human condition with an associated state of society into which people agreed to enter; recognizing the disadvantages of scattered life, they accepted society's constraints in return for its greater benefits. It would follow that isolation and independence still represent the natural human state. But the very recognition of the pluses and minuses of the two condition, and equally the existence of the linguistic and conceptual tools with which to compare and negotiate over them could only have originated in a state that was already social: "man is naturally a being that lives in association with others in communities possessing language" and not one who entered into such a condition out of an earlier and more natural one of isolation.[35] Human nature has been social as long as it has been human.

Another argument is that we can infer the unnaturalness of city life from the deterioration that supposedly takes place in human conduct in highly urban settings; cities must represent a pathologically abnormal habitat for human beings because they foster pathological forms of behavior. High population density, their foremost defining characteristic, has been the one most often blamed, in profoundly flawed arguments that have nonetheless won wide circulation and acceptance. A recent study by the historians of science Edmund Ramsden and Jon Adams examines the work and influence of the US animal ecologist John B. Calhoun (1917–1995), long associated with the National Institutes of Mental Health and a specialist in the effects of density on rodent physiology and behavior.[36] Calhoun conducted many experiments with mammals, especially rats, which he confined in pens with full protection from disease and predators and with an ample supply of food and other necessities. He was interested in the changes that would occur in their behavior as their numbers expanded but the space available to them did not. He found that once population reached a certain point, not only did it then cease growing, despite the availability of subsistence to support much larger numbers, but the behavior of the rats also deteriorated, to the point of sometimes producing what Calhoun named a *behavioral sink*. Violence broke out; infant mortality skyrocketed; many individuals, excluded and isolated, became pathologically withdrawn; incidents of cannibalism occurred; and "sexual perversions" of various forms became frequent.

An article that Calhoun published in 1962 in *Scientific American* titled "Population Density and Social Pathology" brought his findings to a large public.[37] Popularizations by other authors proceeded to draw some morals from the story. Overwhelmingly they took the lesson to be that high density is inimical to a healthy life for animals in general and for *Homo sapiens* in particular. Overwhelmingly they identified the rat pens with human cities and then used the analogy to explain various manifestations of social decay observed in US urban areas of the post–World War II era.[38] The urban historian Lewis Mumford offered one of the more restrained extensions of Calhoun's findings to people when he noted that rats, "when they are placed in equally congested quarters, exhibit the same symptoms of stress, alienation, hostility, sexual perversions, parental incompetence, and rabid violence that we now find in Megalopolis."[39] Those inclined to think badly of cities could find pretexts in the rat studies—best of all, ones firmly grounded in "science" or "nature"—for doing so.

Calhoun himself had given some warrant for such uses of his work. For the most part, though, and increasingly as time went on, he avoided any easy analogy between rat pen and human city. Indeed, when he drew it, he often called attention to its more positive implications. Even among rats, he observed, especially among some of the excluded isolates, the stress of crowding sometimes produced not apathetic withdrawal but active innovation. New forms of behavior occasionally emerged that pointed the way to effective means of coping with the challenges of restricted space. If such creative and constructive responses could arise among rodents, Calhoun argued, they were much more likely to do so among human beings.[40]

This side of Calhoun's work had some affinities with a subsequent line of social science research into the effects of density in human societies, whose chief conclusion, in brief, was that "the rat-cage image of urban life probably is wrong and probably is irrelevant." One of its key results was to establish a distinction between density, a mere physical measure of the numbers of individuals within a given spatial area, and crowding, a judgment of space as inadequate. Higher density by itself did not produce a sense of crowding, which was mediated by many cultural and social factors, including differences in the organization of space, such that a given number of people per unit area might in one case be seen as intolerable overcrowding but not so in another. Assessing the claim that too-close proximity to others caused distress by exceeding a basic human limit, the anthropologist E. T. Hall concluded, "Observations, interviews, analysis of art and literature all point to the fact that there is *no* fixed distance-sensing mechanism (or mechanisms) in man that is universal for all cultures" (emphasis in the original).[41]

These findings captured nothing like the attention given to the simpler and more pessimistic interpretations of what Calhoun's results meant for urbanized human beings. Americans looked at the rat pens, and saw Manhattan; they looked at the quarrelling or withdrawn rats, and saw New Yorkers. But it was a gigantic optical illusion generated by a false analogy. A good deal of loose talk notwithstanding, human beings do not possess any quality or display any behavior that can be equated in more than a superficial way with the phenomena called territoriality in animals. We have already encountered the species discussed in Calhoun's *Scientific American* article: the Norway rat. Its rigidly bioterritorial behavior, similar to that of most rats, helps to account, as we have seen, for the surprisingly greater virulence of the bubonic plague in rural areas than in congested cities. That same behavior explains why conduct and well-being among Calhoun's rats deteriorated so markedly when their numbers increased without a corresponding growth in the space available to them. One of the ablest critics of Calhoun-inspired antiurbanism conceded altogether too much when he wrote that the experiments had shown that "animals" suffered from crowding.[42] Calhoun showed only that certain animals did so. To say that ants or schooling fish, for example, suffer from life at high densities and would be happier and healthier alone by themselves would be ludicrous. The absence of the same kind of territoriality in some other species, the widespread occurrence of gregarious or colonial behavior, makes the results invalid even as a zoological generalization and its absence in human beings makes them sociologically irrelevant.

Social scientists often do speak of human territorial behavior but for most of them the term has a fundamentally different meaning from its use by human sociobiologists. It refers not to a set of inherited instincts but rather to actions taken to declare and exert control over space through reasoned, consciously formulated purposes and procedures. The geographer Robert Sack notes the potential for confusion created by the two distinct uses of the term: "the popular image of territoriality is drawn from works emphasizing biological links," yet the word remains useful and almost indispensable for describing human actions that do not have such roots.[43] The nonbiological usage is not, as some might suppose, an illegitimate attempt by social scientists to trade for their own purposes on the prestige of a word that belonged originally to the natural sciences; the reverse would be closer to the truth. According to the *Oxford English Dictionary*, the original meanings of *territory* were approximately the ones used in the social sciences, and the word's appropriation by natural scientists for an inherited trait found in nonhuman creatures came quite late in its history (the same, of course, is true of the word *inherited* itself). If either usage is parasitic on the other, it is the natural science one on the social science one (as is the case too with *parasitic*).[44] The pattern is not an uncommon one; words have often, perhaps even usually, originated to describe human and social phenomena, which after all tend to be people's chief concerns, and have only later been extended by analogy, more or less properly, to cover phenomena in the realms studied by natural scientists.

The usual understanding of Calhoun's findings erred further in overlooking a basic fact of urban history, as the sociologist Amos Hawley pointed out in 1972. Population densities in US cities of the 1960s, so high as to cause serious and worsening social pathologies if one believes the urban historian Mumford, had been in decline for some decades—indeed, for the better part of a century.[45] They had been substantially higher in US cities of the late nineteenth and early twentieth centuries before the deconcentration promoted first by the electric trolley and then by the automobile. The Jewish immigrant districts of the Lower East Side of Manhattan circa 1900 had population densities previously unheard of in the United States and never duplicated there since. They also had strikingly low levels of violent crime, the problem above all of the 1960s that Calhoun's interpreters so glibly attributed to overcrowding. Indeed, leading nineteenth- and early twentieth-century European and American sociologists thought violent crime more typical of rural than of urban areas (and the reverse for crimes against property).[46]

Calhoun's interpreters were as short on geographical as on historical perspective. Some simple comparisons across space should have shown even moderately critical observers some additional weaknesses of the claimed link between density and pathology. The central parts of US cities of the 1960s, the prime exhibit for the prosecution, had population densities that were low by world urban standards along with social problems that were severe on the same scale. Research published early in the decade contrasted them with a city near the other end of the density continuum, Hong Kong, where despite much higher population densities, problems of crime, social disorganization, and ill-health turned out to be less acute than in US cities.[47] Plainly, densities of human occupation as such had no simple and necessary relation grounded in human biology to the pathologies so often blamed on them.

Nor did the uncritical use of evidence stop even there. If the alleged basic conflict between urban life and human needs truly existed, certain other signs of maladaptation should have offered compelling evidence of it. If one had to choose a single indicator for an unbearably stressful environment for the human organism, there could hardly be a better one than suicide rates. Suicide, on the whole, was indeed more common in urban than rural settings in western Europe in the nineteenth century, and in an era of rapid urbanization it was the object of worried speculation by social theorists such as Emile Durkheim. Today there is no such pattern in either the developed or the developing countries. Age-adjusted rural suicide rates in many places substantially exceed urban ones.[48] There cannot, then, be a simple connection between population density and suicide or the stresses to which it responds. The rural advantage in the United States had already disappeared by the time that Mumford and others drew their conclusions about US cities from Calhoun's work.[49] If urban suicide rates had indeed been higher in the 1960s, surely the decade's detractors of cities would have seized on them as supporting evidence for their claims. Their failure even to discuss them again suggests a state of mind too dominated by antiurban preconceptions to notice strong evidence on the other side.

If, as it appears, high population densities are not necessarily at war with the deepest promptings of human nature, what about the other defining traits of urbanness? Inasmuch as agriculture originated very late in the development of human beings as a species—not notably earlier than cities themselves and perhaps, if Jane Jacobs was correct, even later—the long span of evolution can hardly have implanted some fundamental attachment to it as a way of life. "The systematic cultivation of plants to create an artificial food supply," two anthropologists write, "has never been an instinctive part of the human repertoire. In fact, it is a comparatively recent human activity, practiced for far less than 1 percent of the time our genus has existed."[50] It would be almost equally difficult to argue that government, in the broadest sense, the restraint and guidance of individual actions by the collectivity, runs contrary to human nature; recognizably human beings most likely have always been governed by one another. Only the built-environment criterion for urbanness offers some plausible opportunities for the antiurban position. Even it suffers from a fundamental implausibility. If human nature contains some clear and strong preferences and aversions regarding the surroundings of life, the kinds of environments people build would naturally tend to be guided by them. Moreover, a sizeable minority of animals—what biologists call *urban synanthropes*—find the built city environment particularly well suited to them and thrive in it, though it was certainly not the setting in which they evolved. That human beings might be among them is not impossible.

The popularity that one claim has enjoyed entitles it to a closer look. It rests on the idea that people, similar to any other animal, would have evolved through natural selection to possess certain preferences that offer an advantage for survival and that some of these preferences today will still affect their habitat selection or the surroundings that they find themselves drawn to or repelled by. It goes on to argue that the characteristic land cover of suburbia, the green lawn in particular, derives from the advantages in the human evolutionary past of the savanna landscape—an open grassland with a scattering of trees—of East Africa.[51] Yet it falls short of being convincing on a number of counts. As a number of authors have pointed out, the history of human landscape practices and preferences shows no such uniform attachment to the lawn type of US suburbia as would be expected if it were indeed a powerful human universal. The ecologist F. H. Bormann and colleagues note that if the genetic explanation is correct, "all cultures throughout history would have made lawns central to their public and domestic spaces. Yet this is not the case. . . . In terms of human history, the lawn is not an old tradition," and geographically, they add, it has been important chiefly in areas of French and especially English cultural backgrounds and not elsewhere.[52] Moreover, this explanation for suburban land cover, as Ted Steinberg and others have pointed out, ignores some substantial biophysical differences between the two landscapes, the East African savanna and the typical US lawn.[53] And the one part of the world that undoubtedly possesses the characteristics in question, the East African savanna itself, is, to put it mildly, not the magnet for human migration from around the world today that one would expect it to be if the theory were valid. Two researchers have argued from the finding that young children display a greater preference than older age groups for scenes of a savanna landscape to the conclusion that an innate and universal trait is overlaid in time by a variety of other, learned ones. But such preferences among younger children might also be the result of their already disproportionate and pleasurable exposure to grassy environments (parks and lawns), as suggested by Elizabeth Lyons; moreover, as an explanation of the US lawn it leaves everything to be desired when one remembers that it was not children but adults who made the lawn a central feature of the landscape.[54] If the finding shows anything, it is that a savanna preference is weakest among those whose preferences would have mattered the most. Some studies of expressed preferences have documented a greater liking among their subjects for landscapes with dense tree cover than for the scattered trees characteristic of a savanna. Indeed, another school of thought holds that human beings evolved in a closed forest rather than a savanna landscape; if true, it would not account for the suburban lawn.[55] On the whole, it is hard to avoid Paul Robbins's conclusion: "the lawn is a historically recent development, specific to certain places and times, and most certainly not natural, hard-wired, or inevitable."[56] Finally, even if the theory can explain why a preference for a savanna environment or a vegetated one more generally might have become rooted in human nature through natural selection, no version of it that I have seen proposes a plausible physiological mechanism by which people are powerfully drawn to the right kind of landscape. But let us suppose that the theory is correct and that there is indeed a basic human need for direct experience of a savanna-type nature. Then under present-day circumstances, unless we disperse population so radically as to guarantee every household a green lawn with trees, there is all the more need for high-density urban settlement to protect such natural areas that remain within reach of the city and its inhabitants—and the most attractive and therefore the most apt to be taken—from being developed and placed off limits to the majority.

We might well feel obliged to do the same if we accepted the findings of another set of studies, ones that document less-specific preferences among their research subjects for scenes containing "natural" elements over ones dominated by a built environment. The thrust of this literature, though, is weakened by its focus, once again, on expressed rather than revealed preferences and by the rather narrow demographic range from which its subjects have been drawn; most are well-to-do residents of well-to-do parts of the world, overwhelmingly from the countries of North America and northwestern Europe. As several authors who have contributed to it observe, "As yet, it remains to be empirically demonstrated that the physical and psychological problems of urban living arouse restoration needs that continuously maintain and reinforce nature-oriented preferences."[57] The evidence to date is suggestive but no more. Some studies focus on children's preferences with the goal of finding natural likes and dislikes that have not yet been distorted by socialization into cultural patterns. Yet it is not easy to believe that any children old enough to respond meaningfully in a study will not already have picked up a good many cues about what to like and dislike from the people and things around them—nor is it easy to see why any culture should develop environmental preferences that conflict with important innate ones.

Going beyond mere expressed preferences, a branch of this literature has offered some harder evidence that physical (and also mental) health, and especially recovery from illnesses and operations, is aided by exposure to natural elements, which can be as simple as potted plants in a hospital room or a view of greenery from a window. It has already in some cases prompted innovative ways of working such "natural" elements into urban health-care settings, which in turn have shown how easily the city and the desired elements can be mingled. In any event, the global urban advantage in health and life expectancy suggests that whatever partial penalty a largely built environment may still impose is more than offset by other benefits that cities provide. And here once again we run into an asymmetry in the ways that more and less urban areas are often treated. When studies find that extreme and unvaried urban conditions produce less satisfaction than when other conditions are mixed in, the conclusion is drawn that urbanness is peculiarly unsatisfying to human beings because that is the implied hypothesis being tested and the evidence seems to confirm it. But no similar body of work has provided the necessary balance by asking whether most people living under comparable circumstances at the other end of the continuum, in settings almost entirely lacking in urban features, would be any less dissatisfied, would recover less slowly from illness, or would not welcome a dash of urban features (the presence of other people or signs of a human footprint amid the wilderness). What may be a mere desire for variety takes on the illusory appearance of a specific dislike of cities when dissatisfaction at only one end of the scale is examined. Yet far fewer people choose to live as hermits than as the inhabitants of megacities. Henry David Thoreau himself had frequent recourse to the village of Concord for company during his time at Walden Pond, which lasted only two years at that.[58] "Hardly a day went by," his biographer writes, "that Thoreau did not visit the village or was not visited at the pond." What even Thoreau required, most people would surely require even more.

9
Conclusion

This book began by defining urbanness as the underlying quality that the places we call cities possess in a high degree. It then examined the principal commonsense arguments for expecting high levels of urbanness to lead to undesirable outcomes in the seven major areas of human-environment interaction. For the most part, it found, the evidence did not support those arguments, many of which turned out to rest to a significant degree on errors, faulty assumptions, and fallacies in reasoning. Cities, indeed, possess many environmental advantages, at least partial or potential ones, that the commonsense view fails to acknowledge.

It is not surprising that urban environmental penalties should so often have been supposed to exist where they do not. Optical illusions in observation and pitfalls in reasoning, as we have seen, abound where cities and environmental concerns meet. The more urban an area, the more attention it and its problems will draw. One must, therefore, judge not on the basis of impressions or of anecdotal evidence but on careful comparisons between outcomes in more and less urban areas. The larger an urban area is, the larger, in absolute terms, its problems will be. One must, therefore, correct for population size in order to assess accurately how much impact a person will have or how much safety a person will enjoy in an urban or a rural setting. Urbanization is associated with many other processes and phenomena whose effects can easily but erroneously be conflated with its own, making it an easy scapegoat for many problems whose real origins lie elsewhere. One can check for this possibility by undertaking correlations at different scales—noting, for example, that though the most urbanized countries have the highest per capita consumption of resources, their most urbanized areas have the lowest—or with variables representing other possible causes. Cities, taken by themselves, certainly display a rich array of environmental impacts and environmental risks, and when looked at by themselves, may well appear to be problem areas even if they are less so than less urban areas are. Treating, as Weeks and colleagues have suggested, urbanness as a continuum and investigating outcomes all the way along it—rather than trying to understand the difference cities make by looking solely at what happens at the high end of the scale—is a useful habit to develop to avoid such pitfalls.

When carefully analyzed, greater degrees of urbanness rarely appear to be linked to poor outcomes in the ways often supposed. Often, and apparently more often than not, they are associated with better ones for a given society at a given level of population and standard of living. Do cities damage the environment? They lessen pressure on ecological systems by confining it in space, they slow population growth, and they make the consumption of major natural resources more sparing and efficient. Though they concentrate many forms of pollution, they often reduce the total pollution load and can better control emissions. Do cities put their residents at greater risk from environmental hazards? On the whole, they offer greater safety than more dispersed settlement does from the dangers of nature and of technology, and in modern times, they have even begun to shield them better from infectious diseases in the parts of the world most affected. Do cities achieve all this at the cost of being inherently unsatisfying places for human beings to live? There is little evidence of it.

There are indeed exceptions: damaging concentration of some forms of air pollution exposure, the concentration of water pollution in urbanized bays and estuaries, the urban heat island, a more hospitable setting for some disease vectors, and levels of HIV/AIDS and drug-resistant TB prevalence, for example. All the same, a first approximation would have to be that commonsense antiurbanism has the matter backward, that an advantage is the rule and urban penalties are exceptions, even if they are numerous and sometimes important.

The characteristics that define cities are the ones widely supposed to lead to penalties in these various nature-society domains. In fact, these very characteristics do much to account for the urban advantages registered in them. Large and dense collections of people contain their residents' environmental impact better than if the same population were more spread out, and they make many improvements more feasible by lowering their cost per person. Disproportionately nonagricultural livelihoods do less harm to people and the environment alike. A largely built environment can be shaped in ways that lessen human impact and improve well-being. Institutions of government possess powers of positive action that more institutionally impoverished areas cannot match.

Much of the case for an urban advantage, where one exists, is at least as commonsensical as the case for an urban penalty, once it has been stated, explained, and documented. It is not as stubbornly paradoxical, as daunting a challenge for the uninitiated, as the physics of relativity or even the economics of comparative advantage. The challenge in overcoming the stereotypes of the antienvironmental city is not one of perpetually insisting on what, however true, must always remain counterintuitive. It is, rather, the simpler and more manageable one of making it clear why what is true makes sense after all.

Extreme cases, even purely hypothetical ones that will never actually occur, can do much to color expectations. The images we form of both ends of the scale of urbanness will have more than their proper share of influence over what we suppose. Those that arise all too readily at the high extreme of the scale of urbanness are nightmares of dystopic cities, visions of social and environmental urban disaster in a setting of standing room only. Reveries on the other end of the scale incline, if anything, toward a note of peacefulness and harmony with nature. But a life in a pure state of nature, as Hobbes observed long ago in a different context, is poor, nasty, brutish, and short. And suppose, as a thought experiment, that we merely took the present population of the United States and spread it evenly across the nation's land area, Frank Lloyd Wright's proposed Broadacre City dispersed even further. What would the result be? Ecologically, it would be a plain disaster and so too for the consumption of natural resources: land, energy, water, and materials. It would concentrate pollution less but would generate a good deal more of it and make it less easy to manage. It would not much, if at all, decrease exposure to natural hazards and would certainly increase vulnerability to them as well as to technological hazards. Infectious disease, not a major health burden in the United States as it currently is, might increase or decline somewhat according to the balance of exposure and vulnerability. Even human residential satisfaction would probably decline. Those who value larger living spaces would gain but they can have them (if willing to pay the cost) today already, whereas those who prefer a dense urban environment would no longer be able to find one. Economically, so dispersed a society would certainly be a poorer one, facing higher costs for most goods and services and less able to pay for them—and a degree of deurbanization that would be costly in the United States would be disastrous in the LDCs. Extreme concentration would have its disadvantages but those of extreme deconcentration, though less obvious, would be at least as bad in their own way.

Such thought experiments are useful but results from ranges common in actual experience carry more weight. This book has focused on what has actually happened, on the record of the past, especially the very recent past. In doing so, it differs from but complements many of the books now appearing on the topic of cities and the environment.[1] These, as a rule, offer proposals and guidelines for what cities can become, an important task given their increasingly characteristic role as the home of human society. I have focused instead on what cities have been, on the actual outcomes registered by modern urban areas compared with those of less urban settlements. To know how realistic an untried possibility is, it helps to know what experience in similar cases has shown. If they conflict with the whole record of experience, claims about what cities can do invite skepticism. Writers who contrast damaging cities of the past with idealized ones of the future ask to have a good deal taken on faith.[2] But what cities have done, cities can do. If their record to date, and especially in recent times, is a good one, and better than it is often thought to be, it is a good bet that they will do well in the future. And of course they might be able to do even better, proceeding along the lines of what they have already done. If the record of the past is at least a moderately encouraging one as urban populations grow, proposals for making cities more sustainable are less likely to have to insist on making them less urban. It is likely that they will have to become, if anything, more so. On the evidence this book has reviewed, secondary deurbanization—especially the spatial dispersion of population and the political fragmentation of metropolitan areas—is a more worrisome trend by far than urbanization proper.[3]

Of course, the urbanness of a given population is not simply an independent variable that we can turn up or down at will on its own to achieve the results that we desire. Nor is it by any means the only factor affecting environmental outcomes. There could be places and populations equally urban but differing in what happens because of other differences. Research should try to identify the roles those differences can play. But if the findings of the research this book has reviewed are correct, the more urban place, all else being equal, is likely to record the better outcomes. And if urbanness cannot be manipulated simply and directly, it can be discouraged by obstacles or facilitated by inducements. All too often in the past it has been obstructed, and at a minimum those obstacles to urbanization that rest on misconceptions about its adverse environmental (or social) impacts should be removed.

Appendix A

William B. Meyer and Santiago Reyes Contreras

The period we examined in *Storm Events* ran for twenty years, from April 1, 1990, through March 31, 2010; it ran for ten years on either side of the April 1, 2000, date of the 2000 census. We used the 2000 census data for the county-level population calculations and classifications so that they would be reasonably reflective of conditions during a period of ten years on either side. *Storm Events* also contains figures for injuries and estimated property damage but the death count represents a much more consistent and reliable measure than either of these, less open to interpretation and less likely to vary in completeness from one setting to another—as well as being the most significant form of loss. We defined *highly urban* counties as ones that at the time of the 2000 census met the traditional Census Bureau criteria for urban core counties: ones containing an incorporated metro-area *central city* with at least fifty thousand residents. We defined *highly rural* counties as those that in 2000 lay outside of Census Bureau–defined metropolitan areas and also outside of the *micropolitan* areas as they were first defined and demarcated in 2003 on the basis of the 2000 census data. Table 5.1 in the text shows the results for the ten states that recorded fifty or more tornado deaths during the study period.[1] With a single exception (most-rural county deaths in Oklahoma), an urban advantage and a rural penalty, presumably due to differences in vulnerability, are apparent. It is unlikely that the results merely reflect either a chance period when tornadoes largely missed major centers of population or a tendency for cities to lie outside the most tornado-prone parts of their states. During the period studied, in the ten states that we examined, tornadoes passed not merely within the city limits but through parts of the downtown areas of cities as large as Atlanta, Fort Worth, Nashville, and Little Rock.

Using the *Storm Events* database as before, we counted deaths attributed to flash floods (including ones attributed to *urban stream flooding*) in the same way. *Storm Events* began distinguishing flash floods from others in the figures only in 1993, so the period covered here is a few years shorter than for tornadoes. Flash floods are much more regionally dispersed across the United States than tornadoes are; in the 1993–2010 period, ones causing at least one death were recorded in forty-three of the fifty states. We compared death tolls between highly urban and highly rural counties in the only two states that recorded fifty or more flash-flood deaths, Texas (198 deaths) and Missouri (69 deaths). In Texas, the most urban counties, with 68 percent of the state's population, had 51 percent of the flash-flood deaths and the most rural counties, with 7 percent of the population, had 15 percent of the flash-flood deaths. In Missouri, the most urban counties, with 43 percent of the state's population, had 23 percent of the flash-flood deaths and the most rural counties, with 16 percent of the population, had 42 percent of the flash-flood deaths.

Notes

Chapter 1

1. The value often given for 1900, 13.6 percent, based on the work of Kingsley Davis from the 1950s, has been challenged by Paul Bairoch in favor of a higher value of 17.2 percent. Other estimates assembled by Bairoch range between 13.2 and 18.0 percent: Paul Bairoch, *Cities and Economic Development: From the Dawn of History to the Present*, trans. Christopher Braider (Chicago: University of Chicago Press, 1988), table 31.1, 495.

2. As emphasized by Martin Brockerhoff, "Urban Growth in Developing Countries: A Review of Projections and Predictions," *Population and Development Review* 25, no. 4 (1999): 757–778; and Barney Cohen, "Urban Growth in Developing Countries: A Review of Current Trends and a Caution Regarding Existing Forecasts," *World Development* 32, no. 1 (2004): 23–51.

3. Ann Dale in collaboration with S. B. Hill, *At the Edge: Sustainable Development in the 21st Century* (Vancouver: UBC Press, 2001), 67.

4. National Research Council, *Cities Transformed: Demographic Change and Its Implications in the Developing World* (Washington, DC: National Academies Press, 2003), 259–260, 270–272.

5. On one such linguistic fault line, see Nancy E. McIntyre, K. Knowles-Yánez, and D. Hope, "Urban Ecology as an Interdisciplinary Field: Differences in the Use of 'Urban' Between the Social and Natural Sciences," *Urban Ecosystems* 4, no. 1 (2000): 5–24.

6. David Satterthwaite, "The Transition to a Predominantly Urban World and Its Underpinnings," *International Institute for Environment and Development, Human Settlements Discussion Paper Series* (London: IIED, 2007), 41–47.

7. On economic beliefs, see Bryan Caplan, *The Myth of the Rational Voter: Why Democracies Choose Bad Policies* (Princeton, NJ: Princeton University Press, 2007), 23–49; on the physics of moving bodies, Audrey B. Champagne, Leopold E. Klopfer, and John H. Anderson, "Factors Influencing the Learning of Classical Mechanics," *American Journal of Physics* 48, no. 12 (1980): 1074–1079; Andrea A. DiSessa, "Unlearning Aristotelian Physics: A Study of Knowledge-Based Learning," *Cognitive Science* 6, no. 1 (1982): 37–75; Michael McCloskey, Alfonso

152   *Notes*

Caramazza, and Bert Green, "Curvilinear Motion in the Absence of External Forces," *Science* 210, no. 4474 (1980): 1138–1141; Michael McCloskey, "Naïve Theories of Motion," in *Mental Models*, ed. Dedre Gentner and Albert L. Stevens (Hillsdale, NJ: Lawrence Erlbaum Associates, 1983), 299–324.

8. The saying comes from the eighteenth-century English poet William Cowper's "The Task" (1785). On cultural antiurban biases, see chapter 8 for more discussion. For interesting explorations of antiurbanism outside the environmental realm, see the chapters in *Fleeing the City: Studies in the Culture and Politics of Antiurbanism*, ed. Michael J. Thompson (New York: Palgrave Macmillan, 2009).

9. Patricia Draper, "Crowding among Hunter-Gatherers: The !Kung Bushmen," *Science* n.s. 182, no. 4109 (1973): 301–303. Likewise, as John R. Weeks observes, people live at very high densities in Egyptian villages but in such small numbers that the label *urban* is inappropriate: "Using Remote Sensing and Geographic Information Systems to Identify the Underlying Patterns of Urban Environments," in *New Forms of Urbanization*, ed. Tony Champion and Graeme Hugo (Aldershot, UK: Ashgate, 2004), 325–345.

10. Ulf Hannerz, *Exploring the City: Inquiries toward an Urban Anthropology* (New York: Columbia University Press, 1980), 67. He adds, "When despite all our hesitation in trying to define urbanism cross-culturally we do throw the term about in a variety of contexts, we undoubtedly have in mind the common-sense notion of towns and cities as sizeable dense settlements" (79).

11. Lisa Benton-Short and John R. Short, *Cities and Nature* (London: Routledge, 2008), 18.

12. The anthropologist Bruce Trigger proposed to define an urban area not as a place of dense settlement but rather one that "performs specialized functions in relation to a broader hinterland": Bruce Trigger, *Understanding Early Civilizations: A Comparative Study* (Cambridge, UK: Cambridge University Press, 2003), 121. Yet to do so would exclude all rural areas engaged in anything but providing for their own immediate wants; it also fails to include many elements (not only population size and density but also land cover and political incorporation) that are essential parts of *city* and *urban* in the words' ordinary usage.

13. For the definitions and procedures used in the 2010 census and the changes since 2000, see "2010 Census Urban and Rural Classification and Urban Area Criteria," available at http://www.census.gov/geo/www/ua/2010urbanruralclass .html. For the USDA's criteria, see "Measuring Rurality: Rural-Urban Continuum Codes," available at http://www.ers.usda.gov/briefing/rurality/ruralurbcon.

14. Even so, of course, the population of an overbounded city will still on the whole be much more urban than the area outside its boundaries and the area outside even an underbounded city much less so.

15. Zhou Yixing and Laurence J. C. Ma, "China's Urbanization Levels: Reconstructing a Baseline for the Fifth Population Census," *China Quarterly* 173 (2003): 176–196.

16. United Nations Human Settlements Programme (UN-HABITAT), *State of the World's Cities, 2006/7* (London: Earthscan, 2006), 5.

17. For instance, Weeks, "Using Remote Sensing," documents close positive correlations among all of the criteria for urbanness discussed previously and of each of them with remote-sensing indicators. For summaries of ongoing work relating remotely sensed built-environment variables to the delimitation of urban areas, see *Global Mapping of Human Settlement: Experiences, Datasets, and Prospects*, ed. Paolo Gamba and Martin Herold (Boca Raton, FL: CRC Press, 2009).

18. John R. Weeks, Dennis P. Larson, and Debbie L. Fugate, "Patterns of Urban Land Use as Assessed by Satellite Imagery: An Application to Cairo, Egypt," in *Population, Land Use, and Environment: Research Directions*, ed. Barbara Entwisle and Paul C. Stern (Washington, DC: National Academies Press, 2005), 266.

19. Data from "World Urbanization Prospects: The 2011 Revision," available at http://esa.un.org/unpd/wup/index.htm. On major trends and patterns, see also Hania Zlotnik, "World Urbanization: Trends and Prospects," in Champion and Hugo, *New Forms of Urbanization*, 43–64.

20. For some discussions of this and related issues that are more or less in accord with the position taken here—especially in understanding urban and rural as multidimensional and as matters of degree rather than of kind—see National Research Council, *Cities Transformed*, 67–74 and several of the essays in Champion and Hugo, *New Forms of Urbanization*, notably Weeks, "Using Remote Sensing," and David L. Brown and John B. Cromartie, "The Nature of Rurality in Postindustrial Society," 269–283. The point is also underlined by the collection's subtitle, "Beyond the Urban-Rural Dichotomy."

21. In 2002 (the last time the necessary data were collected), farm production in the United States accounted for only 6.5 percent of employment in nonmetropolitan areas (and 1 percent in metropolitan areas): USDA/ERS, "United States Farm and Farm-Related Employment, 2002," available at http://www.ers.usda.gov/Data/FarmandRelatedEmployment/ViewData.asp?GeoAreaPick=STAUS_United%20States. On agriculture in the LDCs, see Dirk Bezemer and Derek Headey, "Agriculture, Development, and Urban Bias," *World Development* 36, no. 8 (2008): 1347.

22. Sabrina Tavernise and Robert Gebeloff, "Once Rare in Rural America, Divorce Is Changing the Face of Its Families," *New York Times*, March 24, 2011: A18; Leonard J. Paulozzi, "Recent Changes in Drug Poisoning Mortality in the United States by Urban-Rural Status and by Drug Type," *Pharmacoepidemiology and Drug Safety* 17, no. 10 (2008): 997–1005.

23. See, for example, Louis Wirth, "Urbanism as a Way of Life," *American Journal of Sociology* 44, no. 1 (1938): 1–24; Robert Redfield, "The Folk Society and Custom," *American Journal of Sociology* 45, no. 5 (1940): 731–742. On the rise and decline of this view, see Peter Saunders, *Social Theory and the Urban Question*, 2nd ed. (New York: Holmes & Meier, 1986), 84–113.

24. For many similar terms in seven other languages, see Christian Topalov et al., *L'aventure des mots de la ville* (Paris: Robert Laffont, 2010).

25. This is particularly so if one regards suburban grass as a crop; in the same way as any other domesticated plant, it is cultivated for the purpose of satisfying

certain wants (though the consumption is visual and symbolic rather than gastronomic) and the processes of cultivation are not essentially different: "the amount of fertilizer applied to American lawns is comparable to or exceeds the nutrient inputs into almost any major U.S. food crop, including wheat, soy, or cotton": Paul Robbins, *Lawn People: How Grasses, Weeds, and Chemicals Make Us Who We Are* (Philadelphia: Temple University Press, 2007), 63. As noted, too, agriculture (in the more usual sense of the term) that occurs within urban areas is usually found on the fringe, the zone of the lowest degree of urbanness: Christopher Boone and Ali Modarres, *City and Environment* (Philadelphia: Temple University Press), 2006.

26. On the US city as a distinct type, see Kenneth T. Jackson, *Crabgrass Frontier: The Suburbanization of the United States* (New York: Oxford University Press, 1985), 3–11. The quotation is from Jorge E. Hardoy, Diana Mitlin, and David Satterthwaite, *Environmental Problems in an Urbanizing World: Finding Solutions in Africa, Asia, and Latin America* (Sterling, VA: Earthscan Publications, 2001), 21. On major world-regional differences in city form, see Stanley D. Brunn, Maureen Hays-Mitchell, and Donald J. Zeigler, eds., *Cities of the World: World Regional Urban Development*, 4th ed. (Lanham, MD: Rowman & Littlefield, 2008); and Michael Pacione, *Urban Geography: A Global Perspective* (London: Routledge, 2001), 447–459. There are many secondary differences between the cities characteristic of different world regions: of western Europe, of Latin America, of the Middle East, of sub-Saharan Africa, of South and East Asia, of the former East Bloc, and for that matter of different regions within the United States. Nor are any of these forms static. Some countertrends in several of the largest US cities have become so marked that one observer even foresees a general "demographic inversion" that will leave an affluent core surrounded by a decaying and impoverished fringe: Alan Ehrenhalt, "Trading Places: The Demographic Inversion of the American City," *The New Republic* (August 13, 2008): 19–22. At the same time, much of western Europe and many LDCs have seen a considerable and even accelerating degree of high-income decentralization on the classic US model: Robert Bruegmann, *Sprawl: A Compact History* (Chicago: University of Chicago Press, 2005), 73–80, 90–91.

27. On these and related terms (including *disurbanization* and *counterurbanization*), see Tony Champion, "Urbanization, Suburbanization, Counterurbanization and Reurbanization," in *Handbook of Urban Studies*, ed. Roman Paddison (London: Sage, 2001), 143–161.

28. Jane Jacobs, *The Death and Life of Great American Cities* (New York: Random House, 1961); see particularly chapter 11, "The Need for Concentration" (200–221), and chapter 22, "The Kind of Problem a City Is" (428–448).

29. Jane Jacobs, *The Economy of Cities* (New York: Random House, 1969), chapter 1, "Cities First—Rural Development Later," 3–48; Edward W. Soja, *Postmetropolis: Critical Studies of Cities and Regions* (Malden, MA: Blackwell, 2000), 12–13. Soja elsewhere (19–49) discusses the continuing relevance of Jacobs's ideas about prehistory in light of more recent archeological work. For

a later and independent argument that sizeable sedentary settlements came before agriculture, see Jacques Cauvin, *The Birth of the Gods and the Origins of Agriculture*, trans. Trevor Watkins (Cambridge, UK: Cambridge University Press, 2000).

30. Robert Lucas, "On the Mechanics of Economic Development," chapter 1 (originally published in 1988), in *Lectures on Economic Development* (Cambridge, MA: Harvard University Press, 2002), 59; Lyndon B. Johnson, "Remarks at Ceremonies Marking the 100th Anniversary of Dallastown, Pennsylvania, September 3, 1966," in *Public Papers of Lyndon B. Johnson, 1966*, Book II (Washington, DC: US Government Printing Office, 1967), 951.

31. Soja, *Postmetropolis*, 13; for other accounts of Jacobs's influence, see David Nowlan, "Jane Jacobs among the Economists," in *Ideas That Matter: The Worlds of Jane Jacobs*, ed. Max Allen (Owen Sound, ON: The Ginger Press, 1997), 111–113; Pierre Desrochers and Gert-Jan Hospers, "Cities and the Economic Development of Nations: An Essay on Jane Jacobs' Contribution to Economic Theory," *Canadian Journal of Regional Science* 30, no. 1 (2007): 115–132; David Warsh, *Knowledge and the Wealth of Nations: A Story of Economic Discovery* (New York: W. W. Norton, 2006), 245–246, 307–308.

32. For overviews, see, for example, National Research Council, *Cities Transformed*, 51–56; Brendan O'Flaherty, *Urban Economics* (Cambridge, MA: Harvard University Press, 2005), 12–33; Edward L. Glaeser, "Are Cities Dying?" *Journal of Economic Perspectives* 100, no. 6 (1998): 139–160; and *Triumph of the City: How Our Greatest Invention Makes Us Richer, Smarter, Greener, Healthier, and Happier* (New York: The Penguin Press, 2011); Brian Knudsen et al., "Density and Creativity in U.S. Regions," *Annals of the Association of American Geographers* 98, no. 2 (2008): 461–478; William McGreevey et al., "Propinquity Matters: How Better Health, Urbanization, and Income Grew Together," *Georgetown Journal on Poverty Law and Policy* 15 (2008): 605–633; Luís A. M. Bettencourt et al., "Growth, Innovation, Scaling, and the Pace of Life in Cities," *Proceedings of the National Academy of Sciences* 104, no. 17 (2007): 7301–7306; and Mario Polèse, *The Wealth and Poverty of Regions: Why Cities Matter* (Chicago: University of Chicago Press, 2009), 29–66. On density and the costs of public service provision, see John I. Carruthers and Gudmundur F. Ulfarsson, "Urban Sprawl and the Cost of Public Services," *Environment and Planning B* 30 (2003): 503–522; and "Does 'Smart Growth' Matter to Public Finance?" *Urban Studies* 45 (2008): 1791–1823; also Miriam Hortas-Rico and Albert Solé-Ollé, "Does Urban Sprawl Increase the Costs of Providing Local Public Services? Evidence from Spanish Municipalities," *Urban Studies* 47, no. 7 (2010): 1513–1540.

33. Glaeser, *Triumph of the City*, 146–147, 152.

34. Jonathan L. Freedman, *Crowding and Behavior* (New York: The Viking Press, 1975), 106–118; Peter Calthorpe, "Redefining Cities," *Whole Earth Review* no. 45 (March 1985): 1; David Engwicht, *Reclaiming Our Cities and Towns: Better Living with Less Traffic* (Philadelphia: New Society Publishing, 1993), 17; see also Richard Register, *Eco-City Berkeley: Building Cities for a Healthy Future*

(Berkeley: North Atlantic Books, 1987). On the Eco-City movement, see Mark Roseland, "The Eco-City Approach to Sustainable Development in Urban Areas," in *How Green Is the City? Sustainability Assessment and the Management of Urban Environments*, ed. Dimitri Devuyst with Luc Hens and Walter De Lannoy (New York: Columbia University Press, 2001), 85–103.

35. Robert C. Paehlke, *Environmentalism and the Future of Progressive Politics* (New Haven, CT: Yale University Press, 1989), 244–251.

36. Ira S. Lowry, "World Urbanization in Perspective," *Population and Development Review* 16, supplement (1990): 148–176.

37. Martin W. Lewis, *Green Delusions: An Environmentalist Critique of Radical Environmentalism* (Durham, NC: Duke University Press, 1992), 87–101.

38. Hardoy, Mitlin, and Satterthwaite, *Environmental Problems in an Urbanizing World*, 20–24.

39. For some notable examples, see David G. Victor, "Seeking Sustainability: Cities, Countryside, and Wilderness," *Population and Development Review* 32, Supplement (2006), 202–221; David Owen, *Green Metropolis: Why Living Smaller, Living Closer, and Driving Less Are the Keys to Sustainability* (New York: Riverhead Books, 2009); Stewart Brand, *Whole Earth Discipline: An Eco-pragmatist Manifesto* (New York, Viking, 2009), 25–73; Glaeser, *Triumph of the City*, 199–222; and "Better, Greener, Smarter Cities," *Scientific American* 305, no. 74/75 (2011).

40. United Nations Population Fund, *State of World Population 2007: Unleashing the Potential of Urban Growth* (New York: UNFPA, 2007), 1, 35, 55.

41. Owen, *Green Metropolis*, 25–26.

42. The original statement is Michael Lipton, *Why Poor People Stay Poor: Urban Bias in World Development* (Cambridge, MA: Harvard University Press, 1977). For a balanced assessment reviewing many of the criticisms of the thesis, see Gareth A. Jones and Stuart Corbridge, "The Continuing Debate about Urban Bias: The Thesis, Its Critics, Its Influence, and Its Implications for Poverty-Reduction Strategies," *Progress in Development Studies* 10, no. 1 (2010): 1–18. One's confidence in the urban-bias thesis would be enhanced if some of its leading proponents could agree on where the phenomenon does and does not exist. According to Lipton himself, First World regions such as North America and western Europe have long since shifted to the opposite pattern, one of rural bias: Michael Lipton, "Urban Bias," in *Encyclopedia of International Development*, ed. Tim Forsyth (London: Routledge, 2005), 724. However, Debra Lyn Bassett asserts that urban bias is the rule in the United States and other First World countries as well as in the LDCs: "Poverty and Global Ruralism," *Journal of Gender, Race & Justice* 13 (2009): 1–25. It might also be argued that greater ability to influence policy, one of the supposed sources of policy bias, is itself a legitimate advantage of urban location in a more or less democratic system.

43. Lowry, "World Urbanization in Perspective," esp. 149, 166–172.

44. Richard Whately, *Elements of Logic*, 7th ed. (London: B. Fellowes, 1831), 250.

Chapter 2

1. Paehlke, *Environmentalism and the Future of Progressive Politics*, 246.

2. John Stuart Mill, *A System of Logic: Books IV–VI*, in *Collected Works of John Stuart Mill*, ed. J. M. Robson, vol. 8 (Toronto: University of Toronto Press, 1974), 780.

3. Patricia Nelson Limerick, *Something in the Soil: Legacies and Reckonings in the New West* (New York: W. W. Norton, 2000), 180.

4. For a thorough review of the ecological impacts of suburban and exurban development in the United States, see the chapters in *Nature in Fragments: The Legacy of Sprawl*, ed. Elizabeth Ann Johnson and Michael W. Klemens (New York: Columbia University Press, 2005), especially Johnson and Klemens, "The Impact of Sprawl on Biodiversity," 18–53; and Seth R. Reice, "Ecosystems, Disturbance, and the Impact of Sprawl," 90–108. On the ecological impacts of further migration to exurban-rural areas, see those in *The Planner's Guide to Natural Resource Conservation: The Science of Land Development beyond the Metropolitan Fringe*, ed. Adrian X. Esparza and Guy McPherson (Dordrecht: Springer, 2009).

5. Glaeser, *Triumph of the City*, 200–201.

6. Bruegmann, *Sprawl: A Compact History*, 149; Adam Rome, *The Bulldozer in the Countryside: Suburban Sprawl and the Rise of American Environmentalism* (New York: Cambridge University Press, 2001).

7. Scott D. Kraus and Rosalind M. Rolland, eds., *The Urban Whale: North Atlantic Right Whales at the Crossroads* (Cambridge, MA: Harvard University Press, 2007), 4. The concluding chapter discusses "the urban whale syndrome" in similar terms, using *urban* or variants of the word to refer to things as disparate as population growth, fishing, the mechanization of shipping, chemical pollution, noise, and habitat alteration, describing the net effects of these processes as "the cumulative effects of urbanization" (497) and offering the following assessment for *Homo sapiens:* "In humans, constant urban living takes a measurable toll on health and survival . . ." (497). As discussed in chapter 7, human beings today seem in fact to enjoy better-than-average health and life expectancy in urban settings.

8. Bruce E. Babbitt, *Cities in the Wilderness: A New Vision of Land Use in America* (Washington, DC: Island Press, 2005), 98–99.

9. Paul Robbins and Julie T. Sharp, "Producing and Consuming Chemicals: The Moral Economy of the American Lawn," *Economic Geography* 79, no. 4 (2003): 432, 438, 442; see also Robert B. Feagan and Michael Ripmeester, "Contesting Natural(ized) Lawns: A Geography of Private Green Space in the Niagara Region," *Urban Geography* 20, no. 7 (1999): 617–634; and Ted Steinberg, *American Green: The Obsessive Quest for the Perfect Lawn* (New York: W. W. Norton, 2006).

10. On changes in species, see Michael L. McKinney, "Urbanization, Biodiversity, and Conservation," *BioScience* 52, no. 10 (2002), 883–890; and "Urbanization

as a Major Cause of Biotic Homogenization," *Biological Conservation* 127, no. 3 (2006): 247–260. For concise natural-science overviews of the various ecological changes associated with urbanization, see Nancy B. Grimm et al., "Global Change and the Ecology of Cities," *Science* 391 (February 8, 2008): 756–760; and Kevin J. Gaston, Zoe G. Davies, and Jill L. Edmondson, "Urban Environments and Ecosystem Functions," in *Urban Ecology*, ed. Kevin J. Gaston (Cambridge, UK: Cambridge University Press, 2010), 35–52.

11. Brian Stone Jr. and Michael O. Rodgers, "Urban Form and Thermal Efficiency: How the Design of Cities Influences the Urban Heat Island Effect," *Journal of the American Planning Association* 67, no. 2 (2001): 186–198.

12. Ron Chepesiuk, "Missing the Dark," *Environmental Health Perspectives* 117, no. 1 (2009): A20–A27.

13. Even the usual assumption that Owens Valley rural interests were unfairly exploited in the division of proceeds from the water transfer has been effectively challenged by Gary D. Libecap, "Chinatown: Owens Valley and Western Water Reallocation—Getting the Record Straight and What It Means for Water Markets," *Texas Law Review* 83, no. 7 (2005): 2055–2089; he also underlines the marginal economic potential of the valley, which would have made the profitability of a subsidized federal reclamation project highly unlikely.

14. Nigel Dudley and Sue Stolton, "The Role of Forest Protected Areas in Supplying Drinking Water to the World's Biggest Cities," in *The Urban Imperative: Urban Outreach for Protected Area Agencies*, ed. Ted Trzyna (Sacramento: California Institute of Public Affairs, 2005), 27–33.

15. On the Massachusetts case, see Thomas Conuel, *Quabbin: The Accidental Wilderness*, rev. ed. (Amherst: University of Massachusetts Press, 1990); on the New York City system as a powerful agent of preservation in the Catskills, if not always an even-handed or popular one, David Stradling, *Making Mountains: New York City and the Catskills* (Seattle: University of Washington Press, 2007); on the urban origins of the Adirondack preserve, Philip G. Terrie, *Contested Terrain: A New History of Nature and People in the Adirondacks*, 2nd ed. (Syracuse, NY: Syracuse University Press, 2008).

16. Samuel P. Hays, *Explorations in Environmental History: Essays* (Pittsburgh: University of Pittsburgh Press, 1998), 89–94, 97.

17. For widely differing perspectives on such conflicts, agreeing only on their importance and severity, see, for example, *Social Change and Conservation: Environmental Politics and Impacts of National Parks and Protected Areas*, ed. Krishna B. Ghimire and Michel P. Pimbert (London: Earthscan, 1997); *Parks in Peril: People, Politics, and Protected Areas*, ed. Katrina Brandon, Kent H. Redford, and Steven M. Sanderson (Washington, DC: Island Press, 1998); and *Making Parks Work: Strategies for Preserving Tropical Nature*, ed. John Terborgh et al. (Washington, DC: Island Press, 2002).

18. Alexander S. Mather, "The Forest Transition," *Area* 24, no. 4 (1992): 367–379; A. S. Mather, C. L. Needle, and J. Fairbairn, "Environmental Kuznets Curves and Forest Transitions," *Geography* 84, no. 1 (1999): 55–65, tying the theory to other studies conducted within the theoretical framework of the "Environmental

Kuznets Curve," which predicts a rise in environmental degradation in the early phases of economic development followed by improvement thereafter. For similar conclusions, see Karen Ehrhardt-Martinez, Edward M. Crenshaw, and J. Craig Jenkins, "Deforestation and the Environmental Kuznets Curve: A Cross-National Investigation of Intervening Mechanisms," *Social Science Quarterly* 83, no. 1 (2002): 226–243, who cite urbanization as an important element of the process. The generality and the theoretical underpinnings of the forest transition and EKC models remain controversial (for a review of the former, see Thomas K. Rudel, Laura Schneider, and Maria Uriarte, eds., "Forest Transitions," special issue of *Land Use Policy* 27, no. 2 [2009]: 95–179). The point here is that both do identify cases in which urbanization contributes to ecological recovery in nonurban areas.

19. Many of the chapters in *Population Distribution Policies in Development Planning* (New York: United Nations, 1979) illustrate the long-supposed urgency of implementing such policies to stave off the dangers either of excessive urban growth or increased rural population densities. On the Indonesian and Brazilian cases respectively, see Peter Dauvergne, "The Politics of Deforestation in Indonesia," *Pacific Affairs* 66, no. 4 (1994): 511–512 (though for a less critical view, see also Anthony Whitten, "Indonesia's Transmigration Program and Its Role in the Loss of Tropical Rain Forests," *Conservation Biology* 1, no. 3 [1987]: 239–246); and Anna Luiza Ozorio de Almeida, *The Colonization of the Amazon* (Austin: University of Texas Press, 1992). National policies aimed specifically at curbing migration to cities are discussed in chapter 8 of this book.

20. See T. Mitchell Aide and H. Ricardo Grau, "Globalization, Migration, and Latin American Ecosystems," *Science* 305, no. 5692 (2004): 1915–1916; H. Ricardo Grau and T. Mitchell Aide, "Are Rural-Urban Migration and Sustainable Development Compatible in Mountain Systems?" *Mountain Research and Development* 27, no. 2 (2007): 119–123; and H. Ricardo Grau and Mitchell Aide, "Globalization and Land-Use Transitions in Latin America," *Ecology & Society* 13, no. 2 (2008): 1 [online].

21. Sandra R. Baptista, "Metropolitanization and Forest Recovery in Southern Brazil: A Multiscale Analysis of the Florianópolis City-Region, Santa Catarina State, 1970 to 2005," *Ecology & Society* 13, no. 2 (2008): 5 [online].

22. Isabel K. Parés-Ramos, William A. Gould, and T. Mitchell Aide, "Agricultural Abandonment, Suburban Growth, and Forest Expansion in Puerto Rico between 1990 and 2000," *Ecology & Society* 13, no. 2 (2008), 1 [online]; see also Thomas K. Rudel and Maria Perez-Lugo, "When Fields Revert to Forests: Development and Spontaneous Reforestation in Post-War Puerto Rico," *The Professional Geographer* 52, no. 3 (2000): 286–297; and H. Ricardo Grau et al., "The Ecological Consequences of Socioeconomic and Land-Use Changes in Postagriculture Puerto Rico," *BioScience* 52, no. 12 (2003): 1159–1168.

23. For these caveats, see H. Ricardo Grau, T. Mitchell Aide, Jess K. Zimmernann, and John R. Thomlinson, "Trends and Scenarios of the Carbon Budget in Postagricultural Puerto Rico (1936–2060)," *Global Change Biology* 10, no. 7 (2004): 1163–1179 (net carbon releases); Grau et al., "Ecological Consequences," 1163–1164 (postrecovery forest composition); Grau and Aide, "Are Rural-Urban Migration and Sustainable Development Compatible in Mountain Systems?"

119–120, and "Globalization and Land-Use Transitions" (rural environmental and social effects); and Grau and Aide, "Are Rural-Urban Migration and Sustainable Development Compatible in Mountain Systems?" 121 (offsetting costs of intensive agriculture on better lands); also Susanna B. Hecht et al., "Globalization, Forest Resurgence, and Environmental Politics in El Salvador," *World Development* 34, no. 2 (2006): 309–311 (questioning the "undisturbed" character of pre-twentieth-century forest).

24. See, for example, Edward L. Kick et al., "Impacts of Domestic Population Dynamics and Foreign Wood Trade on Deforestation: A World-Systems Perspective," *Journal of Developing Societies* 12, no. 1 (1996): 68–87; Ehrhardt-Martinez, Crenshaw, and Jenkins, "Deforestation and the Environmental Kuznets Curve"; Andrew K. Jorgenson, "Unequal Ecological Exchange and Environmental Degradation: A Theoretical Proposition and Cross-National Study of Deforestation," *Rural Sociology* 71, no. 4 (2006): 696, 702–703; Andrew K. Jorgenson and Thomas J. Burns, "Effects of Rural and Urban Population Dynamics and National Development on Deforestation in Less-Developed Countries, 1990–2000," *Sociological Inquiry* 77, no. 3 (2006): 460–482; and John M. Shandra, Christopher Leckband, and Bruce London, "Ecologically Unequal Exchange and Deforestation: A Cross-National Analysis of Forestry Export Flows," *Organization & Environment* 22, no. 3 (2009): 293–310. One study has found, however, that deforestation was significantly associated at the national level with the rate of urban population growth in the LDCs between 2000 and 2005: Ruth DeFries et al., "Deforestation Driven by Urban Population Growth and Agricultural Trade in the Twenty-First Century," *Nature Geoscience* 3 (2010): 178–181. As the authors themselves note, their results conflict with the prevailing findings in the literature and thus may not apply for periods other than the five years they examine. They note too that "we cannot infer causal relationships based on the associations between forest loss and the independent variables" without further and deeper inquiry (179). It may not be urban growth itself, in any meaningful sense, that drove forest loss in their study period but other changes that more or less paralleled it. Finally, as noted in chapter 1, rates of urbanization, which tend to correlate negatively with the urban level of a country's population, are not usually the best measures of urbanness (the same caveat applies to several of the other studies cited previously).

25. George A. Ball, *Diplomacy for a Crowded World: An American Foreign Policy* (Boston: Little, Brown and Company, 1976), 253–254. Similarly, the report of a committee of Third World leaders simultaneously insisted on the undesirability of city growth and of rural-to-urban migration and on the importance of reducing population growth: *The Challenge to the South: Report of the South Commission* (New York: Oxford University Press, 1990), 106, 281–282.

26. National Research Council, *Cities Transformed*, 125–127, 209–231.

27. For figures on urban-rural differences in sub-Saharan Africa, see David Shapiro and B. O. Tambashe, "Fertility Transition in Urban and Rural Sub-Saharan Africa," *Journal of African Policy Studies* 8, nos. 2/3 (2002): 103–127; Michel Garenne and Veronique Joseph, "The Timing of the Fertility Transition in Sub-Saharan Africa," *World Development* 30, no. 10 (2002): 1835–1843; David Shapiro and Tesfayi Gebreselassie, "Fertility Transitions in Sub-Saharan

Africa: Falling and Stalling," *African Population Studies* 23, no. 1 (2008): 3–23; on variation with city size, National Research Council, *Cities Transformed*, 209–211.

28. For a suggestive study to this effect, see John R. Weeks et al., "The Fertility Transition in Egypt: Intraurban Patterns in Cairo," *Annals of the Association of American Geographers* 94, no. 1 (2004): 74–93.

29. Classic analyses of the incentives to fertility in rural India are Mahmood Mamdani, *The Myth of Population Control: Family, Caste, and Class in an Indian Village* (New York: Monthly Review Press, 1972); and S. K. Rao, "Population Growth and Economic Development: A Counter-Argument," *Economic and Political Weekly* 11, no. 31/33 (1976): 1149–1158.

30. For discussions and analyses of these factors in particular countries, see, for example, Bun Song Lee and Louis G. Pohl, "The Influence of Rural-Urban Migration on Migrants' Fertility in Korea, Mexico, and Cameroon," *Population Research and Policy Review* 12, no. 1 (1993): 3–26; David P. Lindstrom, "Rural-Urban Migration and Reproductive Behavior in Guatemala," ibid. 22, no. 4 (2003): 351–372; and Arpita Chattopadhyay, Michael J. White, and Cornelius Debpuur, "Migrant Fertility in Ghana: Selection versus Adaptation and Disruption as Causal Mechanisms," *Population Studies* 60, no. 2 (2006): 189–203.

31. On Fascist antiurbanism, see Diane Ghirardo, *Building New Communities: New Deal America and Fascist Italy* (Princeton, NJ: Princeton University Press, 1989), 39–43; David G. Horn, "Constructing the Sterile City: Pronatalism and Social Sciences in Interwar Italy," *American Ethnologist* 18, no. 3 (1991): 581–601; and Carl Ipsen, *Dictating Demography: The Problem of Population in Fascist Italy* (New York: Cambridge University Press, 1996). Even in Rome, superficially a symbol and showplace for the regime, fascist policy was essentially deurbanizing: Paul Baxa, *Roads and Ruins: The Symbolic Landscape of Fascist Rome* (Toronto: University of Toronto Press, 2010), 156. For detailed analyses of the land reclamation initiatives and their practical and symbolic significance for fascist attitudes toward cities, rural life, and nature, see Federico Caprotti, *Mussolini's Cities: Internal Colonialism in Italy, 1930–1939* (Youngstown, NY: Cambria Press, 2007) and Steen Bo Frandsen, "'The War that We Prefer': The Reclamation of the Pontine Marshes and Fascist Expansion," in *International Fascism, 1919–1945*, edited by Gert Sørenson and Robert Mallett (London: Frank Cass, 2002), 69–82.

32. Philip Verwimp, "Development Ideology, the Peasantry, and Genocide: Rwanda Represented in Habyarimana's Speeches," *Journal of Genocide Research* 2, no. 3 (2000): 338–339, 341–344; Karol C. Boudreaux, "Land Conflict and Genocide in Rwanda," *Electronic Journal of Sustainable Development* 1, no. 3 (2009).

Chapter 3

1. Boone and Modarres, *City and Environment*, 74; Lester R. Brown, "The Urban Prospect: Reexamining the Basic Assumptions," *Population and Development Review* 2, no. 2 (1976): 267–277; Shannon M. Sweeney, "A Comparison

of Resource Consumption for Rural, Suburban, and Urban Environments," senior honors thesis, Department of Geography, Colgate University, 2007.

2. Peter Newman and Jeffrey Kenworthy, *Sustainability and Cities: Overcoming Automobile Dependence* (Washington, DC: Island Press, 1999), 14.

3. Jesper Stage, Jørn Stage, and Gordon McGranahan, "Is Urbanization Contributing to Higher Food Prices?" *IIED/UNFPA Human Settlements Working Paper Series, Urban and Emerging Population Issues-1,* August 2009, 32.

4. Center for Neighborhood Technology, http://www.cnt.org, maps of "Household Auto Greenhouse Gas Emissions" within "Housing + Transportation Affordability Index."

5. Owen, *Green Metropolis,* 7.

6. Lewis, *Green Delusions,* 93; on elevators, see Owen, *Green Metropolis,* 207–208.

7. Peter W. G. Newman and Jeffrey R. Kenworthy, "Gasoline Consumption and Cities: A Comparison of U.S. Cities with a Global Survey," *Journal of the American Planning Association 55,* no. 1 (1989): 24–37.

8. Jihoon Min, Zeke Hausfather, and Qi Feng Lin, "A High-Resolution Spatial Model of Residential Energy End Use Characteristics for the United States," *Journal of Industrial Ecology 14,* no. 5 (2010): 791–807. For similar results from Canada combining household operating energy, transportation energy, and the energy embodied in construction, see Jonathan Norman, Heather L. MacLean, and Christopher A. Kennedy, "Comparing High and Low Residential Density: Life-Cycle Analysis of Energy Use and Greenhouse Gas Emissions," *Journal of Urban Planning and Development 132,* no. 1 (2006): 10–21; and Jared R. VandeWeghe and Christopher Kennedy, "A Spatial Analysis of Residential Greenhouse Gas Emissions in the Toronto Metropolitan Area," *Journal of Industrial Ecology 11,* no. 2 (2007): 133–144. However, a study from Australia found higher per capita emissions from apartments than from detached dwellings once two factors were taken into account: the energy embodied in construction and the longer periods in which the apartment space was vacant: Alan Perkins et al., "Transport, Housing, and Urban Form: The Life-Cycle Energy Consumption and Emissions of City Centre Apartments Compared with Suburban Dwellings," *Urban Policy and Research 27,* no. 4 (2009): 377–396. Calculating emissions per household may also somewhat exaggerate an urban advantage if the average urban household contains fewer members than the average suburban or rural ones; using simple per capita emissions, though, creates another set of distortions.

9. "Inventory of New York City Greenhouse Gas Emissions, September 2009" (New York: Mayor's Office of Long-Term Planning and Sustainability, 2009), 5.

10. Owen, *Green Metropolis,* 4–6.

11. Edward L. Glaeser and Matthew E. Kahn, "The Greenness of Cities: Carbon Dioxide Emissions and Urban Development," *Journal of Urban Economics 67,* no. 3 (2010): 404–418. On ways in which the benefits of density may be offset by other elements of urban structure, see Austin Troy, *The Very Hungry City:*

Urban Energy Efficiency and the Economic Fate of Cities (New Haven, CT: Yale University Press, 2012), 59–82.

12. Peter Newman and Jeff Kenworthy, "Greening Urban Transportation," in *State of the World 2007: Our Urban Future: A Worldwatch Institute Report on Progress Toward a Sustainable Society* (New York: W. W. Norton, 2007), 69, 72; Sabine Barles, "Urban Metabolism of Paris and Its Region," *Journal of Industrial Ecology* 13, no. 6 (2009): 909.

13. David Satterthwaite, "Cities' Contributions to Global Warming: Notes on the Allocation of Greenhouse Gas Emissions," *Environment and Urbanization* 20, no. 2 (2008): 539–549; David Dodman, "Blaming Cities for Climate Change? An Analysis of Urban Greenhouse Gas Emissions," *Environment and Urbanization* 21, no. 1 (2009): 191–196. The 2009 New York City report cited here excludes aviation fuel but includes emissions from energy generated outside the city for its use and those from business (including industry) conducted in buildings in the city. By the same token, the national figure it uses for comparison does not include agricultural emissions.

14. Satterthwaite, "Cities' Contribution," 540–543, 547; David Dodman and David Satterthwaite, "Are Cities Really to Blame?," *Urban World* 1, no. 2 (2009): 12–13; Daniel Hoornweg, Lorraine Sugar, and Claudia Lorena Trejos Gómez, "Cities and Greenhouse Gas Emissions: Moving Forward," *Environment and Urbanization* 23, no. 1 (2011): 207–227.

15. David Satterthwaite, "How Urban Societies Can Adapt to Resource Shortage and Climate Change," *Philosophical Transactions of the Royal Society A* 369, no. 1942 (2011): 1762–1783.

16. Dodman, "Blaming Cities"; Satterthwaite, "Cities' Contribution"; Hoornweg et al., "Cities and Greenhouse Gas Emissions."

17. Oleg Dzioubinski and Ralph Chipman, "Trends in Consumption and Production: Household Energy Consumption," *DESA Discussion Paper No. 6* (New York: United Nations Department of Social and Economic Affairs, 1999), 9–10; Stockholm Environmental Institute, *China Human Development Report 2002: Making Green Development a Priority* (Oxford: Oxford University Press, 2002), 57; Yukata Tonooka et al., "Energy Consumption in Residential House and Emissions Inventory of GHGs, Air Pollutants in China," *Journal of Asian Architecture and Building Engineering* 2, no. 1 (2003): 93–100; and Shonali Pachauri and Leiwen Jiang, "The Household Energy Transition in India and China," *Energy Policy* 36, no. 11 (2008): 4022–4035 (reporting the same pattern for India as well). It has sometimes been suggested that urbanization up to a certain point may increase per capita energy use and then decrease it beyond that point. For somewhat conflicting evidence (based on national-level correlations, which, as noted, may obscure the effect of urbanization itself), see Phetkeo Poumanyvong and Shinji Kaneko, "Does Urbanization Lead to Less Energy Use and CO_2 Emissions? A Cross-Country Analysis," *Ecological Economics* 70, no. 2 (2010): 434–444; and Immaculada Martínez-Zarzoso and Antonello Maruotti, "The Impact of Urbanization on CO_2 Emissions: Evidence from Developing Countries," *Ecological Economics* 70, no. 7 (2011): 1344–1353.

18. *The Challenge of Rural Electrification: Strategies for Developing Countries,* ed. Douglas F. Barnes (Washington, DC: Resources for the Future, 2007).

19. On the rising cost of public services as density decreases in developed countries, see Carruthers and Ulfarsson: "Urban Sprawl and the Cost of Public Services" and "Does 'Smart Growth' Matter to Public Finance?" On the tendency for cities to subsidize networked public services for the rest of the country, see Laurent Devezies and Rémy Prud'homme, "The Redistributive Role of Mega-Cities," in *Mega-City Growth and the Future,* ed. Roland B. Fuchs et al. (Tokyo: United Nations University Press, 1994), 156–162. For a case study from the United States, see Billie Geyer et al., "Slanted Pavement: How Ohio's Highway Spending Shortchanges Cities and Suburbs," *Discussion Paper,* Brookings Institution Center on Urban and Metropolitan Policy, March 2003. In Africa, costs of providing basic infrastructure are dramatically higher in rural than urban areas: see *Africa's Infrastructure: A Time for Transformation,* ed. Vivien Foster and Cecelia Briceño-Garmendia (Washington, DC: The World Bank, 2010), 128–142; and Sudeshina Ghosh Banerjee and Elvira Morella, *Africa's Water and Sanitation Infrastructure: Access, Affordability, and Alternatives* (Washington, DC: The World Bank, 2011), 197–199.

20. Barles, "Urban Metabolism of Paris," 899.

21. Ibid., 909; see 909–911 for a discussion of the methodological problems for construction materials. Monetary cost, used in the infrastructure studies noted previously, is a reasonable surrogate here for physical materials, given that their cost will be the same, whereas land and labor will be more expensive in urban than in rural areas (though the hours of labor may be fewer) so that any apparent urban cost advantage is likely to be a genuine one in physical or material inputs.

22. I. G. Simmons, *Global Environmental History* (Chicago: University of Chicago Press, 2008), 137; Benton-Short and Short, *Cities and Nature,* 6. See also Owen, *Green Metropolis,* 14, on the prevalence of the same perception regarding New York City.

23. On the development, character, and magnitude of agricultural water subsidies in the United States, see Richard W. Wahl, *Markets for Federal Water: Subsidies, Property Rights, and the Bureau of Reclamation* (Washington, DC: Resources for the Future, 1989); and Terry L. Anderson and Donald R. Leal, *Free Market Environmentalism,* 2nd ed. (New York: Palgrave, 2001), 89–92.

24. National Research Council, *Colorado River Basin Water Management: Evaluating and Adjusting to Hydroclimatic Variability* (Washington, DC: National Academies Press, 2007), 56, 58; Joan F. Kenny et al., *Estimated Use of Water in the United States, 2005,* USGS Circular 1344 (Reston, VA: USGS, 2009), 6–7; *State and Metropolitan Area Data Book 2006* (Washington, DC: United States Census Bureau, 2006), 54, 70.

25. The data are from "Irrigation in the Middle East Region in Figures: AQUASTAT Survey–2008," ed. Karen Frenken, *FAO Water Reports 34* (Rome: FAO, 2009), 29, 37. On the pro-agricultural bias of policies in the region, see David B. Brooks, "Between the Great Rivers: Water in the Heart of the Middle East,"

International Journal of Water Resources Development 13, no. 3 (1997): 291–309; J. A. Allan, *The Middle East Water Question: Hydropolitics and the Global Economy* (London: I. B. Tauris, 2001); and Philipp Stucki, "Water Wars or Water Peace? Rethinking the Nexus between Water Scarcity and Armed Conflict," *PSIS Occasional Paper 3/2005* (Geneva: PSIS, 2005), 29–34.

26. On the USGS data for self-supplied consumers, see Susan S. Hutson, compiler, *Guidelines for Preparation of State Water-Use Estimates for 2005* (Reston, VA: USGS Office of Ground Water, 2007), 12.

27. Sweeney, "A Comparison of Resource Consumption," 20–21.

28. Colin Polsky et al., "The Mounting Risk of Drought in a Humid Landscape: Structure and Agency in Suburbanizing Massachusetts," in *Sustainable Communities on a Sustainable Planet: The Human-Environment Regional Observatory Project*, ed. Brent Yarnal, Colin Polsky, and James O'Brien (New York: Cambridge University Press, 2009), 229–249. For similar results, see Bradfield Lyon, Nicholas Christie-Black, and Yekaterina Gluzberg, "Water Shortages, Development, and Drought in Rockland County, New York," *Journal of the American Water Resources Association* 41, no. 6 (2005): 1457–1469; and, on the role of reduced recharge, Betsy Otto et al., "Paving Our Way to Water Shortages: How Sprawl Aggravates the Effects of Drought," American Rivers/Natural Resources Defense Council/Smart Growth America, 2002.

29. Elena Domenec and David Sauri, "Urbanisation and Water Consumption: Influencing Factors in the Metropolitan Region of Barcelona," *Urban Studies* 43, no. 9 (2006): 1625–1633; Hug March and David Sauri, "The Suburbanization of Water Scarcity in the Barcelona Metropolitan Region: Sociodemographic and Urban Changes Influencing Domestic Water Consumption," *The Professional Geographer* 62, no. 1 (2010): 32–45.

30. "Per capita water consumption in cities [in the LDCs] is higher than in rural areas. . . . Although some see this as a negative factor, it is in fact a positive contribution to the general quest for improved health. In urban areas, both water and sanitation services can be provided at a lower per capita cost and have higher coverage than in rural areas . . . . Rural people of the developing world often take untreated water from polluted sources and suffer the health consequences": Stephen Brichieri-Colombi, *The World Water Crisis: The Failures of Resource Management* (London: I. B. Tauris, 2009), 176–177. On the disparities in urban and rural water access, see John Thompson et al., *Drawers of Water II: 30 Years of Changes in Domestic Water Use and Environmental Health in East Africa* (London: IIED, 2001).

31. Robert I. McDonald et al., "Global Urban Growth and the Geography of Water Availability, Quality, and Delivery," *Ambio* 40, no. 5 (2011): 437–446. The effect of urbanization in reducing population growth itself is also not considered.

32. Mathis Wackernagel and William Rees, *Ecological Footprint: Reducing Human Impact on the Earth* (Philadelphia: New Society Publications, 1996). The ecological footprint measures resource demand in a broad sense that includes demand on the environment for the assimilation of wastes emitted.

33. See, for example, Andrew Light, "The Urban Blind Spot in Environmental Ethics," *Environmental Politics* 10, no. 1 (2001): 26–27; Hardoy, Mitlin, and Satterthwaite, *Environmental Problems in an Urbanizing World*, 195n; Hari Srinivas with Iván Villarrubia Lorenzo, "Footnote on Footprints," available at http://www.gdrc.org/uem/footprints/tokyo-fprint.html; Jason P. Kaye et al., "A Distinct Urban Biogeochemistry?" *Trends in Ecology and Evolution* 21, no. 4 (2006): 192–193; and Dodman, "Blaming Cities for Climate Change?" 185.

34. Timothy Beatley, *Green Urbanism: Learning from European Cities* (Washington, DC: Island Press, 2000), 3. The most influential early study in this vein likewise announced that cities in the Baltic region of Europe relied on the resources of land areas from five hundred to more than one thousand times their own areas: Carl Folke et al., "Ecosystem Appropriation by Cities," *Ambio* 26, no. 3 (1997): 167–172. But it provided no comparisons with nonurban levels or ratios of consumption in the same countries.

35. United Nations Population Fund, *State of World Population 2007*, 57.

36. For collections of such ratios between cities' areas and their ecological footprints, see William E. Rees, "Global Change, Ecological Footprints, and Urban Sustainability," in *How Green Is the City? Sustainability Assessment and the Management of Urban Environments*, ed. Dimitri Devuyst with Luc Hens and Walter De Lannoy (New York: Columbia University Press, 2001), 346–347; and Global Development Research Center, "Urban and Ecological Footprints," available at http://www.gdrc.org/uem/footprints/index.html.

37. Brand, *Whole Earth Discipline*, 68.

38. Boone and Modarres, *City and Environment*, 81.

39. Weeks et al., "The Fertility Transition in Egypt," 75.

40. Rutherford H. Platt, "The 2020 Water Supply Study for Metropolitan Boston," *Journal of the American Planning Association* 61, no. 2 (1995): 185–199.

41. A positive correlation between the size and capacities of municipal governments in the United States and their actions to reduce greenhouse gas emissions is documented by Rachel M. Krause, "Political Decision-Making and Local Provision of Public Goods: The Case of Municipal Climate Protection in the US," *Urban Studies*, forthcoming.

42. David W. Orr, "Re-Ruralizing Education," in *Rooted in the Land: Essays on Community and Place*, ed. William Vitek and Wes Jackson (New Haven, CT: Yale University Press, 1996), 227.

43. J. Lawrence Broz and Daniel Maliniak, "Malapportionment, Gasoline Taxes, and Climate Change," *APSA 2010 Annual Meeting Paper*, available at http://papers.ssrn.com/sol3/papers.cfm?abstract_id=1642499.

44. Boone and Modarres, *City and Environment*, figure 2.3, 48.

Chapter 4

1. H. E. S. Mestl et al., "Urban and Rural Exposure to Indoor Air Pollution from Domestic Biomass and Coal Burning across China," *Science of the Total Environ-*

ment no. 377 (2007): 12–26; see also Ruoting Jiang and Michelle L. Bell, "A Comparison of Particulate Matter from Biomass-Burning Rural and Non-Biomass Burning Urban Households in Northeastern China," *Environmental Health Perspectives* 116, no. 7 (2008): 907–914. On urban-rural differences in the Third World generally, see Kirk R. Smith, "Fuel Combustion, Air Pollution Exposure, and Health: The Situation in Developing Countries," *Annual Review of Energy and the Environment* 18 (1993): 529–566.

2. Kirk R. Smith, "WHO Air Quality Guidelines: Moving Indoors," *Air Quality, Atmosphere and Health* 1, no. 1 (2008): 17; Peter Brimblecombe, *The Big Smoke: Air Pollution in London since Medieval Times* (London: Methuen, 1987), 3.

3. Benton-Short and Short, *Cities and Nature*, 92.

4. E. A. Rehfuss, N. G. Bruce, and K. R. Smith, "Solid Fuel Use: Health Effects," in *Encyclopedia of Environmental Health*, vol. 5, ed. J. O. Nriagu (Burlington, MA: Elsevier, 2011), 156–159.

5. Benton-Short and Short, *Cities and Nature*, 92.

6. David Hackett Fischer, *Historians' Fallacies: Toward a Logic of Historical Thought* (New York: Harper & Row, 1970), 42, 42n, 223–224.

7. Carlos Torres-Duque et al., "Biomass Fuels and Respiratory Diseases: A Review of the Evidence," *Proceedings of the American Thoracic Society* 5, no. 5 (2008): 577, 578.

8. Victor, "Seeking Sustainability: Cities, Countryside, and Wilderness," 211.

9. Kirk R. Smith, "In Praise of Petroleum?" *Science* 298, no. 5600 (2002): 1847, anticipates and answers one possible objection by noting how the added emissions of greenhouse gases from replacing biomass with cleaner but fossil-fuel-based household fuels in the less-developed countries would be small (especially when compared to the magnitude of luxury emissions in the First World) and the human health benefits large.

10. Smith, "Fuel Combustion, Air Pollution Exposure, and Health."

11. Lewis, *Green Delusions*, 94.

12. Brian Stone Jr. et al., "Is Compact Growth Good for Air Quality?" *Journal of the American Planning Association* 73, no. 4 (2007): 404–418; Reid Ewing, Rolf Pendall, and Don Chen, "Measuring Sprawl and Its Impact," *Technical Report,* vol. 1 (Washington, DC: Smart Growth America, 2002).

13. Richard S. Mack and Peter V. Schaeffer, "Nonmetropolitan Manufacturing in the United States and Product Cycle Theory: A Review of the Literature," *Journal of Planning Literature* 8, no. 2 (1993): 124–139; David A. McGranahan, "How People Make a Living in Rural Areas," in *Challenges for Rural America in the Twenty-First Century*, ed. David L. Brown and Louis E. Swanson (University Park: Pennsylvania State University Press, 2003), 138; Polèse, *The Wealth and Poverty of Regions*, 61–64. Proximity to a large labor force is an advantage for industry of an urban setting that has become less important in the developed world as automobile ownership, especially in rural areas, has become all but universal and the mobility of workers has increased.

14. Dennis Roth, "Thinking about Rural Manufacturing: A Brief History," *Rural America* 15, no. 1 (2000): 19, table 2.

15. Chris Bramall, *The Industrialization of Rural China* (Oxford: Oxford University Press, 2007), 322.

16. Victoria Lawson, Lucy Jarosz, and Anne Bonds, "Articulations of Place, Poverty, and Race: Dumping Grounds and Unseen Grounds in the Rural American Northwest," *Annals of the Association of American Geographers* 100, no. 3 (2010): 664.

17. Barbara Allen, *Uneasy Alchemy: Citizens and Experts in Louisiana's Chemical Corridor Disputes* (Cambridge, MA: MIT Press, 2003), quotation from 2.

18. Bryan Tilt, "The Political Ecology of Pollution Enforcement in China: A Case from Sichuan's Rural Industrial Sector," *China Quarterly* 192 (2007): 916; Chunbo Ma and Ethan D. Schoolman, "Who Bears the Environmental Burden in China: An Analysis of the Distribution of Industrial Pollution Sources," *Ecological Economics* 69, no. 9 (2010): 1874.

19. Tilt, "The Political Ecology of Pollution Enforcement," 926; Ma and Schoolman, "Who Bears the Environmental Burden in China," 1874.

20. On the last, see *METROMEX: A Review and Summary*, ed. Stanley A. Changnon (Boston: American Meteorological Society, 1981). The net effects on agriculture downwind appear to have been beneficial, the result of increased summer showers over fields mainly devoted to growing corn.

21. Michael Hendryx, Evan Fedorko, and Joel Halverson, "Pollution Sources and Mortality Rates across Rural-Urban Areas in the United States," *Journal of Rural Health* 26, no. 4 (2010): 383–391; Innocent M. Aprioku, "Oil-Spill Disasters and the Rural Hazardscape of Eastern Nigeria," *Geoforum* 34, no. 1 (2003): 99–112.

22. Angus Wright, *The Death of Ramón González: The Modern Agricultural Dilemma* (Austin: University of Texas Press, 1990), xii, 16–19, 201.

23. On pesticide risks in agriculture, see International Labour Office, *Safety and Health in Agriculture*, Report VI (1) (Geneva: ILO, 1999), 57–61.

24. Yi-Fu Tuan, *Landscapes of Fear* (New York: Pantheon Books, 1979), 142.

25. M. Celeste Murphy-Greene, "The Occupational Safety and Health of Florida Farm Workers," *Journal of Health and Human Services Administration* 25, no. 3 (2002): 281–314.

26. International Labour Office, *Safety and Health in Agriculture*, 60. For assessments of the United States focusing on children's exposure in agricultural areas, see Gina M. Solomon, *Trouble on the Farm: Growing Up with Pesticides* (New York: National Resources Defense Council, 1998); and Susan E. Carozza, Bo Li, Kai Elgethun, and Ryan Whitworth, "Risk of Childhood Cancers Associated with Residence in Agriculturally Intense Areas in the United States," *Environmental Health Perspectives* 116, no. 4 (2008): 559–565.

27. On California, see Jill Lindsey Harrison, *Pesticide Drift and the Pursuit of Environmental Justice* (Cambridge, MA: MIT Press, 2011); for examples from

Florida, see Barry Estabrook, *Tomatoland* (Kansas City, MO: Andrews McMeel, 2011), 50–51.

28. Robbins, *Lawn People: How Grasses, Weeds, and Chemicals Make Us Who We Are*, chapter 4, "Are Lawn Inputs a Hazard?" 45–71.

29. EPA, "National Water Quality Inventory: Report to Congress, 2004 Reporting Cycle" (Washington, DC: EPA Office of Water, 2009), 16, 19, 23. See also Marc Ribaudo and Robert Johansson, "Water Quality Impacts of Agriculture," in *Agricultural Resources and Environmental Indicators*, ed. Keith Wiebe and Noel Gollehon (New York: Nova Science Publishers, 2007), 39–47.

30. Steward T. A. Pickett et al., "Beyond Urban Legends: An Emerging Framework of Urban Ecology, as Illustrated by the Baltimore Ecosystem Study," *BioScience* 58, no. 2 (2008): 143–144. Two other authors also note that "exurban development . . . is nearly always serviced by private wells and septic systems . . . extend[ing] the possible range and associated environmental impacts of rural-residential development such as sedimentation but also temperature, organic wastewater contaminants, and nutrient loading from septic systems well beyond the urban fringe": Kathleen A. Lohse and Adina M. Merenlender, "Impacts of Exurban Development on Water Quality," in *The Planner's Guide to Natural Resource Conservation: The Science of Land Development beyond the Metropolitan Fringe*, ed. Adrian X. Esparza and Guy McPherson (New York: Springer, 2009), 160.

31. Lowry, "World Urbanization in Perspective," 172.

32. On problems typical of domestic well water, see CDC-NCEH, "Healthy Housing Reference Manual," chapter 8, "Rural Water Supplies and Water Quality Issues," 2008. A recent study found levels of contaminants exceeding health standards in more than 20 percent of household wells sampled: Leslie A. DeSimone, Pixie A. Hamilton, and Robert J. Gilliom, "Quality of Water from Domestic Wells in Principal Aquifers of the United States," *USGS Circular 1332* (2009); as the authors note, private wells are not subject to the federal regulations and testing requirements that govern public systems. On the advantages of larger systems over smaller ones in meeting national standards for drinking water quality and waste releases, see Claudia Copeland, "Rural Water Supply and Sewer Systems: Background Information," *CRS Report to Congress 98–64* (Washington, DC: Congressional Research Service, 2010).

33. Michael G. Rupert, "Decadal-Scale Changes of Nitrate in Ground Water of the United States, 1988–2004," *Journal of Environmental Quality* 37, supplement 5 (2008): S240–S248.

34. For a discussion citing these and other challenges, see the transcript of a United States Environmental Protection Agency seminar, "Rural Recycling: Bridging the Gaps," available at http://www.epa.gov/smm/web-academy/2010/videos/apr/apr10_trans.htm.

35. Jacobs, *The Economy of Cities*, 110–111.

36. Martin Medina, *The World's Scavengers: Salvaging for Sustainable Consumption and Production* (Lanham, MD: Altamira Press, 2007).

37. Ibid., viii, 250–254.

38. Ibid., 86–107.

39. Ibid., chapter 7, "Case Study: Colombia," 152–166.

40. David R. Lighthall and Steven Kopecky, "Confronting the Problem of Backyard Burning," *Society and Natural Resources* 13, no. 2 (2000): 157–167.

41. Lawson et al., "Articulations of Place, Poverty, and Race," 667.

42. "An Analysis of Illegal Dumpsites in Rural Pennsylvania" (Harrisburg: Center for Rural Pennsylvania, 2009).

43. Smith, "Fuel Combustion"; Mestl et al., "Urban and Rural Exposure"; Hardoy, Mitlin, and Satterthwaite, *Environmental Problems in an Urbanizing World*, 89–107; Mario J. Molina and Luisa T. Molina, "Megacities and Air Pollution," *Journal of the Air and Waste Management Association* 54, no. 6 (2004): 644–680.

Chapter 5

1. US Global Change Research Program, 1997, "Natural Hazards, Human Impacts, and Disaster Reduction," available at http://www.usgcrp.gov/usgcrp/seminars/97514DD.html.

2. John A. Cross, "Megacities and Small Towns: Different Perspectives on Hazard Vulnerability," *Environmental Hazards* 3, no. 2 (2001): 63–80, reviews many such claims from the 1980s and 1990s. For some recent examples, see Mary B. Anderson, "Vulnerability to Disaster and Sustainable Development: A General Framework for Assessing Vulnerability," in *Storms*, vol. 1, ed. R. Pielke Jr. and R. Pielke Sr. (New York: Routledge, 2000), 17–18; David Alexander, *Confronting Catastrophe: New Perspectives on Natural Disasters* (New York: Oxford University Press, 2000), 94–95; Hans Günter Brauch, "Urbanization and Natural Disasters in the Mediterranean: Population Growth and Climatic Change in the 21st Century," in *Building Safer Cities: The Future of Disaster Risk*, ed. A. Kreimer, M. Arnold, and A. Carlin (Washington, DC: The World Bank Disaster Management Facility, 2003), 149–164; United Nations Human Settlements Programme, *Enhancing Urban Safety and Security: Global Report on Human Settlements 2007* (London: Earthscan, 2007), 169–171; Zoë Chafe, "Reducing Natural Disaster Risk in Cities," chapter 6, *State of the World 2007: Our Urban Future* (Washington, DC: Worldwatch Institute, 2007), 112–129; Franke Kraus, "Megacities as Global Risk Areas" (originally published in 2003), reprinted in *Urban Ecology: An International Perspective on the Interaction between Humans and Nature*, ed. John M. Marzluff et al. (New York: Springer, 2008), 583–596; Robin M. Leichenko and Karen L. O'Brien, *Environmental Change and Globalization: Double Exposures* (New York: Oxford University Press, 2008), 76–79; and Roberto Sánchez-Rodríguez, "Urban Sustainability and Global Environmental Change: Reflections for a Research Agenda," in *The New Global Frontier: Urbanization, Poverty and Environment in the 21st Century*, ed. George Martine et al. (Sterling, VA: Earthscan, 2008), 155. Mark Pelling, *The Vulnerability of Cities: Natural Disasters and Social Resilience* (Sterling, VA: Earthscan, 2003),

14, claims however that cities have always been viewed as safer from natural hazards than rural areas but offers no evidence in support.

3. "Joplin's Tornado," *Wall Street Journal*, May 24, 2011: A18. An earlier writer asserted that "vulnerability increases exponentially with the concentration of people and property": C. W. Gusewelle, "The Winds of Ruin: Tornadoes on the American Land," *American Heritage* 29, no. 3 (1978): 96. Ted Steinberg, *Acts of God: The Unnatural History of Natural Disaster in America* (New York: Oxford University Press, 2000), 71, 226–227, likewise suggests that urbanization (as distinct from mere population growth) increased danger from tornadoes in the central United States.

4. *Cities at Risk—Making Cities Safer . . . Before Disaster Strikes* (United Nations International Strategy for Disaster Reduction Secretariat [UNISDR]/ International Decade for Natural Disaster Reduction [IDNDR], 1996), 10. For similar assertions, see William B. Meyer, *Human Impact on the Earth* (New York: Cambridge University Press, 1996), 76; and Lee Clarke, *Worst Cases: Terror and Catastrophe in the Popular Imagination* (Chicago: University of Chicago Press, 2006), 32, 33.

5. E. L. Quarantelli, "Urban Vulnerability to Disasters in Developing Countries: Managing Risks," in *Building Safer Cities*, ed. Kreimer et al., 212.

6. The term was introduced by Amos Tversky and Daniel Kahneman, "Judgment under Uncertainty: Heuristics and Biases," *Science* 185, no. 4157 (1974): 1124–1131.

7. Snowden D. Flora, *Tornadoes of the United States* (Norman: University of Oklahoma Press, 1953), 62, 66, see also 32, 55. The United States National Oceanic and Atmospheric Administration likewise observes that "an urban tornado will have a lot more debris to toss around than a rural twister": "Tornado Myths, Facts, and Safety," available at http://www.ncdc.noaa.gov/oa/ climate/severeweather/tornadosafety.html.

8. Ben Wisner, Piers Blaikie, Terry Cannon, and Ian Davis, *At Risk: Natural Hazards, People's Vulnerability and Disasters*, 2nd ed. (New York: Routledge, 2004), 11.

9. The quoted phrase is the title of *There Is No Such Thing as a Natural Disaster: Race, Class, and Hurricane Katrina*, ed. Chester Hartman and Gregory D. Squires (New York: Routledge, 2006). For a sample of important pre-Katrina works from various perspectives in the social sciences making a similar point, see Kenneth Hewitt, ed., *Interpretations of Calamity from the Viewpoint of Human Ecology* (Boston: Allen & Unwin, 1983); Ian Burton, Robert W. Kates, and Gilbert F. White, *The Environment as Hazard*, 2nd ed. (New York: Guilford Press, 1993); Kenneth Hewitt, *Regions of Risk: A Geographical Introduction to Disasters* (Harlow: Longman, 1997); Steinberg, *Acts of God*; and Eric Klinenberg, *Heat Wave: A Social Autopsy of Disaster in Chicago* (Chicago: University of Chicago Press, 2002).

10. R. R. Dynes, "The Dialogue between Voltaire and Rousseau on the Lisbon Earthquake: The Emergence of a Social Science View," *International Journal of Mass Emergencies and Disasters* 18, no. 1 (2000): 97–115.

11. Available at http://wiki.answers.com/Q/Why_is_it_safer_to_live_in_a_rural _area_during_an_earthquake.

12. Susan Elizabeth Hough and Roger G. Bilham, *After the Earth Quakes: Elastic Rebound on an Urban Planet* (New York: Oxford University Press, 2006), chapter 13, "Demonic Demographics," 255–276.

13. E. G. Gutiérrez et al., "Analysis of Worldwide Earthquake Mortality Using Multivariate Demographic and Seismic Data," *American Journal of Epidemiology* 161, no. 12 (2005): 1151–1158.

14. Hough and Bilham, *After the Earth Quakes*, 257–260.

15. Global Seismic Hazard Assessment Program, "Global Seismic Hazard Map," available at http://www.seismo.ethz.ch/static/GSHAP.

16. See, for example, M. Degg, "Natural Disasters: Recent Trends and Future Prospects," *Geography* 77, no. 3 (1992): 198–209; Peter Timmerman and Rodney White, "Megahydropolis: Coastal Cities in the Context of Global Environmental Change," *Global Environmental Change* 7, no. 3 (1997): 205–234.

17. Christopher Small and Robert J. Nicholls, "A Global Analysis of Human Settlement in Coastal Zones," *Journal of Coastal Research* 19, no. 3 (2003): 584–599; Gordon McGranahan, Deborah Balk, and Bridget Anderson, "The Rising Tide: Assessing the Risks of Climatic Change to Human Settlements in Low-Elevation Coastal Zones," *Environment and Urbanization* 19, no. 1 (2007): 17–37.

18. Guoqing Hu, Susan P. Baker, and Timothy D. Baker, "Urban-Rural Disparities in Injury Mortality in China, 2006," *Journal of Rural Health* 26, no. 1 (2010): 73–77; Connie Peek-Asa, Craig Zwerling, and Lorann Stallones, "Acute Traumatic Injuries in Rural Populations," *American Journal of Public Health* 94, no. 10 (2004): 1689.

19. Cormac Ó Gráda, *Famine: A Short History* (Princeton, NJ: Princeton University Press, 2009), 15–16.

20. Wisner et al., *At Risk*, 3.

21. The social science literature on famine is enormous but for useful overviews see Frances D'Souza, "Democracy as a Cure for Famine," *Journal of Peace Research* 31, no. 4 (1994): 369–373; Stephen Devereux, "Famine in the Twentieth Century," *IDS Working Paper #105* (2000); and Gráda, *Famine: A Short History*.

22. Bezemer and Headey, "Agriculture, Development, and Urban Bias," 1347.

23. Ó Gráda, *Famine*, 82–85. Wisner et al., *At Risk*, 93, observe that "urban people of all wealth categories almost never starve." Michel Garenne et al., "The Demographic Impact of a Mild Famine in an African City: The Case of Antananarivo, 1985–7," in *Famine Demography: Perspectives from the Past and Present*, ed. Tim Dyson and Cormac Ó Gráda (Oxford: Oxford University Press, 2002), 204–217, establish a substantial (and overlooked) degree of excess urban mortality in connection with one case of scarcity and a rise in food prices but do not compare it with the rural effects of the same event.

24. Alex de Waal, *Famine Crimes: Politics & the Disaster Relief Industry in Africa* (Bloomington: Indiana University Press, 1997), 31, also 42, 95, 103, 110; Jeremy Swift, "Why Are Rural People Vulnerable to Famine?" *IDS Bulletin* 20, no. 2 (1989): 8–15.

25. Debra Lyn Bassett, "Distancing Rural Poverty," *Georgetown Journal on Poverty Law and Policy* 13 (2006): 3.

26. John McQuaid, "The Levees," in Jenni Bergal et al., *City Adrift: New Orleans Before and After Katrina* (Baton Rouge: Louisiana State University Press, 2007), 20–31.

27. Benton-Short and Short, *Cities and Nature*, 120.

28. None of the four deadliest coastal storms by far of the past half-century—the Bangladesh cyclones of 1970 and 1991, Typhoon Nina in China in 1975, and Cyclone Nargis in Myanmar in 2008—was chiefly an urban, still less a large-city, disaster.

29. United Nations Development Programme, *Reducing Disaster Risk: A Challenge for Development* (New York: UNDP Bureau for Crisis Prevention and Recovery, 2004), 39–40, 42; Saleemul Haq, "Environmental Hazards in Dhaka," in *Crucibles of Hazard: Mega-Cities and Disasters in Transition*, ed. James K. Mitchell (New York: United Nations University Press, 1999), 130.

30. IDNDR, *Cities at Risk*, 7; Wisner et al., *At Risk*, 5, 59.

31. David Satterthwaite, "Urban Myths and the Mis-Use of Data to Underpin Them," United Nations University World Institute for Development Economics Research, *Working Paper No. 2010/28,* 2010, 8–10.

32. See, for example, Hamish Main and Stephen Wyn Williams, "Marginal Urban Environments as Havens for Low-Income Housing," in *Environment and Housing in Third World Cities*, ed. Hamish Main and Stephen Wyn Williams (Chichester, UK: John Wiley, 1994), 151–170; Wisner et al., *At Risk*, 70–71; World Resources Institute, *World Resources 1996–97* (New York: Oxford University Press, 1996), 15, 59, 60.

33. Iwan Matsuda, "Loss of Human Lives Induced by the Cyclone of 29–30 April 1991 in Bangladesh," *GeoJournal* 31, no. 4 (1993): 321; Gabriel A. Ondetti, *Land, Protest, and Politics: The Landless Movement and the Struggle for Agrarian Reform in Brazil* (University Park: Pennsylvania State University Press, 2008).

34. The UNDP report, *Reducing Disaster Risk*, 67, notes that the rural poor often occupy marginal and hazardous lands just as the urban poor do; Wisner et al., *At Risk*, 69, themselves note the same phenomenon with reference to Bangladesh.

35. See, for example, Pelling, *The Vulnerability of Cities*, 27–28; Leichenko and O'Brien, *Environmental Change and Globalization*, 79–80; James K. Mitchell, "Natural Disasters in the Context of Mega-Cities," in *Crucibles of Hazard*, 27.

36. Eve Gruntfest, "Flash Floods in the United States," in *Storms*, vol. 2, ed. R. Pielke Jr. and R. Pielke Sr. (New York: Routledge, 1999), 192, 193; Eve Gruntfest

and A. Ripps, "Flash Floods: Warning and Mitigation Efforts and Prospects," in *Floods*, vol. 1, ed. D. J. Parker (New York: Routledge, 2000), 377; Christopher P. Konrad, "Effects of Urban Development on Floods," *USGS Fact Sheet FS-876–03*, 2003; Peter J. Robinson, *North Carolina Weather & Climate* (Chapel Hill: University of North Carolina Press, 2005), 131; and Edward Bryant, *Natural Hazards*, 2nd ed. (Cambridge, UK: Cambridge University Press, 2005), 127–131.

37. On the Chicago and Peshtigo fires, see Cross, "Megacities and Small Towns," 75; on loss of life in the latter, Denise Gess and William Lutz, *Firestorm at Peshtigo: A Town, Its People, and the Deadliest Fire in American History* (New York: Henry Holt and Company, 2002), 211–215; on the post-Peshtigo response, Janet Kreger, "Fire and Failure," *Michigan History Magazine* 82, no. 1 (1998): 15–20.

38. Stephen J. Pyne, "The New American Fire," *New York Times*, October 28, 1991: 17; Cross, "Megacities and Small Towns," 69. For a particularly vivid discussion of suburban and exurban fire, see Mike Davis, "The Case for Letting Malibu Burn," *Environmental History Review* 19, no. 2 (1995): 1–36. The Central Park case, which occurred on August 2, 2002, is described in the *Storm Events* database. On the heavy rural penalty in US lightning safety, see Raúl E. López and Ronald L. Holle, "Changes in the Number of Lightning Deaths in the United States during the Twentieth Century," *Journal of Climate* 11, no. 8 (1998): 2070–2077.

39. The urban penalty is widely documented; for a review, see Michael A. McGeehin and Maria Mirabelli, "The Potential Impacts of Climate Variability and Change on Temperature-Related Morbidity and Mortality in the United States," *Environmental Health Perspectives* 109, supplement 2 (2001): 185–189; for some recent studies, see Susanna Conti et al., "Epidemiologic Study of Mortality during the Summer 2003 Heat Wave in Italy," *Environmental Research* 98, no. 3 (2005): 390–399; Andreas Matzaraki, Manuela de Rocco, and Georges Naijar, "Thermal Bioclimate in Strasbourg: The 2003 Heat Wave," *Theoretical and Applied Climatology* 98, no. 3/4 (2009): 209–220; and Katharina M. A. Gabriel and Wilfried R. Endlicher, "Urban and Rural Mortality Rates during Heat Waves in Berlin and Brandenburg, Germany," *Environmental Pollution* 159, no. 8/9 (2011): 2044–2050.

40. Maria T. F. Thacker et al., "Overview of Deaths Associated with Natural Events, United States, 1979–2004," *Disasters* 32, 2 (2008): 303–315.

41. Robert E. Davis et al., "Changing Heat-Related Mortality in the United States," *Environmental Health Perspectives* 111, no. 14 (2003): 1712–1718; for a case study of unequal impacts on different groups of the same event, see Klinenberg, *Heat Wave*.

42. Kevin A. Borden and Susan L. Cutter, "Spatial Patterns of Natural Hazards Mortality in the United States," *International Journal of Health Geographies* 7 (2008): 64 cf. The authors themselves emphasize the tentativeness of their findings imposed by the limitations of the available data.

Chapter 6

1. "In short, by the work of our hands we strive to create a sort of second nature within the world of nature": Cicero, *The Nature of the Gods*, trans. P. G. Walsh (Oxford: Clarendon Press, 1997), 103.

2. The phrase is from Edward Tenner, *Why Things Bite Back: Technology and the Revenge of Unintended Consequences* (New York: Knopf, 1996).

3. Pollution hazards, which might also be classed as ones of technology, are discussed separately in chapter 4 of this book.

4. United Nations Human Settlements Programme, *Enhancing Urban Safety and Security: Global Report on Human Settlements 2007* (London: Earthscan, 2007), 223.

5. M. E. Eberhardt et al., *Urban and Rural Health Chartbook: Health, United States, 2001* (Hyattsville, MD: National Center for Health Statistics, 2001), 54–55; National Highway Traffic Safety Administration, *Traffic Safety Facts: 2007 Data, Urban-Rural Comparison* (DOT HS 810 996, 2009); Craig Zwerling et al., "Fatal Motor Vehicle Crashes in Rural and Urban Areas: Decomposing Rates into Contributing Factors," *Injury Prevention* 11, no. 1 (2005): 24–28.

6. Leanne Kmet, Penny Brasher, and Colin Macarthur, "A Small Area Study of Motor Vehicle Crashes in Alberta, Canada," *Accident Analysis and Prevention* 35, no. 2 (2003): 177–182; Leanne Kmet and Colin Macarthur, "Urban-Rural Differences in Motor Vehicle Crash Fatality and Hospitalization Rates among Children and Youth," *Accident Analysis and Prevention* 38, no. 1 (2006): 122–127; H. Y. Chen et al., "Fatal Crash Trends for Australian Young Drivers, 1997–2007," *Journal of Safety Research* 41, no. 2 (2010): 123–128; Sylvain Lassarre and Isabelle Thomas, "Exploring Road Mortality Ratios in Europe: National versus Regional Realities," *Journal of the Royal Statistical Society A* 168, pt. 1 (2005): 127–144. Statistics from developing countries generally do not permit equally rigorous comparisons but higher ratios of vehicles to people may lead to a larger urban toll as a percentage of population (though apparently not, as noted in the text, in Latin America, and not necessarily per vehicle mile traveled).

7. National Highway Traffic Safety Administration, *Traffic Crashes Take Their Toll on America's Rural Roads* (DOT HS 810 658, 2006); on the importance of this factor, see Richard P. Gonzalez et al., "Does Increased Emergency Medical Services Prehospital Time Affect Patient Mortality in Rural Motor Vehicle Crashes? A Statewide Analysis," *American Journal of Surgery* 197, no. 1 (2009): 30–34.

8. William H. Lucy, "Mortality Risk Associated with Leaving Home," *American Journal of Public Health* 93, no. 9 (2003): 1564–1569.

9. Reid H. Ewing, Richard A. Schieber, and Charles V. Zegeer, "Urban Sprawl as a Risk Factor in Motor Vehicle Occupant and Pedestrian Fatalities," *American Journal of Public Health* 93, no. 9 (2003): 1541–1545; David E. Clark, "Effect

of Population Density on Mortality after Motor Vehicle Collisions," *Accident Analysis & Prevention* 35, no. 6 (2003): 965–971; Thomas E. Lambert and Peter B. Meyer, "Ex-Urban Sprawl as a Factor in Traffic Fatalities and EMS Response Times in the Southeastern United States," *Journal of Economic Issues* 40, no. 4 (2006): 941–953.

10. Nick Paumgarten, "Up and Then Down: The Lives of Elevators," *New Yorker*, April 21, 2008: 107.

11. Paul Slovic, Baruch Fischoff, and Sarah Lichtenstein, "Rating the Risks," *Environment* 21, no. 3 (1979): 36–37.

12. Ibid.

13. Stephen Keane, *Disaster Movies: The Cinema of Catastrophe*, 2nd ed. (London: Wallflower, 2006), 82. America's largest city has been a particularly favored location for US films dealing with natural and technological hazards alike; see Max Page, *The City's End: Two Centuries of Fantasies, Fears, and Premonitions of New York's Destruction* (New Haven, CT: Yale University Press, 2008). So has its second-largest city: Mike Davis, *Ecology of Fear: Los Angeles and the Imagination of Disaster* (New York: Henry Holt and Company, 1998), 275–355.

14. "Creating larger jumbo jets creates a bigger body count when one crashes": Clarke, *Worst Cases*, 32. So it does but jumbo jets have exceptionally good safety records and if they had not been built the same amount of travel occurring in smaller and less safe aircraft would have meant a higher toll of accidents. Again a focus on disaster hides the net toll from a hazard.

15. Cross, "Megacities and Small Towns," 69–76; on motor vehicle accidents, 69–70. On distinctive elements of rural vulnerability to toxic chemical accidents in the United States, see William D. Solecki, "Rural Places and the Circumstances of Acute Chemical Disasters," *Journal of Rural Studies* 8, no. 1 (1992): 1–13.

16. Judith Holt, Sue Hotto, and Kevin Cole, "Demographic Aspects of Hearing Impairment: Questions and Answers," 3rd ed., Center for Assessment and Demographic Studies, Gallaudet University, 1994. The same rural penalty appears in India, though there it seems to have less to do with noise exposure than with a greater prevalence and poorer treatment of ear inflammation and infection: S. B. S. Mann et al., "Incidence of Hearing Impairment among Rural and Urban School Going Children: A Survey," *Indian Journal of Pediatrics* 65, no. 1 (1998): 141–145; Suneela Garg et al., "Deafness: Burden, Prevention and Control in India," *National Medical Journal of India* 22, no. 2 (2009): 79–81.

17. "The Rural Fire Problem in the United States," Federal Emergency Management Administration, United States Fire Administration, August 1997, 20, 43–44. For similar conclusions from more recent data, see also Corinne Peek-Asa, Craig Zwerling, and Loranne Stallone, "Acute Traumatic Injuries in Rural Populations," *American Journal of Public Health* 94, no. 10 (2004): 1691; and Jennifer D. Flynn, "Characteristics of Home Fire Victims," National Fire Protection Association, Fire Analysis and Research Division, 2010, 9. These studies do not differentiate city and suburb, lumping them together into the urban category. It is possible that within metropolitan areas, the dwelling fire risk increases with the

level of urbanness and is higher in cities than in suburbs. To conclude, though, that a penalty inheres in a high degree of urbanness is to err in a way discussed in the chapter 1 because the reason may well be (and probably is) the distinctive spatial pattern of the US city that concentrates poverty and deprivation in the core rather than anything necessarily involved in the definition of urbanness. Moreover, in naturally fire-prone parts of the world, suburbs may be substantially more at risk. "In the industrial world, what passes for urban 'conflagrations' center on just such scenes—from the urban brush of Sydney to the tourist-cluttered slopes of the Côte d'Azur to subdivisions crowded amid the chaparral of Sierran foothills. . . . More incredibly, many such communities sport—even promote and advertise—wooden roofing": Stephen J. Pyne, *Fire: A Brief History* (Seattle: University of Washington Press, 2001), 111.

18. G. Gururaj, "Injuries in India: A National Perspective," *NCMH Background Papers: Burden of Disease in India* (New Delhi: NCMH, 2005), 333; Shobha Chamania, "Training and Burn Care in Rural India," *Indian Journal of Plastic Surgery* 43, supplement (2010): S126; United Nations Development Programme, *Reducing Disaster Risk: A Challenge for Development* (New York: UNDP Bureau for Crisis Prevention and Recovery, 2004), 45.

19. Karly B. Smith, John S. Humphreys, and Murray G. A. Wilson, "Addressing the Health Disadvantage of Rural Populations: How Does Epidemiological Evidence Inform Rural Health Policies and Research?" *Australian Journal of Rural Health* 16, no. 2 (2008): 58.

20. Cross, "Megacities and Small Towns," 69; US Department of Labor, Bureau of Labor Statistics, "Number and Rate of Fatal Occupational Injuries, by Industry Sector, 2010," available at http://www.bls.gov/iif/oshwc/cfoi/cfch0009.pdf.

21. Craig Veitch, "Impact of Rurality on Environmental Determinants and Hazards," *Australian Journal of Rural Health* 17, no. 1 (2009): 18; Adarsh Kumar, Mathew Varghese, and Dinesh Mohan, "Equipment-Related Injuries in Agriculture: An International Perspective," *Injury Control & Safety Promotion* 7, no. 3 (2000): 175–186. For an African study finding rural occupational injury rates four times greater than urban (with the hazards of agriculture accounting for most of the difference), see Charles Mock et al., "Occupational Injuries in Ghana," *International Journal of Occupational and Environmental Health* 11, no. 3 (2005): 238–245.

22. Philip D. Somervell and George A. Conway, "Does the Small Farm Exemption Cost Lives?" *American Journal of Industrial Medicine* 54, no. 6 (2011): 461–466.

23. David Harvey, *Justice, Nature, and the Geography of Difference* (Cambridge, MA: Blackwell, 1996), 334–341. On the Triangle Fire's regulatory consequences, see Richard A. Greenwald, *The Triangle Fire, the Protocols of Peace, and Industrial Democracy in Progressive Era New York* (Philadelphia: Temple University Press, 2005).

24. L. T. Dresang, "Gun Deaths in Rural and Urban Settings: Recommendations for Prevention," *Journal of the American Board of Family Practice* 14, no. 2 (2001): 107–115; Michael L. Nance et al., "Variation in Pediatric and Adolescent

Firearm Mortality Rates in Rural and Urban US Counties," *Pediatrics* 125, no.6 (2010): 1112–1118.

25. Vanessa Costilla and David Bishai, "Lawn Mower Injuries in the United States, 1996–2004," *Annals of Emergency Medicine* 47, no. 6 (2006): 567–573.

26. Ya Fang et al., "Child Drowning Deaths in Xiamen City and Suburbs, People's Republic of China," *Injury Prevention* 13, no. 5 (2007): 339–343; A. Rahman et al., "Analysis of the Childhood Fatal Drowning Situation in Bangladesh," *Injury Prevention* 15: 75–79.

27. On the United States, see Peek-Asa et al. "Acute Traumatic Injuries in Rural Populations," 1689–1693; for a European study, M. Boland, A. Staines, P. Fitzpatrick, and E. Scanlan, "Urban-Rural Variation in Mortality and Hospital Admission Rates for Unintentional Injury in Ireland," *Injury Prevention* 11, no. 1 (2005): 38–42. For India, see Gururaj, "Injuries in India." For China, see Guoqing Hu, Susan P. Baker, and Timothy D. Baker, "Urban-Rural Disparities in Injury Mortality in China, 2006," *Journal of Rural Health* 26, no. 1 (2010): 73–77; Jixiang Ma et al., "Epidemiological Analysis of Injury in Shandong Province, China," *BMC Public Health* 8 (2008): 122; Le Cai and Virasakdi Changsuvivatwong, "Rural-Urban Differentials of Premature Mortality Burden in South-West China," *International Journal for Equity in Health* 5 (2006): 13; and Guohong Jiang et al., "Leading Causes of Death from Injuries and Poisoning by Age, Sex, and Urban/Rural Areas in Tianjin Province, China, 1999–2006," *Injury* 42, no. 5 (2011): 501–506.

28. As noted by Hu, Baker, and Baker, "Urban-Rural Disparities in Injury Mortality," 74.

29. For an exploration of some of the possibilities, see William J. Mitchell and Anthony M. Townsend, "Cyborg Agonistes: Disaster and Reconstruction in the Digital Electronic Era," in *The Resilient City: How Modern Cities Recover from Disaster*, ed. Lawrence J. Vale and Thomas J. Campanella (New York: Oxford University Press, 2005), 313–334.

30. Alexander, *Confronting Catastrophe*, 99.

31. Michael Marmor and Nicholas E. Marmor, "Slippery Road Conditions and Fatal Motor Vehicle Crashes in the Northeastern United States, 1998–2002," *American Journal of Public Health* 96, no. 5 (2006): 914–920.

32. Harrison, *Pesticide Drift and the Pursuit of Environmental Justice*.

Chapter 7

1. Richard Horton, "The Infected Metropolis," *The Lancet* 347, no. 8995 (1996): 134–135; Anthony J. McMichael, *Planetary Overload: Global Environmental Change and the Health of the Human Species* (Cambridge, UK: Cambridge University Press, 1993), 264; Ronak B. Patel and Thomas F. Burke, "Urbanization: A Humanitarian Disaster," *New England Journal of Medicine* 361 (2009): 741–743. For similar statements, see Eugene Linden, "The Exploding Cities of

the Developing World," *Foreign Affairs* 75, no. 1 (1996): 52–65; Jennifer Brower and Peter Chalk, *The Global Threat of New and Reemerging Infectious Disease: Reconciling U.S. National Security and Public Health Policy* (Santa Monica, CA: RAND, 2003), 21–23; L. Scott Chavers and Sten H. Vermund, "An Introduction to Emerging and Reemerging Infectious Diseases," in *Emerging Infectious Diseases: Trends and Issues*, 2nd ed., ed. Felissa R. Lashley and Jerry D. Durham (New York: Springer, 2007), 8–10; and Emilie Alirol et al., "Urbanisation and Infectious Diseases in a Globalising World," *Lancet Infectious Diseases* 11 (2011): 131–141.

2. National Research Council, *Cities Transformed*, 259–260.

3. On the earliest of these writers, see Chris Galley, "A Model of Early Modern Urban Demography," *Economic History Review*, n.s. 48, no. 3 (1995): 448; later ones include Thomas Short, *New Observations, Natural, Moral, Civil, Political, and Medical, on City, Town, and Country Bills of Mortality* (London: T. Longman, 1750), 94–95, 120, 234; and Richard Price, *Observations on Reversionary Payments . . .* , 2nd ed. (London: T. Cadell, 1772), 176, 197–199, 201–202. The quotation is from Thomas Robert Malthus, *An Essay on the Principle of Population*, 6th ed. (originally published in 1826), ed. E. A. Wrigley and David Souden, in *The Works of Thomas Robert Malthus*, vol. 2 (London: William Pickering, 1986), 243.

4. Jan de Vries, *European Urbanization, 1500–1800* (Cambridge, MA: Harvard University Press, 1984), 180.

5. Elio Lo Cascio, "Did the Population of Imperial Rome Reproduce Itself?" in *Urbanism in the Preindustrial World: Cross-Cultural Approaches*, ed. Glenn R. Storey (Tuscaloosa: University of Alabama Press, 2006), 53–54.

6. De Vries, *European Urbanization*, 181.

7. Allan Sharlin, "Natural Decrease in Early Modern Cities: A Reconsideration," *Past and Present* 79 (1978): 126–138.

8. Galley, "A Model of Early Modern Urban Demography," 448–469; Robert Woods, "Urban-Rural Mortality Differentials: An Unresolved Debate," *Population and Development Review* 29, no. 1 (2003): 29–46.

9. Ibid., 31–32; Susan B. Hanley, *Everyday Things in Premodern Japan: The Hidden Legacy of Material Culture* (Berkeley: University of California Press, 1997), chapter 5, "Urban Sanitation and Physical Well-Being," 104–128. Hanley (106) cites an earlier work to the effect that even in premodern Japan, the urban graveyard effect prevailed but the only substantial inquiry given in that work failed to do what de Vries and Lo Cascio point out must be done before reaching such a conclusion, that is, correct for the distortion of crude birth and death rates by migration: Susan B. Hanley and Kozo Yamamura, *Economic and Demographic Change in Preindustrial Japan, 1600–1868* (Princeton, NJ: Princeton University Press, 1977), 304–305.

10. Lo Cascio, "Did the Population of Imperial Rome Reproduce Itself?" 52–68; Angelo Celli, *Malaria According to the New Researches*, trans. John Joseph Eyre (London: Longmans, Green, and Co., 1900), 236–237.

11. Paul R. Ehrlich and Anne H. Ehrlich, *One with Nineveh: Politics, Consumption, and the Human Future* (Washington, DC: Island Press, 2004), 103–104.

12. Amir Afkhami, "Compromised Constitutions: The Iranian Experience with the 1918 Influenza Pandemic," *Bulletin of the History of Medicine* 77, no. 2 (2003): 367–392; Kirsten McSweeny et al., "Was Rurality Protective in the 1918 Influenza Pandemic in New Zealand?" *New Zealand Medical Journal* 120, no. 1256 (2007): 44–49; Niall Johnson, *Britain and the 1918–19 Influenza Pandemic: A Dark Epilogue* (New York: Routledge, 2006), 62–63; Gerardo Chowell et al., "The 1918–1919 Influenza Pandemic in England and Wales: Spatial Patterns in Transmissibility and Mortality Impact," *Proceedings of the Royal Society B: Biological Sciences* 275, no. 1634 (2008): 504–505.

13. Svenn-Erik Mamelund, "Geography May Explain Adult Mortality from the 1918–20 Influenza Pandemic," *Epidemics* 3, no. 1 (2011): 46–60.

14. Ole J. Benedictow, *The Black Death, 1346–1353: The Complete History* (Woodbridge, UK: Boydell Press, 2004).

15. Ibid., 31–33. The original study was E. H. Hankin, "On the Epidemiology of Plague," *Journal of Hygiene* 5 (1905): 48–83. The direct relevance of Hankin's and other studies to the Black Death depends on the latter's identity with the plague, which has been challenged (see, for example, Samuel K. Cohn, *The Black Death Transformed: Disease and Culture in Early Renaissance Europe* (New York: Oxford University Press, 2002) but seems now to have been solidly established: Stephanie Haensch et al., "Distinct Clones of *Yersinia pestis* Caused the Black Death," *PLoS Pathogens* 6, no. 10 (2010): e1001134.

16. Benedictow, *The Black Death*, 32.

17. On the urban advantage in life expectancy, see National Research Council, *Cities Transformed*. In China, an urban advantage exists in every province of the country and is highest in the westernmost and least-developed provinces, approaching or exceeding ten years in several of them: UNDP China, *China Human Development Report 2005*, 9. Though the United States has overall higher mortality rates in urban than rural areas, countries as culturally and socioeconomically similar as Canada and Australia show the opposite: Raymond W. Pong, Marie DesMeules, and Claudia Lagacé, "Rural-Urban Disparities in Health: How Does Canada Fare and How Does Canada Compare with Australia," *Australian Journal of Rural Health* 17 (2009): 58–64.

18. See National Research Council, *Cities Transformed*, 264–265; Ashok Vikhe Patil, K. V. Sonasundaram, and R. C. Goyal, "Current Health Scenario in Rural India," *Australian Journal of Rural Health* 10, no. 2 (2002): 129–135; and Trevor J. B. Dummer and Ian G. Cook, "Health in China and India: A Cross-Country Comparison in a Context of Rapid Globalisation," *Social Science & Medicine* 67, no. 4 (2008): 590–605. For a recent household-based study in Africa comparing urban slum with rural rates of three major common manifestations of infectious illness (and finding the rural rates to be higher), see Daniel R. Feikin et al., "The Burden of Common Infectious Disease Syndromes at the Clinic and Household Level from Population-Based Surveillance in Rural and Urban Kenya," *PLoS* 6, no. 1 (2011): e16085.

19. A decline in deaths from communicable diseases as a country develops is also sometimes more narrowly called the *epidemiological transition,* a term introduced by Abdel R. Omran, "The Epidemiological Transition: A Theory of the Epidemiology of Population Change," *Milbank Quarterly* 49, no. 4 (1971): 509–538. On the general parallelism of all the transitions mentioned, see McGreevey et al., "Propinquity Matters."

20. Vincent Robert et al., "Malaria Transmission in Urban Sub-Saharan Africa," *American Journal of Tropical Medicine and Hygiene* 68, no. 2 (2003): 169–176; Simon I. Hay et al., "Urbanization, Malaria Transmission, and Disease Burden in Africa," *Nature Reviews in Microbiology* 3, no. 1 (2005): 81–90; Julie I. Thwing et al., "How Much Malaria Occurs in Urban Luanda, Angola? A Health Facility-Based Assessment," *American Journal of Tropical Medicine and Hygiene* 80, no. 3 (2009): 487–491.

21. William R. Brieger, "Urban Malaria: Myth and Reality," *Africa Health* 33, no. 2 (2011): 14–17.

22. See Joseph William Bastien, *The Kiss of Death: Chagas' Disease in the Americas* (Salt Lake City: University of Utah Press, 1998).

23. *Ecosystems and Human Well-Being: Current State and Trends,* vol. 1, ed. Rashid Hassan, Robert Scholes, and Neville Ash (Washington, DC: Island Press, 2005), 397–400. For examples of other, mostly rural, land uses promoting infectious disease reemergence, see Jonathan A. Patz et al., "Unhealthy Landscapes: Policy Recommendations on Land Use Change and Infectious Disease Emergence," *Environmental Health Perspectives* 112, no. 10 (2004): 1092–1098.

24. Peter Hotez, *Forgotten People, Forgotten Diseases: The Neglected Tropical Diseases and Their Impact on Global Health and Development* (Washington, DC: ASM Press, 2008), 103.

25. Melinda S. Meade and Michael Emch, *Medical Geography,* 3rd ed. (New York: Guilford Press, 2010), 131–135.

26. Barbara J. Holtzclaw, "Dengue Fever," in Lashley and Durham, *Emerging Infectious Diseases,* 129; Hotez, *Forgotten People, Forgotten Diseases,* 105–108.

27. On yellow fever, *Aedes* mosquitoes, and the pre-twentieth century urban penalty, see John R. McNeill, *Mosquito Empires: Ecology and War in the Greater Caribbean, 1620–1914* (New York: Cambridge University Press, 2010). Today, as McNeill notes (47), western hemisphere yellow fever is endemic now only in forested areas, from which its sporadic reintroduction to cities produces occasional outbreaks.

28. George W. Beran, "Urban Rabies," in *The Natural History of Rabies,* 2nd ed., ed. George M. Baer (Boca Raton, FL: CRC Press, 1991), 439.

29. Darryn L. Knobel et al., "Re-Evaluating the Burden of Rabies in Africa and Asia," *Bulletin of the World Health Organization* 83, no. 5 (2005): 360–368, find rural death rates higher than urban overall and in most regions, with China an exception; Sowath Ly et al., "Rabies Situation in Cambodia," *PLoS Neglected Tropical Diseases* 3, no. 9 (2009): e511.

30. Tim Dyson, "HIV/AIDS and Urbanization," *Population and Development Review* 29, no. 3 (2003): 427–442.

31. World Health Organization, "Hepatitis B: Fact Sheet #204," available at http://www.who.int/mediacentre/factsheets/fs204/en; Chien-Jen Chen, Li-Yu Wang, and Ming-Whei Yu, "Epidemiology of Hepatitis B Virus Infection in the Asia-Pacific Region," *Journal of Gastroenterology and Hepatology* 15, supplement (2000): E4; Laurentius A. Lesmana et al., "Hepatitis B: Overview of the Burden of Disease in the Asia-Pacific Region," *Liver International* 26, supplement (2006): 5.

32. Timothy Lahey et al., "Increased Mortality in Rural Patients with HIV in New England," *AIDS Research and Human Retroviruses* 23, no. 5 (2007): 693–698; Michael Ohl et al., "Rural Residence Is Associated with Delayed Care Entry and Increased Mortality among Veterans with Human Immunodeficiency Virus Infection," *Medical Care* 48, no. 12 (2010): 1064–1070.

33. E. Fuller Torrey and Robert H. Yolken, *Beasts of the Earth: Animals, Humans, and Disease* (New Brunswick, NJ: Rutgers University Press, 2005), 131. For a similar assessment, see Mark S. Smolinski, Margaret A. Hamburg, and Joshua Lederberg, eds., *Microbial Threats to Health: Emergence, Detection, and Response* (Washington, DC: National Academies Press, 2003), 83.

34. World Health Organization, *World Health Statistics 2011* (Geneva: WHO, 2011), 104–113.

35. National Research Council, *Cities Transformed*, chapter 7, "Mortality and Morbidity: Is City Life Good for Your Health?" 259–299. On the water-related rural penalty in diarrheal disease in Africa, see Dean T. Jamison et al., *Disease and Mortality in Sub-Saharan Africa*, 2nd ed. (Washington, DC: The World Bank, 2006), 114–116.

36. René Borroto and Ramon Martinez-Piedra, "Geographical Patterns of Cholera in Mexico, 1991–1996," *International Journal of Epidemiology* 29, no. 4 (2000): 764–772; Hossein-Ali Khazaei et al., "The Epidemiology of *Vibrio cholerae* in Zabol City, Southeast of Iran," *Archives of Iranian Medicine* 8, no. 3 (2005): 197–201.

37. Marcus Cueto, "Stigma and Blame during an Epidemic: Cholera in Peru, 1991," in *Disease in the History of Modern Latin America: From Malaria to AIDS*, ed. Diego Armus (Durham, NC: Duke University Press, 2003), 269; Eliseu Alves Waldman et al., "Cholera in Brazil during 1991–98: Socioeconomic Characteristics of Affected Areas," *Journal of Health, Population and Nutrition* 20, no. 1 (2002): 85–92; Jaime Sepúlveda, José Luis Valdespino, and Lourdes García-García, "Cholera in Mexico: The Paradoxical Benefits of the Last Pandemic," *International Journal of Infectious Diseases* 10 (2006): 4–13.

38. As well as the UN-HABITAT report discussed in chapter 2, many of the studies of health differentials cited in National Research Council, *Cities Transformed*, 284–289, "A Penalty for the Urban Poor?" commit this error by generalizing on the basis of figures that only compare urban poor or slum populations with the entire rural population of the same country. It is sometimes suggested that urban slum mortality and morbidity (from disease and also from natural

and technological hazards) will tend to be underrecorded but it can hardly be taken for granted that they will be so to a greater degree than cases in remote rural regions will.

39. Feikin et al., "The Burden of Common Infectious Disease Syndromes at the Clinic and Household Level," e16085.

40. Ellen van de Poel, Owen O'Donnell, and Eddy Van Doorslaer, "Are Urban Children Really Healthier? Evidence from 47 Developing Countries," *Social Science & Medicine* 65, no. 10 (2007): 1986–2003. Another study by the same authors likewise underlines the importance of clean water and sanitation: "What Explains the Rural-Urban Gap in Infant Mortality: Household or Community Characteristics?" *Demography* 46, no. 4 (2009): 827–850. Philippe Bocquier, Nyovani Madise, and Eliya Zulu, "Is There an Urban Advantage in Child Survival in Sub-Saharan Africa? Evidence from 18 Countries in the 1990s," *Demography* 48, no. 2 (2011): 531–558, conclude that the urban advantage apparent in overall statistics is largely accounted for, not by urban residence itself but by such factors as "parental education, access to water and sanitation, and household wealth status" (553)—but these, again, are factors that are not higher in urban areas simply by chance. The studies covered in a recent review of the literature at most suggest that the urban poor and the rural poor sometimes suffer similar levels of ill-health rather than supporting the thesis of a genuine urban slum penalty: Alice Sverdlik, "Ill-Health and Poverty: A Literature Review on Health in Informal Settlements," *Environment and Urbanization* 23, no. 1 (2011): 140–142.

41. See, for example, Deepak Almeida et al., "Incidence of Multidrug-Resistant Tuberculosis in Urban and Rural India and Implications for Prevention," *Clinical Infectious Diseases* 36, no. 12 (2003): e152–e154.

42. David A. Leon, "Cities, Urbanization, and Health," *International Journal of Epidemiology* 37, no. 1 (2008): 4.

Chapter 8

1. David Orr, "Refugees or Homecomers? Conjectures about the Future of Rural America," chapter 23, *Earth in Mind: On Education, Environment, and the Human Prospect* (Washington, DC: Island Press, 1994), 187.

2. Roland J. Fuchs and George J. Demko, "Rethinking Population Distribution Policies," *Population Research and Policy Review* 2, no. 2 (1983): 164; *World Urban Prospects: The 2005 Revision* (New York: United Nations, 2006), 24. See also Charles M. Becker and Andrew R. Morrison, "Public Policy and Rural-Urban Migration," in *Cities in the Developing World: Issues, Theory, and Policy*, ed. Josef Gugler (Oxford: Oxford University Press, 1997), 88–105.

3. Kevin McIntyre, "Geography as Destiny: Cities, Villages, and Khmer Rouge Orientalism," *Comparative Studies in Society and History* 38, no. 4 (1996): 730–758; Nicholas Eberstadt, "Poverty in South Africa," chapter 7, in *The Tyranny of Numbers: Mismeasurement and Misrule* (Washington, DC: AEI Press, 1995), 150–169; Alan B. Simmons, "A Review and Evaluation of Attempts to

Constrain Migration to Selected Urban Centres and Regions," in *Population Distribution Policies in Development Planning* (New York: The United Nations, 1981), 87–100.

4. On the role of development restrictions in First World urban cores, see Glaeser, *Triumph of the City*, 135–163. For subsidies to suburbanization in the United States, see Jackson, *Crabgrass Frontier*, especially chapter 11, "Federal Subsidy and the Suburban Dream," 190–218.

5. The quotation is from David Turnock, "The Planning of Rural Settlement in Romania," *Geographical Journal* 157, no. 3 (1991): 260; Rodger Yeager, "Demography and Development Policy in Tanzania," *Journal of Developing Areas* 16, no. 4 (1982): 489–510, makes the same point about Tanzania's policy of villagization. The principal modern example of what properly could be called *forced urbanization* was a short-lived United States initiative during the Vietnam War: Robert K. Brigham, "Vietnamese Society at War," in *The Columbia History of the Vietnam War*, ed. David L. Anderson (New York: Columbia University Press, 2011), 323–329.

6. Polèse, *The Wealth and Poverty of Regions*, 139–140; for a similar assessment, see Victor, "Seeking Sustainability," 206.

7. On the prevalence of overall urban economic and social advantages in well-being, assessed by a wide range of indicators, see National Research Council, *Cities Transformed*.

8. Cecelia Tacoli, Gordon McGranahan, and David Satterthwaite, "Urbanization, Poverty and Inequity: Is Rural-Urban Migration a Poverty Problem, or Part of the Solution?" in *The New Global Frontier: Urbanization, Poverty and Environment in the 21st Century*, ed. George Martine et al. (London: Earthscan, 2008), 42; see also Hardoy, Mitlin, and Satterthwaite, *Environmental Problems in an Urbanizing World*, 315–317.

9. On this point, see National Research Council, *Cities Transformed*, 183–184.

10. David E. Sahn and David C. Stifel, "Urban-Rural Inequality in Living Standards in Africa," *Journal of African Economies* 12, no. 4 (2003): 564–597 (quotation from 583).

11. National Research Council, *Cities Transformed*, emphasizes this point: "Although no one would dismiss the possibility of an urban bias in expenditures, the element of bias is more difficult to isolate than is commonly recognized. The spatial concentration of urban populations allows economies of scale and scope to be exploited in urban infrastructural investments [and in other services, one might add], and these economies are not readily captured in dispersed rural settings" (318).

12. United Nations Human Settlements Program, *The Challenge of Slums: Global Report on Human Settlements, 2003* (London: Earthscan, 2003); and *State of the World's Cities Report 2006/7* (London: Earthscan, 2006), x–xi. I have drawn chiefly on the latter report as the more detailed of the two. In some places, it uses total urban as a second category instead of urban nonslum, with the same results.

13. *State of the World's Cities Report 2006/7*, 19, for the five criteria used.

14. On the rural disadvantage on most of the measures, see the research reviewed in National Research Council, *Cities Transformed*; on land tenure, Klaus W. Deininger, *Land Policies for Growth and Poverty Reduction* (Washington, DC: World Bank with Oxford University Press, 2003), xviii.

15. Neil MacFarquahar, "African Farmers Displaced as Investors Move In," *New York Times*, December 22, 2010: A1, A4 (quotation). See also the materials in Transnational Institute, "Debating the Global Land Grab," available at http://www.tni.org/article/debating-global-land-grab.

16. Compare UN-HABITAT, *State of the World's Cities 2008/9* (London: Earthscan, 2008) 68, 73, 77; with Sahn and Stifel, "Urban-Rural Inequality," 587. Studies do more often than not show a greater inequality in urban than in rural areas of the Third World but as most use monetary measures rather than (as Sahn and Stifel did) direct consumption or well-being, they may err in failing to include other components whose net effect is to raise the relative standard of living of the urban poor.

17. Cynthia B. Lloyd, ed., *Growing Up Global: The Changing Transitions to Adulthood in Developing Countries* (Washington, DC: National Academies Press, 2005), 78–79, 156–159; Maureen A. Lewis and Marlaine E. Lockheed, eds., *Exclusion, Gender and Education: Case Studies from the Developing World* (Washington, DC: Center for Global Development, 2007).

18. Jack London, *The People of the Abyss* (New York: Macmillan, 1904), 45.

19. Orr, "Refugees or Homecomers?" 186.

20. Orr, "Re-Ruralizing Education," 227.

21. Claude S. Fischer, "Urban Malaise," *Social Forces* 52, no. 2 (1973): 224, 233. "Surveys carried out in Third World cities have time and again arrived at the same conclusion: in almost all cases, individuals who had left the countryside for the city stated that their condition had improved": Polèse, *The Wealth and Poverty of Regions*, 139.

22. Brian J. L. Berry and Adam Okulicz-Kozaryn, "Dissatisfaction with City Life: A New Look at Some Old Questions," *Cities* 26, no. 3 (2009): 117–124. A later study by the same authors explores the distinctively US pattern of antiurbanism: "An Urban-Rural Gradient in Happiness," *Urban Geography* 32, no. 6 (2011): 871–883.

23. Satterthwaite, "How Urban Societies Can Adapt to Resource Shortage and Climate Change."

24. The most ambitious case for a US antiurban tradition, Morton and Lucia White, *The Intellectual versus the City, from Thomas Jefferson to Frank Lloyd Wright* (Cambridge, MA: Harvard University Press, 1962), has been subjected to much criticism but for later persuasive arguments along the same lines, see, for example, Wilbur Zelinsky, *The Cultural Geography of the United States* (Englewood Cliffs, NJ: Prentice-Hall, 1973), 49; Jackson, *Crabgrass Frontier*, 68–72; and Garry Wills, *John Wayne's America: The Politics of Celebrity* (New York: Simon and Schuster, 1997), 302–309. Owen, *Green Metropolis*, 18–28, in turn notes the pervasive influence of US antiurbanism on some of the longstanding characteristics and concerns of US environmentalism.

25. Herbert J. Gans, *The Urban Villagers: Group and Class in the Life of Italian-Americans* (New York: The Free Press, 1962), 22–23.

26. See, for example, Mike Davis, *Magical Urbanism: Latinos Reinvent the US City* (London: Verso, 2000); Michael Mendez, "Latin New Urbanism: Building on Cultural Preferences," *Opolis* 1, no. 1 (2005): 33–48.

27. See, for example, Donald Pitkin, "Mediterranean Europe," *Anthropological Quarterly* 36, no. 3 (1963): 120–129; Jeremy Boissevain, "Foreword," in *Urban Life in Mediterranean Europe: Anthropological Perspectives*, ed. Michael Kenny and David I. Kertzer (Urbana: University of Illinois Press, 1983), vii–viii; Richard L. Kagan with Fernando Marías, *Urban Images of the Hispanic World, 1493–1793* (New Haven, CT: Yale University Press, 2000), especially 24–28, 43–44; Lila Leontidou, "Cultural Representations of Urbanism and Experiences of Urbanisation in Mediterranean Europe," in *Geography, Environment and Development in Mediterranean Europe*, ed. Russell King, Paolo de Mas, and J. Mansvelt-Beck (Brighton, UK: Sussex Academic Press, 2001), 85–90. Likewise, Marvin Harris, *Town and Country in Brazil* (New York: Columbia University Press, 1956), 281, describes an "urban ethos" as "probably a fundamental part of Mediterranean and Latin American culture." How valid these characterizations are overall is less important for the present purpose than the evidence they afford that cities have been far from universally disliked.

28. Theodore Roszak, *The Voice of the Earth* (New York: Simon and Schuster, 1992), 217.

29. Torsten Malmberg, *Human Territoriality: Survey of Behavioral Territories in Man with Preliminary Analysis and Discussion of Meaning* (The Hague, The Netherlands: Mouton, 1980), 198.

30. Orr, "Re-Ruralizing Education," 226.

31. Martin V. Melosi, *Effluent America: Cities, Industry, Energy, and the Environment* (Pittsburgh: University of Pittsburgh Press, 2001), 1.

32. Freedman, *Crowding and Behavior*, 7.

33. Jacobs, *The Death and Life of Great American Cities*, 443–444.

34. John Stuart Mill, *Utilitarianism* (originally published in 1863), ed. Roger Crisp (Oxford: Oxford University Press, 1998), 76–77.

35. John Dewey, *Logic: The Theory of Inquiry* (originally published 1938), vol. 12, Jo Ann Boydston, ed., *John Dewey: The Later Works, 1925–1953* (Carbondale: Southern Illinois University Press, 1986), 26.

36. Edmund Ramsden and Jon Adams, "Escaping the Laboratory: The Rodent Experiments of John B. Calhoun and Their Cultural Influence," *Journal of Social History* 42, no. 3 (2009): 761–792.

37. John B. Calhoun, "Population Density and Social Pathology," *Scientific American* 206, no. 2 (1962): 139–148.

38. Ramsden and Adams, "Escaping the Laboratory," 768–773.

39. Lewis Mumford, *The Urban Prospect* (New York: Harcourt, Brace & World, 1968), 210.

40. Ramsden and Adams, "Escaping the Laboratory," 776–779.

41. Claude S. Fischer, *The Urban Experience*, 2nd ed. (San Diego: Harcourt Brace Jovanovich, 1984), 175; for substantiating material, see 174–186; Freedman, *Crowding and Behavior*; Mark Baldassare, "Human Spatial Behavior," *Annual Review of Sociology* 4 (1978): 29–56; and Peter Newman and Trevor Hogan, "A Review of Urban Density Models: Toward a Resolution of the Conflict between Populace and Planner," *Human Ecology* 9, no. 3 (1981): 269–303; Edward T. Hall, "Proxemics," *Current Anthropology* 9, no. 2/3 (1968): 94; Ramsden and Adams, "Escaping the Laboratory," 774–775.

42. David Levinson, "Population Density in Cross-Cultural Perspective," *American Ethnologist* 6, no. 4 (1979): 742.

43. Robert David Sack, *Human Territoriality: Its Theory and History* (New York: Cambridge University Press, 1986), 1–2. For social science dissections of claims about human territoriality as a biological phenomenon, see Freedman, *Crowding and Behavior*, 50–54; and Claude S. Fischer, "The 'Myth of Territoriality' in Van Den Berghe's "Bringing Beasts Back In," *American Sociological Review* 40, no. 5 (1975): 674–676.

44. *The Oxford English Dictionary*, 2nd ed. (Oxford: Clarendon Press, 1989), vol. XVII, 818–820; vol. VII, 969–970; vol. XI, 207–208.

45. Amos Hawley, "Population Density and the City," *Demography* 9, no. 4 (1972): 527.

46. Kenneth T. Jackson, "Urban Deconcentration in the Nineteenth Century: A Statistical Inquiry," in *The New Urban History: Quantitative Explorations by American Historians*, ed. Leo T. Schnore (Princeton, NJ: Princeton University Press, 1975), 120; Irving Howe with Kenneth Libo, *World of Our Fathers* (New York: Harcourt Brace Jovanovich, 1976), 98–99; Eric H. Monkkonen, *Murder in New York City* (Berkeley: University of California Press, 2001), 16. On earlier beliefs about rural violent crime, see Emile Durkheim, *On Suicide* (originally published in 1897), trans. Robin Buss (New York: Penguin Books, 2006), 393; Cesare Lombroso, *Crime: Its Causes and Remedies*, trans. Henry B. Horton (Boston: Little, Brown, and Company, 1911), 72–75; Paul L. Vogt, *Introduction to Rural Sociology* (New York: D. Appleton and Company, 1917), 224, 226; Maurice Parmelee, *Criminology* (New York: Macmillan, 1918), 59; Stephen P. Frank, *Crime, Cultural Conflict, and Justice in Rural Russia, 1856–1914* (Berkeley: University of California Press, 1999), 58–59, 60–61, 65–66. In "The Adventure of the Copper Beeches" (1892), Sherlock Holmes explains to Dr. Watson why violent crime is necessarily more prevalent in rural than in urban areas. For research casting plenty of doubt on the belief that crime, violent or not, always increases with the degree of urbanness, see, for example, Frank, op. cit.; James Buchanan Given, *Society and Homicide in Thirteenth-Century England* (Stanford, CA: Stanford University Press, 1977), chapters 8 and 9; Roger Lane, "Crime and Criminal Statistics in Nineteenth-Century Massachusetts," *Journal of Social History* 2, no. 2 (1968): 156–163; Eric A. Johnson, *Urbanization and Crime: Germany, 1871–1914* (New York: Cambridge University Press, 1995); Monkkonen, *Murder in New York City*; and several of the essays in Eric A. Johnson

and Eric H. Monkkonen, eds., *The Civilization of Crime: Violence in Town and Country since the Middle Ages* (Urbana: University of Illinois Press, 1996).

47. Robert C. Schmitt, "Implications of Density in Hong Kong," *Journal of the American Institute of Planners* 29, no. 3 (1963): 210–216. For a later and broader overview reaching similar conclusions, see Levinson, "Population Density in Cross-Cultural Perspective," 742–751.

48. Jameson K. Hirsch, "A Review of the Literature on Rural Suicide: Risks and Protective Factors, Incidence, and Prevention," *Crisis: The Journal of Crisis Intervention and Suicide Prevention* 27, no. 4 (2006): 189–199. The belief in an earlier urban penalty as a general rule in western Europe may also be oversimplified: Olive Anderson, "Did Suicide Increase with Industrialization in Victorian England?" *Past and Present* no. 86 (1980): 149–173.

49. James T. Massey, "Suicide in the United States, 1950–1964," National Center for Health Statistics series 20, no. 5 (Washington, DC: U.S. Government Printing Office, 1967), 6–7.

50. Robert J. Wenke and Deborah I. Olszewski, *Patterns in Prehistory: Humankind's First Three Million Years*, 5th ed. (New York: Oxford University Press, 2007), 228. The point is bolstered by the well-documented reluctance within historic times of many hunter-gatherers to adopt sedentary agriculture as a way of life, and on a different note by the apparent deterioration in human health and well-being that occurred in prehistory following the shift to farming: Jared Diamond, "The Worst Mistake in the History of the Human Race" (originally published in 1987), reprinted in *The Introductory Reader in Human Geography: Contemporary Debates and Classic Writings*, ed. William G. Moseley, David A. Lanegran, and Kavita Pandit (Malden, MA: Blackwell, 2007), 116–121.

51. Gordon H. Orians, "Habitat Selection: General Theory and Application to Human Behavior," in *The Evolution of Human Social Behavior*, ed. Joan S. Lockard (New York: Elsevier, 1980), 56–58; Gordon H. Orians and Judith H. Heerwagen, "Evolved Responses to Landscapes," in Jerome H. Barkow, Leda Cosmides, and John Tooby, eds., *The Adapted Mind: Evolutionary Psychology and the Generation of Culture* (New York: Oxford University Press, 1992), 555–579; John D. Balling and John H. Falk, "Development of Visual Preference for Natural Environments," *Environment and Behavior* 14, no. 1 (1982): 5–28. The idea has become widely disseminated; see, for example, Tony Hiss, *The Experience of Place* (New York: Alfred A. Knopf, 1990), 36–37; Steven Pinker, *How the Mind Works* (New York: W. W. Norton, 1997), 374–378; Bruce Bridgeman, *Psychology and Evolution: The Origins of Mind* (Thousand Oaks, CA: Sage, 2003), 62–63.

52. F. Herbert Bormann, Diana Balmori, and Gordon T. Geballe, *Redesigning the American Lawn: A Search for Environmental Harmony* (New Haven, CT: Yale University Press, 1993), 12; see also Robbins, *Lawn People*, 18–21; and Steinberg, *American Green*, 9–10.

53. Steinberg, *American Green*, 10.

54. Balling and Falk, "Development of Visual Preference for Natural Environments"; Elizabeth Lyons, "Demographic Correlates of Landscape Preference,"

Environment and Behavior 15, no. 4 (1983): 507. For a discussion of some of the difficulties of inferring natural human responses from children's behavior, see Bernard Mergen, "Children and Nature in History," *Environmental History* 8, no. 4 (2003): 643–669.

55. See Ke-Tsung Han, "Responses to Six Major Terrestrial Biomes in Terms of Scenic Beauty, Preference, and Restorativeness," *Environment and Behavior* 39, no. 4 (2007): especially 545–547, and studies cited therein; also Patrick Hartmann and Vanessa Apaolaza-Ibáñez, "Beyond Savanna: An Evolutionary and Environmental Psychology Approach to Behavioral Effects of Nature Scenery in Green Advertising," *Journal of Environmental Psychology* 30, no. 1 (2010): 119–128.

56. Robbins, *Lawn People*, 19; see also Steinberg, *American Green*, 9.

57. For reviews, see Agnes van den Berg, Terry Hartig, and Henk Staats, "Preference for Nature in Urbanized Societies: Stress, Restoration, and the Pursuit of Sustainability," *Journal of Social Issues* 63, no. 1 (2007): 79–96 (quotation from 92); Jo Barton and Jules Pretty, "Urban Ecology and Human Health and Wellbeing," in *Urban Ecology*, ed. Kevin J. Gaston (Cambridge, UK: Cambridge University Press, 2010), 202–229; and Jon Sadler et al., "Bringing Cities Alive: The Importance of Urban Green Spaces for People and Biodiversity," in ibid., 230–260.

58. Walter Harding, *The Days of Henry Thoreau*, rev. ed. (New York: Dover Publications, 1982), 190; for details, see 184, 190–196.

Chapter 9

1. Good recent examples (the list is far from exhaustive) include Timothy Beatley, *Biophilic Cities: Integrating Nature into Urban Design and Planning* (Washington, DC: Island Press, 2011); Peter Calthorpe, *Urbanism in the Age of Climate Change* (Washington, DC: Island Press, 2011); Joan Fitzgerald, *Emerald Cities: Urban Sustainability and Economic Development* (New York: Oxford University Press, 2010); and Steffen Lehmann, *The Principles of Green Urbanism: Transforming the City for Sustainability* (London: Earthscan, 2010).

2. For an extreme example, see Herbert Girardet, *The Gaia Atlas of Cities* (London: Gaia, 1996).

3. On these trends, see, for example, William D. Solecki and Robin M. Leichenko, "Urbanization and the Metropolitan Environment: Lessons from New York and Shanghai," *Environment* 48, no. 4 (2006): 8–23.

Appendix A

1. *Storm Events* lists twenty-five deaths in Florida from the tornado outbreak of March 12, 1993, but does not indicate what counties they occurred in. The data used were obtained from "County-by-County Damage Report," *Miami Herald*, March 14, 1993: 25A.

Bibliography

Afkhami, Amir. "Compromised Constitutions: The Iranian Experience with the 1918 Influenza Pandemic." *Bulletin of the History of Medicine* 77 (2) (2003): 367–392.

Aide, T. Mitchell and H. Ricardo Grau. "Globalization, Migration, and Latin American Ecosystems." *Science* 305 (5692) (2004): 1915–1916.

Alexander, David. *Confronting Catastrophe: New Perspectives on Natural Disasters.* New York: Oxford University Press, 2000.

Alirol, Emilie, Laurent Getaz, Beat Stoll, François Chappuis, and Louis Loutan. "Urbanisation and Infectious Diseases in a Globalising World." *Lancet Infectious Diseases* 11 (2) (2011): 131–141.

Allan, J. A. *The Middle East Water Question: Hydropolitics and the Global Economy.* London: I. B. Tauris, 2001.

Allen, Barbara. *Uneasy Alchemy: Citizens and Experts in Louisiana's Chemical Corridor Disputes.* Cambridge, MA: MIT Press, 2003.

Almeida, Deepak, Camilla Rodrigues, Zarir F. Udwadia, Ajit Lalvani, G. D. Gothi, Pravin Mehta, and Ajita Mehta. "Incidence of Multidrug-Resistant Tuberculosis in Urban and Rural India and Implications for Prevention." *Clinical Infectious Diseases* 36 (12) (2003): e152–e154.

Anderson, Mary B. "Vulnerability to Disaster and Sustainable Development: A General Framework for Assessing Vulnerability." In *Storms.* vol. 1, ed. R. Pielke Jr. and R. Pielke Sr., 11–25. New York: Routledge, 2000.

Anderson, Olive. "Did Suicide Increase with Industrialization in Victorian England?" *Past & Present* 86 (1) (1980): 149–173.

Anderson, Terry L., and Donald R. Leal. *Free Market Environmentalism.* 2nd ed. New York: Palgrave, 2001.

Aprioku, Innocent M. "Oil-Spill Disasters and the Rural Hazardscape of Eastern Nigeria." *Geoforum* 34 (1) (2003): 99–112.

Babbitt, Bruce E. *Cities in the Wilderness: A New Vision of Land Use in America.* Washington, DC: Island Press, 2005.

Bairoch, Paul. *Cities and Economic Development: From the Dawn of History to the Present.* Trans. Christopher Braider. Chicago: University of Chicago Press, 1988.

Baldassare, Mark. "Human Spatial Behavior." *Annual Review of Sociology* 4 (1978): 29–56.

Ball, George A. *Diplomacy for a Crowded World: An American Foreign Policy.* Boston: Little, Brown and Company, 1976.

Balling, John D., and John H. Falk. "Development of Visual Preference for Natural Environments." *Environment and Behavior* 14 (1) (1982): 5–28.

Banerjee, Sudeshina Ghosh, and Elvira Morella. *Africa's Water and Sanitation Infrastructure: Access, Affordability, and Alternatives.* Washington, DC: The World Bank, 2011.

Baptista, Sandra R. "Metropolitanization and Forest Recovery in Southern Brazil: A Multiscale Analysis of the Florianópolis City-Region, Santa Catarina State, 1970 to 2005." [online] *Ecology & Society* 13 (2) (2008): 5.

Barles, Sabine. "Urban Metabolism of Paris and Its Region." *Journal of Industrial Ecology* 13 (6) (2009): 898–913.

Barnes, Douglas F., ed. *The Challenge of Rural Electrification: Strategies for Developing Countries.* Washington, DC: Resources for the Future, 2007.

Barton, Jo, and Jules Pretty. "Urban Ecology and Human Health and Wellbeing." In *Urban Ecology*, ed. Kevin J. Gaston, 202–229. Cambridge, UK: Cambridge University Press, 2010.

Bassett, Debra Lyn. "Distancing Rural Poverty." *Georgetown Journal on Poverty Law and Policy* 13 (2006): 3–32.

Bassett, Debra Lyn. "Poverty and Global Ruralism." *Journal of Gender, Race & Justice* 13 (2009): 1–25.

Bastien, Joseph William. *The Kiss of Death: Chagas' Disease in the Americas.* Salt Lake City: University of Utah Press, 1998.

Baxa, Paul. *Roads and Ruins: The Symbolic Landscape of Fascist Rome.* Toronto: University of Toronto Press, 2010.

Beatley, Timothy. *Biophilic Cities: Integrating Nature into Urban Design and Planning.* Washington, DC: Island Press, 2011.

Beatley, Timothy. *Green Urbanism: Learning from European Cities.* Washington, DC: Island Press, 2000.

Becker, Charles M., and Andrew R. Morrison. "Public Policy and Rural-Urban Migration." In *Cities in the Developing World: Issues, Theory, and Policy*, ed. Josef Gugler, 88–105. Oxford: Oxford University Press, 1997.

Benedictow, Ole J. *The Black Death, 1346–1353: The Complete History.* Woodbridge, UK: Boydell Press, 2004.

Benton-Short, Lisa, and John R. Short. *Cities and Nature.* London: Routledge, 2008.

Beran, George W. "Urban Rabies." In *The Natural History of Rabies*. 2nd ed., ed. George M. Baer, 427–443. Boca Raton, FL: CRC Press, 1991.

Berry, Brian J. L., and Adam Okulicz-Kozaryn. "An Urban-Rural Gradient in Happiness." *Urban Geography* 32 (6) (2011): 871–883.

Berry, Brian J. L., and Adam Okulicz-Kozaryn. "Dissatisfaction with City Life: A New Look at Some Old Questions." *Cities* 26 (3) (2009): 117–123.

Bettencourt, Luís A. M., José Lobo, Dirk Helbing, Christian Kühnert, and Geoffrey B. West. "Growth, Innovation, Scaling, and the Pace of Life in Cities." *Proceedings of the National Academy of Sciences of the United States of America* 104 (17) (2007): 7301–7306.

"Better, Greener, Smarter Cities." *Scientific American* 305, no. 74/75 (2011).

Bezemer, Dirk, and Derek Headey. "Agriculture, Development, and Urban Bias." *World Development* 36 (8) (2008): 1342–1364.

Bocquier, Philippe, Nyovani Madise, and Eliya Zulu. "Is There an Urban Advantage in Child Survival in Sub-Saharan Africa? Evidence from 18 Countries in the 1990s." *Demography* 48 (2) (2011): 531–558.

Boissevain, Jeremy. "Foreword." In *Urban Life in Mediterranean Europe: Anthropological Perspectives*, ed. Michael Kenny and David I. Kertzer, vii–x. Urbana: University of Illinois Press, 1983.

Boland, M., A. Staines, P. Fitzpatrick, and E. Scanlan. "Urban-Rural Variation in Mortality and Hospital Admission Rates for Unintentional Injury in Ireland." *Injury Prevention* 11 (1) (2005): 38–42.

Boone, Christopher, and Ali Modarres. *City and Environment*. Philadelphia: Temple University Press, 2006.

Borden, Kevin A., and Susan L. Cutter. "Spatial Patterns of Natural Hazards Mortality in the United States." *International Journal of Health Geographies* 7 (2008): 64.

Bormann, F. Herbert, Diana Balmori, and Gordon T. Geballe. *Redesigning the American Lawn: A Search for Environmental Harmony*. New Haven, CT: Yale University Press, 1993.

Borroto, René, and Ramon Martinez-Piedra. "Geographical Patterns of Cholera in Mexico, 1991–1996." *International Journal of Epidemiology* 29 (4) (2000): 764–772.

Boudreaux, Karol C. "Land Conflict and Genocide in Rwanda." *Electronic Journal of Sustainable Development* 1 (3) (2009).

Bramall, Chris. *The Industrialization of Rural China*. Oxford: Oxford University Press, 2007.

Brand, Stewart. *Whole Earth Discipline: An Ecopragmatist Manifesto*. New York: Viking, 2009.

Brandon, Katrina, Kent H. Redford, and Steven M. Sanderson, eds. *Parks in Peril: People, Politics, and Protected Areas*. Washington, DC: Island Press, 1998.

Brauch, Hans Günter. "Urbanization and Natural Disasters in the Mediterranean: Population Growth and Climatic Change in the 21st Century." In *Building Safer Cities: The Future of Disaster Risk*, ed. A. Kreimer, M. Arnold, and A. Carlin, 149–164. Washington, DC: The World Bank Disaster Management Facility, 2003.

Brichieri-Colombi, Stephen. *The World Water Crisis: The Failures of Resource Management*. London: I. B. Tauris, 2009.

Bridgeman, Bruce. *Psychology and Evolution: The Origins of Mind.* Thousand Oaks, CA: Sage, 2003.

Brieger, William R. "Urban Malaria: Myth and Reality." *Africa Health* 33 (2) (2011): 14–17.

Brigham, Robert K. "Vietnamese Society at War." In *The Columbia History of the Vietnam War,* ed. David L. Anderson, 317–332. New York: Columbia University Press, 2011.

Brimblecombe, Peter. *The Big Smoke: Air Pollution in London since Medieval Times.* London: Methuen, 1987.

Brockerhoff, Martin. "Urban Growth in Developing Countries: A Review of Projections and Predictions." *Population and Development Review* 25 (4) (1999): 757–778.

Brooks, David B. "Between the Great Rivers: Water in the Heart of the Middle East." *International Journal of Water Resources Development* 13 (3) (1997): 291–309.

Brower, Jennifer, and Peter Chalk. *The Global Threat of New and Reemerging Infectious Disease: Reconciling U.S. National Security and Public Health Policy.* Santa Monica, CA: RAND, 2003.

Brown, David L., and John B. Cromartie. "The Nature of Rurality in Postindustrial Society." In *New Forms of Urbanization,* ed. Tony Champion and Graeme Hugo, 269–283. Aldershot, UK: Ashgate, 2004.

Brown, Lester R. "The Urban Prospect: Reexamining the Basic Assumptions." *Population and Development Review* 2 (2) (1976): 267–277.

Broz, J. Lawrence and Daniel Maliniak. "Malapportionment, Gasoline Taxes, and Climate Change." APSA 2010 Annual Meeting Paper. http://papers.ssrn.com/sol3/papers.cfm?abstract_id=1642499.

Bruegmann, Robert. *Sprawl: A Compact History.* Chicago: University of Chicago Press, 2005.

Brunn, Stanley D., Maureen Hays-Mitchell, and Donald J. Zeigler, eds. *Cities of the World: World Regional Urban Development.* 4th ed. Lanham, MD: Rowman & Littlefield, 2008.

Bryant, Edward. *Natural Hazards.* 2nd ed. Cambridge, UK: Cambridge University Press, 2005.

Burton, Ian, Robert W. Kates, and Gilbert F. White. *The Environment as Hazard.* 2nd ed. New York: Guilford Press, 1993.

Cai, Le, and Virasakdi Changsuvivatwong. "Rural-Urban Differentials of Premature Mortality Burden in South-West China." *International Journal for Equity in Health* 5 (2006): 13.

Calhoun, John B. "Population Density and Social Pathology." *Scientific American* 206 (2) (1962): 139–148.

Calthorpe, Peter. "Redefining Cities." *Whole Earth Review* (45) (March 1985): 1.

Calthorpe, Peter. *Urbanism in the Age of Climate Change.* Washington, DC: Island Press, 2011.

Caplan, Bryan. *The Myth of the Rational Voter: Why Democracies Choose Bad Policies.* Princeton, NJ: Princeton University Press, 2007.

Caprotti, Federico. *Mussolini's Cities: Internal Colonialism in Italy, 1930–1939.* Youngstown, NY: Cambria Press, 2007.

Carozza, Susan E. Bo Li, Kai Elgethun, and Ryan Whitworth: "Risk of Childhood Cancers Associated with Residence in Agriculturally Intense Areas in the United States." *Environmental Health Perspectives* 116 (4) (2008): 559–565.

Carruthers, John I., and Gudmundur F. Ulfarsson. "Does 'Smart Growth' Matter to Public Finance?" *Urban Studies* 45 (9) (2008): 1791–1823.

Carruthers, John I., and Gudmundur F. Ulfarsson. "Urban Sprawl and the Cost of Public Services." *Environment and Planning B* 30 (4) (2003): 503–522.

Cauvin, Jacques. *The Birth of the Gods and the Origins of Agriculture.* Trans. Trevor Watkins. Cambridge, UK: Cambridge University Press, 2000.

Celli, Angelo. *Malaria According to the New Researches.* Trans. John Joseph Eyre. London: Longmans, Green, and Co., 1900.

Center for Rural Pennsylvania. *An Analysis of Illegal Dumpsites in Rural Pennsylvania.* Harrisburg: Author, 2009.

Chafe, Zoë. "Reducing Natural Disaster Risk in Cities." In *State of the World 2007: Our Urban Future,* 112–129. Washington, DC: Worldwatch Institute, 2007.

Chamania, Shobha. "Training and Burn Care in Rural India." *Indian Journal of Plastic Surgery* 43 (supplement) (2010): 126–130.

Champagne, Audrey B., Leopold E. Klopfer, and John H. Anderson. "Factors Influencing the Learning of Classical Mechanics." *American Journal of Physics* 48 (12) (1980): 1074–1079.

Champion, Tony. "Urbanization, Suburbanization, Counterurbanization and Reurbanization." In *Handbook of Urban Studies,* ed. Roman Paddison, 143–161. London: Sage, 2001.

Changnon, Stanley A., ed. *METROMEX: A Review and Summary.* Boston: American Meteorological Society, 1981.

Chattopadhyay, Arpita, Michael J. White, and Cornelius Debpuur. "Migrant Fertility in Ghana: Selection versus Adaptation and Disruption as Causal Mechanisms." *Population Studies* 60 (2) (2006): 189–203.

Chavers, L. Scott and Sten H. Vermund. "An Introduction to Emerging and Reemerging Infectious Diseases." In *Emerging Infectious Diseases: Trends and Issues.* 2nd ed., ed. Felissa R. Lashley and Jerry D. Durham, 3–24. New York: Springer, 2007.

Chen, Chien-Jen, Li-Yu Wang, and Ming-Whei Yu. "Epidemiology of Hepatitis B Virus Infection in the Asia-Pacific Region." *Journal of Gastroenterology and Hepatology* 15 (supplement) (2000): E3–E6.

Chen, H. Y., T. Senserrick, A. L. Martiniuk, R. Q. Ivers, S. Boufous, H. Y. Chang, and R. Norton. "Fatal Crash Trends for Australian Young Drivers, 1997–2007." *Journal of Safety Research* 41 (2) (2010): 123–128.

Chepesiuk, Ron. "Missing the Dark." *Environmental Health Perspectives* 117 (1) (2009): A20–A27.

Chowell, Gerardo, Luís A. M. Bettencourt, Niall Johnson, Wladimir J. Alonso, and Cécile Viboud. "The 1918–1919 Influenza Pandemic in England and Wales: Spatial Patterns in Transmissibility and Mortality Impact." *Proceedings of the Royal Society B:: Biological Sciences* 275 (1634) (2008): 501–509.

Cicero, Marcus Tullius. *The Nature of the Gods.* Trans. P. G. Walsh. Oxford: Clarendon Press, 1997.

Clark, David E. "Effect of Population Density on Mortality after Motor Vehicle Collisions." *Accident Analysis and Prevention* 35 (6) (2003): 965–971.

Clarke, Lee. *Worst Cases: Terror and Catastrophe in the Popular Imagination.* Chicago: University of Chicago Press, 2006.

Cohen, Barney. "Urban Growth in Developing Countries: A Review of Current Trends and a Caution Regarding Existing Forecasts." *World Development* 32 (1) (2004): 23–51.

Cohn, Samuel K. *The Black Death Transformed: Disease and Culture in Early Renaissance Europe.* New York: Oxford University Press, 2002.

Conti, Susanna, Paola Meli, Giada Minelli, Renata Solimini, Virgilia Toccaceli, Monica Vichi, Carmen Beltrano, and Luigi Perini. "Epidemiologic Study of Mortality during the Summer 2003 Heat Wave in Italy." *Environmental Research* 98 (3) (2005): 390–399.

Conuel, Thomas. *Quabbin: The Accidental Wilderness.* Rev. ed. Amherst: University of Massachusetts Press, 1990.

Copeland, Claudia. "Rural Water Supply and Sewer Systems: Background Information." *CRS Report to Congress* 98–64. Washington, DC: Congressional Research Service, 2010.

Costilla, Vanessa, and David Bishai. "Lawn Mower Injuries in the United States, 1996–2004." *Annals of Emergency Medicine* 47 (6) (2006): 567–573.

Cross, John A. "Megacities and Small Towns: Different Perspectives on Hazard Vulnerability." *Environmental Hazards* 3 (2) (2001): 63–80.

Cueto, Marcus. "Stigma and Blame during an Epidemic: Cholera in Peru, 1991." In *Disease in the History of Modern Latin America: From Malaria to AIDS,* ed. Diego Armus, 268–289. Durham, NC: Duke University Press, 2003.

Dale, Ann, in collaboration with S. B. Hill. *At the Edge: Sustainable Development in the 21st Century.* Vancouver: UBC Press, 2001.

Dauvergne, Peter. "The Politics of Deforestation in Indonesia." *Pacific Affairs* 66 (4) (1994): 497–518.

Davis, Mike. "The Case for Letting Malibu Burn." *Environmental History Review* 19 (2) (1995): 1–36.

Davis, Mike. *Ecology of Fear: Los Angeles and the Imagination of Disaster.* New York: Henry Holt and Company, 1998.

Davis, Mike. *Magical Urbanism: Latinos Reinvent the US City.* London: Verso, 2000.

Davis, Robert E., Paul C. Knappenberger, Patrick J. Michaels, and Wendy M. Novicoff. "Changing Heat-Related Mortality in the United States." *Environmental Health Perspectives* 111 (14) (2003): 1712–1718.

DeFries, Ruth, Thomas Rudel, Maria Uriarte, and Matthew Hansen. "Deforestation Driven by Urban Population Growth and Agricultural Trade in the Twenty-First Century." *Nature Geoscience* 3 (2010): 178–181.

Degg, M. "Natural Disasters: Recent Trends and Future Prospects." *Geography (Sheffield, England)* 77 (3) (1992): 198–209.

Deininger, Klaus W. *Land Policies for Growth and Poverty Reduction*. Washington, DC: World Bank with Oxford University Press, 2003.

DeSimone, Leslie A., Pixie A. Hamilton, and Robert J. Gilliom. "Quality of Water from Domestic Wells in Principal Aquifers of the United States." *USGS Circular 1332*, 2009.

Desrochers, Pierre, and Gert-Jan Hospers. "Cities and the Economic Development of Nations: An Essay on Jane Jacobs' Contribution to Economic Theory." *Canadian Journal of Regional Science* 30 (1) (2007): 115–132.

Devereux, Stephen. "Famine in the Twentieth Century." *IDS Working Paper 105*, 2000.

Devezies, Laurent, and Rémy Prud'homme. "The Redistributive Role of Mega-Cities." In *Mega-City Growth and the Future*, ed. Roland B. Fuchs et al., 149–171. Tokyo: United Nations University Press, 1994.

De Vries, Jan. *European Urbanization, 1500–1800*. Cambridge, MA: Harvard University Press, 1984.

de Waal, Alex. *Famine Crimes: Politics & the Disaster Relief Industry in Africa*. Bloomington: Indiana University Press, 1997.

Dewey, John. *Logic: The Theory of Inquiry* (originally published in 1938). vol. 12, Jo Ann Boydston, ed., *John Dewey: The Later Works, 1925–1953*. Carbondale: Southern Illinois University Press, 1986.

Diamond, Jared. "The Worst Mistake in the History of the Human Race." In *The Introductory Reader in Human Geography: Contemporary Debates and Classic Writings*, ed. William G. Moseley, David A. Lanegran, and Kavita Pandit, 116–121. Malden, MA: Blackwell, 2007.

DiSessa, Andrea A. "Unlearning Aristotelian Physics: A Study of Knowledge-Based Learning." *Cognitive Science* 6 (1) (1982): 37–75.

Dodman, David. "Blaming Cities for Climate Change? An Analysis of Urban Greenhouse Gas Emissions." *Environment and Urbanization* 21 (1) (2009): 185–201.

Dodman, David, and David Satterthwaite. "Are Cities Really to Blame?" *Urban World* 1 (2) (2009): 12–13.

Domenec, Elena, and David Sauri. "Urbanisation and Water Consumption: Influencing Factors in the Metropolitan Region of Barcelona." *Urban Studies (Edinburgh, Scotland)* 43 (9) (2006): 1625–1633.

Draper, Patricia. "Crowding among Hunter-Gatherers: The !Kung Bushmen." *Science* 182 (4109) (1973): 301–303.

Dresang, L. T. "Gun Deaths in Rural and Urban Settings: Recommendations for Prevention." *Journal of the American Board of Family Practice* 14 (2) (2001): 107–115.

D'Souza, Frances. "Democracy as a Cure for Famine." *Journal of Peace Research* 31 (4) (1994): 369–373.

Dudley, Nigel, and Sue Stolton. "The Role of Forest Protected Areas in Supplying Drinking Water to the World's Biggest Cities." In *The Urban Imperative: Urban Outreach for Protected Area Agencies*, ed. Ted Trzyna, 27–33. Sacramento: California Institute of Public Affairs, 2005.

Dummer, Trevor J. B., and Ian G. Cook. "Health in China and India: A Cross-Country Comparison in a Context of Rapid Globalisation." *Social Science & Medicine* 67 (4) (2008): 590–605.

Durkheim, Emile. *On Suicide* (originally published in 1897). Trans. Robin Buss. New York: Penguin Books, 2006.

Dynes, R. R. "The Dialogue between Voltaire and Rousseau on the Lisbon Earthquake: The Emergence of a Social Science View." *International Journal of Mass Emergencies and Disasters* 18 (1) (2000): 97–115.

Dyson, Tim. "HIV/AIDS and Urbanization." *Population and Development Review* 29 (3) (2003): 427–442.

Dzioubinski, Oleg, and Ralph Chipman. "Trends in Consumption and Production: Household Energy Consumption." *DESA Discussion Paper No. 6.* New York: United Nations Department of Social and Economic Affairs, 1999.

Eberhardt, M. E., D. D. Ingram, D. M. Makuc, et al. *Urban and Rural Health Chartbook: Health, United States, 2001.* Hyattsville, MD: National Center for Health Statistics, 2001.

Eberstadt, Nicholas. *The Tyranny of Numbers: Mismeasurement and Misrule.* Washington, DC: AEI Press, 1995.

Ehrenhalt, Alan. "Trading Places: The Demographic Inversion of the American City." *The New Republic* (August 13, 2008): 19–22.

Ehrhardt-Martinez, Karen, Edward M. Crenshaw, and J. Craig Jenkins. "Deforestation and the Environmental Kuznets Curve: A Cross-National Investigation of Intervening Mechanisms." *Social Science Quarterly* 83 (1) (2002): 226–243.

Ehrlich, Paul R., and Anne H. Ehrlich. *One with Nineveh: Politics, Consumption, and the Human Future.* Washington, DC: Island Press, 2004.

Engwicht, David. *Reclaiming Our Cities and Towns: Better Living with Less Traffic.* Philadelphia: New Society Publishing, 1993.

EPA. *National Water Quality Inventory: Report to Congress, 2004 Reporting Cycle.* Washington, DC: EPA Office of Water, 2009.

Esparza, Adrian X., and Guy McPherson, eds. *The Planner's Guide to Natural Resource Conservation: The Science of Land Development beyond the Metropolitan Fringe.* Dordrecht, Germany: Springer, 2009.

Estabrook, Barry. *Tomatoland.* Kansas City, MO: Andrews McMeel, 2011.

Ewing, Reid, Rolf Pendall, and Don Chen. "Measuring Sprawl and Its Impact." *Technical Report* 1. Washington, DC: Smart Growth America, 2002.

Ewing, Reid H., Richard A. Schieber, and Charles V. Zegeer. "Urban Sprawl as a Risk Factor in Motor Vehicle Occupant and Pedestrian Fatalities." *American Journal of Public Health* 93 (9) (2003): 1541–1545.

Fang, Ya, Long Dai, Michael S. Jaung, Xiaoxuan Chen, Songlin Yu, and Huiyun Xiang. "Child Drowning Deaths in Xiamen City and Suburbs, People's Republic of China." *Injury Prevention* 13 (5) (2007): 339–343.

Feagan, Robert B., and Michael Ripmeester. "Contesting Natural(ized) Lawns: A Geography of Private Green Space in the Niagara Region." *Urban Geography* 20 (7) (1999): 617–634.

Federal Emergency Management Administration. "The Rural Fire Problem in the United States," FEMA/United States Fire Administration, August 1997.

Feikin, Daniel R., Beatrice Olack, Godfrey M. Bigogo, Allan Audi, Leonard Cosmas, Barrack Aura, Heather Burke, M. Kariuki Njenga, John Williamson, and Robert F. Breiman. "The Burden of Common Infectious Disease Syndromes at the Clinic and Household Level from Population-Based Surveillance in Rural and Urban Kenya." *PloS* 6 (1) (2011): e16085.

Fischer, Claude S. "The 'Myth of Territoriality' in Van Den Berghe's 'Bringing Beasts Back In.'" *American Sociological Review* 40 (5) (1975): 674–676.

Fischer, Claude S. *The Urban Experience.* 2nd ed. San Diego: Harcourt Brace Jovanovich, 1984.

Fischer, Claude S. "Urban Malaise." *Social Forces* 52 (2) (1973): 221–235.

Fischer, David Hackett. *Historians' Fallacies: Toward a Logic of Historical Thought.* New York: Harper & Row, 1970.

Fitzgerald, Joan. *Emerald Cities: Urban Sustainability and Economic Development.* New York: Oxford University Press, 2010.

Flora, Snowden D. *Tornadoes of the United States.* Norman: University of Oklahoma Press, 1953.

Flynn, Jennifer D. "Characteristics of Home Fire Victims." Quincy, MA: National Fire Protection Association, Fire Analysis and Research Division, 2010.

Folke, Carl, Åsa Jansson, Jonas Larsson, and Robert Costanza. "Ecosystem Appropriation by Cities." *Ambio* 26 (3) (1997): 167–172.

Foster, Vivien, and Cecelia Briceño-Garmendia, eds. *Africa's Infrastructure: A Time for Transformation.* Washington, DC: The World Bank, 2010.

Frandsen, Steen Bo. "'The War that We Prefer': The Reclamation of the Pontine Marshes and Fascist Expansion." In *International Fascism, 1919–1945,* ed. Gert Sørensen and Robert Mallett, 69–82. London: Frank Cass, 2002.

Frank, Stephen P. *Crime, Cultural Conflict, and Justice in Rural Russia, 1856–1914.* Berkeley: University of California Press, 1999.

Freedman, Jonathan L. *Crowding and Behavior.* New York: The Viking Press, 1975.

Frenken, Karen. "Irrigation in the Middle East Region in Figures: AQUASTAT Survey: 2008." In *FAO Water Reports 34*. Rome: FAO, 2009.

Fuchs, Roland J., and George J. Demko. "Rethinking Population Distribution Policies." *Population Research and Policy Review* 2 (2) (1983): 161–187.

Gabriel, Katharina M. A., and Wilfried R. Endlicher. "Urban and Rural Mortality Rates during Heat Waves in Berlin and Brandenburg, Germany." *Environmental Pollution* 159 (8/9) (2011): 2044–2050.

Galley, Chris. "A Model of Early Modern Urban Demography." *Economic History Review*, 48 (3) (1995): 448–469.

Gamba, Paolo, and Martin Herold, eds. *Global Mapping of Human Settlement: Experiences, Datasets, and Prospects*. Boca Raton, FL: CRC Press, 2009.

Gans, Herbert J. *The Urban Villagers: Group and Class in the Life of Italian-Americans*. New York: The Free Press, 1962.

Garenne, Michel, and Veronique Joseph. "The Timing of the Fertility Transition in Sub-Saharan Africa." *World Development* 30 (10) (2002): 1835–1843.

Garenne, Michel, et al. "The Demographic Impact of a Mild Famine in an African City: The Case of Antananarivo, 1985–7." In *Famine Demography: Perspectives from the Past and Present*, ed. Tim Dyson and Cormac Ó Gráda, 204–217. Oxford: Oxford University Press, 2002.

Garg, Suneela, Shelly Chadha, Sumit Malhotra, and A. K. Agarwal. "Deafness: Burden, Prevention, and Control in India." *National Medical Journal of India* 22 (2) (2009): 79–81.

Gaston, Kevin J., Zoe G. Davies, and Jill L. Edmondson. "Urban Environments and Ecosystem Functions." In *Urban Ecology*, ed. Kevin J. Gaston, 35–52. Cambridge, UK: Cambridge University Press, 2010.

Gess, Denise, and William Lutz. *Firestorm at Peshtigo: A Town, Its People, and the Deadliest Fire in American History*. New York: Henry Holt and Company, 2002.

Geyer, Billie, Claudette Robey, Edward W. Hill, John Brennan, Kevin O'Brien, and Robert Puentes. "Slanted Pavement: How Ohio's Highway Spending Short-changes Cities and Suburbs." Discussion Paper, Brookings Institution Center on Urban and Metropolitan Policy, March 2003.

Ghimire, Krishna B., and Michel P. Pimbert, eds. *Social Change and Conservation: Environmental Politics and Impacts of National Parks and Protected Areas*. London: Earthscan, 1997.

Ghirardo, Diane. *Building New Communities: New Deal America and Fascist Italy*. Princeton, NJ: Princeton University Press, 1989.

Girardet, Herbert. *The Gaia Atlas of Cities*. London: Gaia, 1996.

Given, James Buchanan. *Society and Homicide in Thirteenth-Century England*. Stanford, CA: Stanford University Press, 1977.

Glaeser, Edward L. "Are Cities Dying?" *Journal of Economic Perspectives* 100 (6) (1998): 139–160.

Glaeser, Edward L. *Triumph of the City: How Our Greatest Invention Makes Us Richer, Smarter, Greener, Healthier, and Happier.* New York: The Penguin Press, 2011.

Glaeser, Edward L., and Matthew E. Kahn. "The Greenness of Cities: Carbon Dioxide Emissions and Urban Development." *Journal of Urban Economics* 67 (3) (2010): 404–418.

Global Development Research Center. "Urban and Ecological Footprints." http://www.gdrc.org/uem/footprints/index.html.

Global Seismic Hazard Assessment Program. "Global Seismic Hazard Map." http://www.seismo.ethz.ch/static/GSHAP.

Gonzalez, Richard P., Glenn R. Cummings, Herbert A. Phelan, Madhuri S. Mulekar, and Charles B. Rodning. "Does Increased Emergency Medical Services Prehospital Time Affect Patient Mortality in Rural Motor Vehicle Crashes? A Statewide Analysis." *American Journal of Surgery* 197 (1) (2009): 30–34.

Grau, H. Ricardo, and T. Mitchell Aide. "Are Rural-Urban Migration and Sustainable Development Compatible in Mountain Systems?" *Mountain Research and Development* 27 (2) (2007): 119–123.

Grau, H. Ricardo, and Mitchell Aide. "Globalization and Land-Use Transitions in Latin America." [online] *Ecology & Society* 13 (2) (2008): 1.

Grau, H. Ricardo, T. Mitchell Aide, Jess K. Zimmermann, and John R. Thomlinson. "Trends and Scenarios of the Carbon Budget in Postagricultural Puerto Rico (1936–2060)." *Global Change Biology* 10 (7) (2004): 1163–1179.

Grau, H. Ricardo, T. Mitchell Aide, Jess K. Zimmerman, John R. Thomlinson, Eileen Helmer, and Xioming Zou. "The Ecological Consequences of Socioeconomic and Land-Use Changes in Postagriculture Puerto Rico." *Bioscience* 52 (12) (2003): 1159–1168.

Greenwald, Richard A. *The Triangle Fire, the Protocols of Peace, and Industrial Democracy in Progressive Era New York.* Philadelphia: Temple University Press, 2005.

Grimm, Nancy B., Stanley H. Faeth, Nancy E. Golubiewski, Charles L. Redman, Jianguo Wu, Xuemei Bai, and John M. Briggs. "Global Change and the Ecology of Cities." *Science* 391 (February 8, 2008): 756–760.

Gruntfest, Eve. "Flash Floods in the United States." In *Storms.* vol. 2. ed. R. Pielke Jr. and R. Pielke Sr., 192–206. New York: Routledge, 1999.

Gruntfest, Eve, and A. Ripps. "Flash Floods: Warning and Mitigation Efforts and Prospects." In *Floods.* vol. 1, ed. D. J. Parker, 377–390. New York: Routledge, 2000.

Gururaj, G. "Injuries in India: A National Perspective." In *NCMH Background Papers: Burden of Disease in India.* New Delhi: NCMH, 2005.

Gusewelle, C. W. "The Winds of Ruin: Tornadoes on the American Land." *American Heritage* 29 (3) (1978): 90–97.

Gutiérrez, E. G., F. Taucer, T. De Groeve, D. H. A. Al-Khudairy, and J. M. Zaldivar. "Analysis of Worldwide Earthquake Mortality Using Multivariate Demographic and Seismic Data." *American Journal of Epidemiology* 161 (12) (2005): 1151–1158.

Haensch, Stephanie, Raffaella Bianucci, Michel Signoli, Minoarisoa Rajerison, Michael Schultz, Sacha Kacki, Marco Vermunt, Darlene A. Weston, Derek Hurst, Mark Achtman, Elisabeth Carniel, and Barbara Bramanti. "Distinct Clones of *Yersinia pestis* Caused the Black Death." *PLoS Pathogens* 6 (10) (2010): e1001134.

Hall, Edward T. "Proxemics." *Current Anthropology* 9 (2/3) (1968): 83–108.

Han, Ke-Tsung. "Responses to Six Major Terrestrial Biomes in Terms of Scenic Beauty, Preference, and Restorativeness." *Environment and Behavior* 39 (4) (2007): 529–556.

Hankin, E. H. "On the Epidemiology of Plague." *Journal of Hygiene* 5 (1) (1905): 48–83.

Hanley, Susan B. *Everyday Things in Premodern Japan: The Hidden Legacy of Material Culture.* Berkeley: University of California Press, 1997.

Hanley, Susan B., and Kozo Yamamura. *Economic and Demographic Change in Preindustrial Japan, 1600–1868.* Princeton, NJ: Princeton University Press, 1977.

Hannerz, Ulf. *Exploring the City: Inquiries toward an Urban Anthropology.* New York: Columbia University Press, 1980.

Haq, Saleemul. "Environmental Hazards in Dhaka." In *Crucibles of Hazard: Mega-Cities and Disasters in Transition,* ed. James K. Mitchell, 119–137. New York: United Nations University Press, 1999.

Harding, Walter. *The Days of Henry Thoreau.* Rev. ed. New York: Dover Publications, 1982.

Hardoy, Jorge E., Diana Mitlin, and David Satterthwaite. *Environmental Problems in an Urbanizing World: Finding Solutions in Africa, Asia, and Latin America.* Sterling, VA: Earthscan Publications, 2001.

Harris, Marvin. *Town and Country in Brazil.* New York: Columbia University Press, 1956.

Harrison, Jill Lindsey. *Pesticide Drift and the Pursuit of Environmental Justice.* Cambridge, MA: MIT Press, 2011.

Hartman, Chester, and Gregory D. Squires, eds. *There Is No Such Thing as a Natural Disaster: Race, Class, and Hurricane Katrina.* New York: Routledge, 2006.

Hartmann, Patrick, and Vanessa Apaolaza-Ibáñez. "Beyond Savanna: An Evolutionary and Environmental Psychology Approach to Behavioral Effects of Nature Scenery in Green Advertising." *Journal of Environmental Psychology* 30 (1) (2010): 119–128.

Harvey, David. *Justice, Nature, and the Geography of Difference.* Cambridge, MA: Blackwell, 1996.

Hassan, Rashid, Robert Scholes, and Neville Ash, eds. *Ecosystems and Human Well-Being: Current State and Trends.* vol. 1. Washington, DC: Island Press, 2005.

Hawley, Amos. "Population Density and the City." *Demography* 9 (4) (1972): 521–529.

Hay, Simon I., Carlos A. Guerra, Andrew J. Tatem, Peter M. Atkinson, and Robert W. Snow. "Urbanization, Malaria Transmission, and Disease Burden in Africa." *Nature Reviews Microbiology* 3 (1) (2005): 81–90.

Hays, Samuel P. *Explorations in Environmental History: Essays.* Pittsburgh: University of Pittsburgh Press, 1998.

Hecht, Susanna B., Susan Kandel, Ileana Gomes, Nelson Cuellar, and Herman Rosa. "Globalization, Forest Resurgence, and Environmental Politics in El Salvador." *World Development* 34 (2) (2006): 308–323.

Hendryx, Michael, Evan Fedorko, and Joel Halverson. "Pollution Sources and Mortality Rates across Rural-Urban Areas in the United States." *Journal of Rural Health* 26 (4) (2010): 383–391.

Hewitt, Kenneth, ed. *Interpretations of Calamity from the Viewpoint of Human Ecology.* Boston: Allen & Unwin, 1983.

Hewitt, Kenneth. *Regions of Risk: A Geographical Introduction to Disasters.* Harlow, UK: Longman, 1997.

Hirsch, Jameson K. "A Review of the Literature on Rural Suicide: Risks and Protective Factors, Incidence, and Prevention." *Crisis: The Journal of Crisis Intervention and Suicide Prevention* 27 (4) (2006): 189–199.

Hiss, Tony. *The Experience of Place.* New York: Alfred A. Knopf, 1990.

Holt, Judith, Sue Hotto, and Kevin Cole. "Demographic Aspects of Hearing Impairment: Questions and Answers." 3rd ed. Washington, DC: Center for Assessment and Demographic Studies, Gallaudet University, 1994.

Holtzclaw, Barbara J. "Dengue Fever." In *Emerging Infectious Diseases: Trends and Issues.* 2nd ed., ed. Felissa R. Lashley and Jerry D. Durham, 123–132. New York: Springer, 2007.

Hoornweg, Daniel, Lorraine Sugar, and Claudia Lorena Trejos Gómez. "Cities and Greenhouse Gas Emissions: Moving Forward." *Environment and Urbanization* 23 (1) (2011): 207–227.

Horn, David G. "Constructing the Sterile City: Pronatalism and Social Sciences in Interwar Italy." *American Ethnologist* 18 (3) (1991): 581–601.

Hortas-Rico, Miriam, and Albert Solé-Ollé. "Does Urban Sprawl Increase the Costs of Providing Local Public Services? Evidence from Spanish Municipalities." *Urban Studies (Edinburgh, Scotland)* 47 (7) (2010): 1513–1540.

Horton, Richard. "The Infected Metropolis." *Lancet* 347 (8995) (1996): 134–135.

Hotez, Peter. *Forgotten People, Forgotten Diseases: The Neglected Tropical Diseases and Their Impact on Global Health and Development.* Washington, DC: ASM Press, 2008.

Hough, Susan Elizabeth, and Roger G. Bilham. *After the Earth Quakes: Elastic Rebound on an Urban Planet.* New York: Oxford University Press, 2006.

Howe, Irving, with Kenneth Libo. *World of Our Fathers*. New York: Harcourt Brace Jovanovich, 1976.

Hu, Guoqing, Susan P. Baker, and Timothy D. Baker. "Urban-Rural Disparities in Injury Mortality in China, 2006." *Journal of Rural Health* 26 (1) (2010): 73–77.

Hutson, Susan S., compiler. *Guidelines for Preparation of State Water-Use Estimates for 2005*. Reston, VA: USGS Office of Ground Water, 2007.

International Labour Office. *Safety and Health in Agriculture. Report VI (1)*. Geneva: ILO, 1999.

Ipsen, Carl. *Dictating Demography: The Problem of Population in Fascist Italy*. New York: Cambridge University Press, 1996.

Jackson, Kenneth T. *Crabgrass Frontier: The Suburbanization of the United States*. New York: Oxford University Press, 1985.

Jackson, Kenneth T. "Urban Deconcentration in the Nineteenth Century: A Statistical Inquiry." In *The New Urban History: Quantitative Explorations by American Historians*, ed. Leo T. Schnore, 110–142. Princeton, NJ: Princeton University Press, 1975.

Jacobs, Jane. *The Death and Life of Great American Cities*. New York: Random House, 1961.

Jacobs, Jane. *The Economy of Cities*. New York: Random House, 1969.

Jamison, Dean T., Richard G. Feachem, Malegapuru W. Makgoba, Eduard R. Bos, Florence K. Baingana, Karen T. Hofman, and Khama O. Rogo. *Disease and Mortality in Sub-Saharan Africa*. 2nd ed. Washington, DC: The World Bank, 2006.

Jiang, Guohong, Bernard C. K. Choi, Dezheng Wang, Hui Zhang, Wenlong Aheng, Tongyu Wu, and Gai Chang. "Leading Causes of Death from Injuries and Poisoning by Age, Sex, and Urban/Rural Areas in Tianjin Province, China, 1999–2006." *Injury* 42 (5) (2011): 501–506.

Jiang, Ruoting, and Michelle L. Bell. "A Comparison of Particulate Matter from Biomass-Burning Rural and Non-Biomass Burning Urban Households in Northeastern China." *Environmental Health Perspectives* 116 (7) (2008): 907–914.

Johnson, Elizabeth Ann, and Michael W. Klemens, eds. *Nature in Fragments: The Legacy of Sprawl*. New York: Columbia University Press, 2005.

Johnson, Elizabeth Ann, and Michael W. Klemens. "The Impact of Sprawl on Biodiversity." In *Nature in Fragments: The Legacy of Sprawl*, ed. Elizabeth Ann Johnson and Michael W. Klemens, 18–53. New York: Columbia University Press, 2005.

Johnson, Eric A. *Urbanization and Crime: Germany, 1871–1914*. New York: Cambridge University Press, 1995.

Johnson, Eric A., and Eric H. Monkkonen, eds. *The Civilization of Crime: Violence in Town and Country since the Middle Ages*. Urbana: University of Illinois Press, 1996.

Johnson, Lyndon B. "Remarks at Ceremonies Marking the 100th Anniversary of Dallastown, Pennsylvania, September 3, 1966." In *Public Papers of Lyndon B.*

Johnson, 1966, Book II, 947–952. Washington, DC: US Government Printing Office, 1967.

Johnson, Niall. *Britain and the 1918–19 Influenza Pandemic: A Dark Epilogue.* New York: Routledge, 2006.

Jones, Gareth A., and Stuart Corbridge. "The Continuing Debate about Urban Bias: The Thesis, Its Critics, Its Influence, and Its Implications for Poverty-Reduction Strategies." *Progress in Development Studies* 10 (1) (2010): 1–18.

"Joplin's Tornado." *Wall Street Journal* (May 24, 2011): A18.

Jorgenson, Andrew K. "Unequal Ecological Exchange and Environmental Degradation: A Theoretical Proposition and Cross-National Study of Deforestation." *Rural Sociology* 71 (4) (2006): 685–712.

Jorgenson, Andrew K., and Thomas J. Burns. "Effects of Rural and Urban Population Dynamics and National Development on Deforestation in Less-Developed Countries, 1990–2000." *Sociological Inquiry* 77 (3) (2006): 460–482.

Kagan, Richard L. with Fernando Marías. *Urban Images of the Hispanic World, 1493–1793.* New Haven, CT: Yale University Press, 2000.

Kaye, Jason P., Peter M. Groffman, Nancy B. Grimm, Lawrence A. Baker, and Richard V. Pouyat. "A Distinct Urban Biogeochemistry?" *Trends in Ecology & Evolution* 21 (4) (2006): 192–199.

Keane, Stephen. *Disaster Movies: The Cinema of Catastrophe.* 2nd ed. London: Wallflower, 2006.

Kenny, Joan F., Nancy L. Baker, Susan S. Hutson, Kristin S. Linsey, John K. Lovelace, and Molly A. Maupin. *Estimated Use of Water in the United States, 2005. USGS Circular 1344.* Reston, VA: USGS, 2009.

Khazaei, Hossein-Ali, Nima Rezaei, Gholam-Reza Bagheri, Maryam Mahmoudi, Abbas-Ali Moin, Mohammed-Ali Dankoub, and Akbardagh Gazeran. "The Epidemiology of *Vibrio cholerae* in Zabol City, Southeast of Iran." *Archives of Iranian Medicine* 8 (3) (2005): 197–201.

Kick, Edward L., Thomas J. Burns, Byron Davis, David A. Murray, and Dixie A. Murray. "Impacts of Domestic Population Dynamics and Foreign Wood Trade on Deforestation: A World-Systems Perspective." *Journal of Developing Societies* 12 (1) (1996): 68–87.

Klinenberg, Eric. *Heat Wave: A Social Autopsy of Disaster in Chicago.* Chicago: University of Chicago Press, 2002.

Kmet, Leanne, Penny Brasher, and Colin Macarthur. "A Small Area Study of Motor Vehicle Crashes in Alberta, Canada." *Accident; Analysis and Prevention* 35 (2) (2003): 177–182.

Kmet, Leanne, and Colin Macarthur. "Urban-Rural Differences in Motor Vehicle Crash Fatality and Hospitalization Rates among Children and Youth." *Accident Analysis and Prevention* 38 (1) (2006): 122–127.

Knobel, Darryn L., Sarah Cleaveland, Paul G. Coleman, Eric M. Fèvre, Martin I. Meltzer, M. Elizabeth G. Miranda, Alexandra Shaw, Jakob Zinsstag, and

François-Xavier Meslin. "Re-Evaluating the Burden of Rabies in Africa and Asia." *Bulletin of the World Health Organization* 83 (5) (2005): 360–368.

Knudsen, Brian, Richard Florida, Kevin Stolarick, and Gary Gates. "Density and Creativity in U.S. Regions." *Annals of the Association of American Geographers* 98 (2) (2008): 461–478.

Konrad, Christopher P. "Effects of Urban Development on Floods." *USGS Fact Sheet FS-876–03*, 2003.

Kraus, Franke. "Megacities as Global Risk Areas." In *Urban Ecology: An International Perspective on the Interaction between Humans and Nature*, ed. John M. Marzluff et al., 583–596. New York: Springer, 2008.

Krause, Rachel M. "Political Decision-Making and Local Provision of Public Goods: The Case of Municipal Climate Protection in the US." *Urban Studies* (forthcoming).

Krauss, Scott D., and Rosalind M. Rolland, eds. *The Urban Whale: North Atlantic Right Whales at the Crossroads*. Cambridge, MA: Harvard University Press, 2007.

Kreger, Janet. "Fire and Failure." *Michigan History Magazine* 82 (1) (1998): 15–20.

Kumar, Adarsh, Mathew Varghese, and Dinesh Mohan. "Equipment-Related Injuries in Agriculture: An International Perspective." *Injury Control and Safety Promotion* 7 (3) (2000): 175–186.

Lahey, Timothy, Michelle Lin, Bryan Marsh, Jim Curtin, Kim Wood, Betsy Eccles, and C. Fordham von Reyn. "Increased Mortality in Rural Patients with HIV in New England." *AIDS Research and Human Retroviruses* 23 (5) (2007): 693–698.

Lambert, Thomas E., and Peter B. Meyer. "Ex-Urban Sprawl as a Factor in Traffic Fatalities and EMS Response Times in the Southeastern United States." *Journal of Economic Issues* 40 (4) (2006): 941–953.

Lane, Roger. "Crime and Criminal Statistics in Nineteenth-Century Massachusetts." *Journal of Social History* 2 (2) (1968): 156–163.

Lassarre, Sylvain, and Isabelle Thomas. "Exploring Road Mortality Ratios in Europe: National versus Regional Realities." *Journal of the Royal Statistical Society A* 168 (pt. 1) (2005): 127–144.

Lawson, Victoria, Lucy Jarosz, and Anne Bonds. "Articulations of Place, Poverty, and Race: Dumping Grounds and Unseen Grounds in the Rural American Northwest." *Annals of the Association of American Geographers* 100 (3) (2010): 655–677.

Lee, Bun Song, and Louis G. Pohl. "The Influence of Rural-Urban Migration on Migrants' Fertility in Korea, Mexico, and Cameroon." *Population Research and Policy Review* 12 (1) (1993): 3–26.

Lehmann, Steffen. *The Principles of Green Urbanism: Transforming the City for Sustainability*. London: Earthscan, 2010.

Leichenko, Robin M., and Karen L. O'Brien. *Environmental Change and Globalization: Double Exposures.* New York: Oxford University Press, 2008.

Leon, David A. "Cities, Urbanization, and Health." *International Journal of Epidemiology* 37 (1) (2008): 4–8.

Leontidou, Lila. "Cultural Representations of Urbanism and Experiences of Urbanisation in Mediterranean Europe." In *Geography, Environment and Development in Mediterranean Europe*, ed. Russell King, Paolo de Mas, and J. Mansvelt-Beck, 83–98. Brighton, UK: Sussex Academic Press, 2001.

Lesmana, Laurentius A., Nancy Wai-Lee Leung, Varocha Mahachai, Pham Hoang Phiet, Dong Jin Suh, Guangbi Yao, and H. Zhuang. "Hepatitis B: Overview of the Burden of Disease in the Asia-Pacific Region." *Liver International* 26 (supplement) (2006): 3–10.

Levinson, David. "Population Density in Cross-Cultural Perspective." *American Ethnologist* 6 (4) (1979): 742–751.

Lewis, Martin W. *Green Delusions: An Environmentalist Critique of Radical Environmentalism.* Durham, NC: Duke University Press, 1992.

Lewis, Maureen A., and Marlaine E. Lockheed, eds. *Exclusion, Gender and Education: Case Studies from the Developing World.* Washington, DC: Center for Global Development, 2007.

Libecap, Gary D. "Chinatown: Owens Valley and Western Water Reallocation—Getting the Record Straight and What It Means for Water Markets." *Texas Law Review* 83 (7) (2005): 2055–2089.

Light, Andrew. "The Urban Blind Spot in Environmental Ethics." *Environmental Politics* 10 (1) (2001): 7–35.

Lighthall, David R., and Steven Kopecky. "Confronting the Problem of Backyard Burning." *Society & Natural Resources* 13 (2) (2000): 157–167.

Limerick, Patricia Nelson. *Something in the Soil: Legacies and Reckonings in the New West.* New York: W. W. Norton, 2000.

Linden, Eugene. "The Exploding Cities of the Developing World." *Foreign Affairs* 75 (1) (1996): 52–65.

Lindstrom, David P. "Rural-Urban Migration and Reproductive Behavior in Guatemala." *Population Research and Policy Review* 22 (4) (2003): 351–372.

Lipton, Michael. "Urban Bias." In *Encyclopedia of International Development*, ed. Tim Forsyth, 724–726. London: Routledge, 2005.

Lipton, Michael. *Why Poor People Stay Poor: Urban Bias in World Development.* Cambridge, MA: Harvard University Press, 1977.

Lloyd, Cynthia B., ed. *Growing Up Global: The Changing Transitions to Adulthood in Developing Countries.* Washington, DC: National Academies Press, 2005.

Lo Cascio, Elio. "Did the Population of Imperial Rome Reproduce Itself?" In *Urbanism in the Preindustrial World: Cross-Cultural Approaches*, ed. Glenn R. Storey, 52–68. Tuscaloosa: University of Alabama Press, 2006.

Lohse, Kathleen A., and Adina M. Merenlender. "Impacts of Exurban Development on Water Quality." In *The Planner's Guide to Natural Resource Conservation: The Science of Land Development beyond the Metropolitan Fringe*, ed. Adrian X. Esparza and Guy McPherson, 159–179. New York: Springer, 2009.

Lombroso, Cesare. *Crime: Its Causes and Remedies*. Trans. Henry B. Horton. Boston: Little, Brown, and Company, 1911.

London, Jack. *The People of the Abyss*. New York: Macmillan, 1904.

López, Raúl E., and Ronald L. Holle. "Changes in the Number of Lightning Deaths in the United States during the Twentieth Century." *Journal of Climate* 11 (8) (1998): 2070–2077.

Lowry, Ira S. "World Urbanization in Perspective." *Population and Development Review* 16 (supplement) (1990): 148–176.

Lucas, Robert. "On the Mechanics of Economic Development." In *Lectures on Economic Development*, 19–62. Cambridge, MA: Harvard University Press, 2002.

Lucy, William H. "Mortality Risk Associated with Leaving Home." *American Journal of Public Health* 93 (9) (2003): 1564–1569.

Ly, Sowath, Philippe Buchy, Nay Yim Heng, Sivuth Ong, Nareth Chhor, Hervé Bourhy, and Sirenda Vong. "Rabies Situation in Cambodia." *PLoS Neglected Tropical Diseases* 3 (9) (2009): e511.

Lyon, Bradfield, Nicholas Christie-Black, and Yekaterina Gluzberg. "Water Shortages, Development, and Drought in Rockland County, New York." *Journal of the American Water Resources Association* 41 (6) (2005): 1457–1469.

Lyons, Elizabeth. "Demographic Correlates of Landscape Preference." *Environment and Behavior* 15 (4) (1983): 487–511.

Ma, Chunbo, and Ethan D. Schoolman. "Who Bears the Environmental Burden in China: An Analysis of the Distribution of Industrial Pollution Sources." *Ecological Economics* 69 (9) (2010): 1869–1876.

Ma, Jixiang, Xiaolei Guo, Aiqiang Xu, Jiyu Zhang, and Chongqi Jia. "Epidemiological Analysis of Injury in Shandong Province, China." *BMC Public Health* 8 (2008): 122.

MacFarquahar, Neil. "African Farmers Displaced as Investors Move In." *New York Times* (December 22, 2010): A1, A4.

Mack, Richard S., and Peter V. Schaeffer. "Nonmetropolitan Manufacturing in the United States and Product Cycle Theory: A Review of the Literature." *Journal of Planning Literature* 8 (2) (1993): 124–139.

Main, Hamish, and Stephen Wyn Williams. "Marginal Urban Environments as Havens for Low-Income Housing." In *Environment and Housing in Third World Cities*, ed. Hamish Main and Stephen Wyn Williams, 151–170. Chichester, UK: John Wiley, 1994.

Malmberg, Torsten. *Human Territoriality: Survey of Behavioural Territories in Man with Preliminary Analysis and Discussion of Meaning*. The Hague, The Netherlands: Mouton, 1980.

Malthus, Thomas Robert. "An Essay on the Principle of Population." 6th ed. (originally published in 1826). In *The Works of Thomas Robert Malthus,* vol. 2, ed. E. A. Wrigley and David Souden. London: William Pickering, 1986.

Mamdani, Mahmood. *The Myth of Population Control: Family, Caste, and Class in an Indian Village.* New York: Monthly Review Press, 1972.

Mamelund, Svenn-Erik. "Geography May Explain Adult Mortality from the 1918–20 Influenza Pandemic." *Epidemics* 3 (1) (2011): 46–60.

Mann, S. B. S., S. C. Sharma, A. K. Gupta, Anu N. Nagarkar, and Dharamvir. "Incidence of Hearing Impairment among Rural and Urban School Going Children: A Survey." *Indian Journal of Pediatrics* 65 (1) (1998): 141–145.

March, Hug, and David Sauri. "The Suburbanization of Water Scarcity in the Barcelona Metropolitan Region: Sociodemographic and Urban Changes Influencing Domestic Water Consumption." *Professional Geographer* 62 (1) (2010): 32–45.

Marmor, Michael, and Nicholas E. Marmor. "Slippery Road Conditions and Fatal Motor Vehicle Crashes in the Northeastern United States, 1998–2002." *American Journal of Public Health* 96 (5) (2006): 914–920.

Martínez-Zarzoso, Immaculada, and Antonello Maruotti. "The Impact of Urbanization on CO_2 Emissions: Evidence from Developing Countries." *Ecological Economics* 70 (7) (2011): 1344–1353.

Massey, James T. "Suicide in the United States, 1950–1964." *National Center for Health Statistics,* Series 20 (5). Washington, DC: US Government Printing Office, 1967.

Mather, Alexander S. "The Forest Transition." *Area* 24 (4) (1992): 367–379.

Mather, A. S., C. L. Needle, and J. Fairbairn. "Environmental Kuznets Curves and Forest Transitions." *Geography* 84 (1) (1999): 55–65.

Matsuda, Iwan. "Loss of Human Lives Induced by the Cyclone of 29–30 April 1991 in Bangladesh." *GeoJournal* 31 (4) (1993): 319–325.

Matzaraki, Andreas, Manuela de Rocco, and Georges Naijar. "Thermal Bioclimate in Strasbourg: The 2003 Heat Wave." *Theoretical and Applied Climatology* 98 (3/4) (2009): 209–220.

Mayor's Office of Long-Term Planning and Sustainability. *Inventory of New York City Greenhouse Gas Emissions, September 2009.* New York: Author, 2009.

McCloskey, Michael. "Naïve Theories of Motion." In *Mental Models,* ed. Dedre Gentner and Albert L. Stevens, 299–324. Hillsdale, NJ: Lawrence Erlbaum, 1983.

McCloskey, Michael, Alfonso Caramazza, and Bert Green. "Curvilinear Motion in the Absence of External Forces." *Science* 210 (4474) (1980): 1138–1141.

McDonald, Robert I., Ian Douglas, Carmen Revenga, Rebecca Hale, Nancy Grimm, Jenny Grönwall, and Balazs Fekete. "Global Urban Growth and the Geography of Water Availability, Quality, and Delivery." *Ambio* 40 (5) (2011): 437–446.

McGeehin, Michael A., and Maria Mirabelli. "The Potential Impacts of Climate Variability and Change on Temperature-Related Morbidity and Mortality in the United States." *Environmental Health Perspectives* 109 (supplement 2) (2001): 185–189.

McGranahan, David A. "How People Make a Living in Rural Areas." In *Challenges for Rural America in the Twenty-First Century*, ed. David L. Brown and Louis E. Swanson, 135–151. University Park: Pennsylvania State University Press, 2003.

McGranahan, Gordon, Deborah Balk, and Bridget Anderson. "The Rising Tide: Assessing the Risks of Climatic Change to Human Settlements in Low-Elevation Coastal Zones." *Environment and Urbanization* 19 (1) (2007): 17–37.

McGreevey, William, Arnab Acharya, Jeffrey S. Hammer, and Landis MacKellar. "Propinquity Matters: How Better Health, Urbanization, and Income Grew Together." *Georgetown Journal on Poverty Law and Policy* 15 (2008): 605–633.

McIntyre, Kevin. "Geography as Destiny: Cities, Villages, and Khmer Rouge Orientalism." *Comparative Studies in Society and History* 38 (4) (1996): 730–758.

McIntyre, Nancy E., K. Knowles-Yánez, and D. Hope. "Urban Ecology as an Interdisciplinary Field: Differences in the Use of 'Urban' Between the Social and Natural Sciences." *Urban Ecosystems* 4 (1) (2000): 5–24.

McKinney, Michael L. "Urbanization as a Major Cause of Biotic Homogenization." *Biological Conservation* 127 (3) (2006): 247–260.

McKinney, Michael L. "Urbanization, Biodiversity, and Conservation." *Bioscience* 52 (10) (2002): 883–890.

McMichael, Anthony. *Planetary Overload: Global Environmental Change and the Health of the Human Species.* Cambridge, UK: Cambridge University Press, 1993.

McNeill, John R. *Mosquito Empires: Ecology and War in the Greater Caribbean, 1620–1914.* New York: Cambridge University Press, 2010.

McQuaid, John. "The Levees." In *City Adrift: New Orleans Before and After Katrina*, by Jenni Bergal, Sarah Shipley Hiles, John McQuaid, Jim Morris, Katy Reckdahl, Curtis Wilkie, and Frank Koughan, 20–31. Baton Rouge: Louisiana State University Press, 2007.

McSweeny, Kirsten, Atalie Colman, Nick Fancourt, Melinda Parnell, Sara Stantiall, Geoffrey Rice, Michael Baker, and Nick Wilson. "Was Rurality Protective in the 1918 Influenza Pandemic in New Zealand?" *New Zealand Medical Journal* 120 (1256) (2007): 44–49.

Meade, Melinda S., and Michael Emch. *Medical Geography.* 3rd ed. New York: Guilford Press, 2010.

Medina, Martin. *The World's Scavengers: Salvaging for Sustainable Consumption and Production.* Lanham, MD: Altamira Press, 2007.

Melosi, Martin V. *Effluent America: Cities, Industry, Energy, and the Environment.* Pittsburgh: University of Pittsburgh Press, 2001.

Mendez, Michael. "Latin New Urbanism: Building on Cultural Preferences." *Opolis* 1 (1) (2005): 33–48.

Mergen, Bernard. "Children and Nature in History." *Environmental History* 8 (4) (2003): 643–669.

Mestl, H. E. S., K. Aunan, H. M. Seip, S. Wang, Y. Zhao, and D. Zhang. "Urban and Rural Exposure to Indoor Air Pollution from Domestic Biomass and Coal Burning Across China." *Science of the Total Environment* 377 (2007): 12–26.

Meyer, William B. *Human Impact on the Earth*. New York: Cambridge University Press, 1996.

Mill, John Stuart. "A System of Logic: Books IV–VI." In *Collected Works of John Stuart Mill*. vol. 8, ed. J. M. Robson. Toronto: University of Toronto Press, 1974.

Mill, John Stuart. *Utilitarianism* (originally published in 1863), ed. Roger Crisp. Oxford: Oxford University Press, 1998.

Min, Jihoon, Zeke Hausfather, and Qi Feng Lin. "A High-Resolution Spatial Model of Residential Energy End Use Characteristics for the United States." *Journal of Industrial Ecology* 14 (5) (2010): 791–807.

Mitchell, James K. "Natural Disasters in the Context of Mega-Cities." In *Crucibles of Hazard: Mega-Cities and Disasters in Transition*, ed. James K. Mitchell, 15–55. New York: United Nations University Press, 1999.

Mitchell, William J., and Anthony M. Townsend. "Cyborg Agonistes: Disaster and Reconstruction in the Digital Electronic Era." In *The Resilient City: How Modern Cities Recover from Disaster*, ed. Lawrence J. Vale and Thomas J. Campanella, 313–334. New York: Oxford University Press, 2005.

Mock, Charles, Samuel Adjei, Frederick Acheampong, Lisa DeRoo, and Kate Simpson. "Occupational Injuries in Ghana." *International Journal of Occupational and Environmental Health* 11 (3) (2005): 238–245.

Molina, Mario J., and Luisa T. Molina. "Megacities and Air Pollution." *Journal of the Air & Waste Management Association* 54 (6) (2004): 644–680.

Monkkonen, Eric H. *Murder in New York City*. Berkeley: University of California Press, 2001.

Mumford, Lewis. *The Urban Prospect*. New York: Harcourt, Brace & World, 1968.

Murphy-Greene, M. Celeste. "The Occupational Safety and Health of Florida Farm Workers." *Journal of Health and Human Services Administration* 25 (3) (2002): 281–314.

Nance, Michael L., Brendan G. Carr, Michael J. Kallam, Charles C. Branas, and Douglas J. Wiebe. "Variation in Pediatric and Adolescent Firearm Mortality Rates in Rural and Urban US Counties." *Pediatrics* 125 (6) (2010): 1112–1118.

National Highway Traffic Safety Administration. "Traffic Crashes Take Their Toll on America's Rural Roads." *DOT HS 810* (2006): 658.

National Highway Traffic Safety Administration. "Traffic Safety Facts: 2007 Data, Urban-Rural Comparison." *DOT HS 810* (2009): 996.

National Research Council. *Cities Transformed: Demographic Change and Its Implications in the Developing World*. Washington, DC: National Academies Press, 2003.

National Research Council. *Colorado River Basin Water Management: Evaluating and Adjusting to Hydroclimatic Variability*. Washington, DC: National Academies Press, 2007.

Newman, Peter, and Trevor Hogan. "A Review of Urban Density Models: Toward a Resolution of the Conflict between Populace and Planner." *Human Ecology* 9 (3) (1981): 269–303.

Newman, Peter W. G., and Jeffrey R. Kenworthy. "Gasoline Consumption and Cities: A Comparison of U.S. Cities with a Global Survey." *Journal of the American Planning Association* 55 (1) (1989): 24–37.

Newman, Peter, and Jeffrey Kenworthy. *Sustainability and Cities: Overcoming Automobile Dependence*. Washington, DC: Island Press, 1999.

Newman, Peter, and Jeff Kenworthy. "Greening Urban Transportation." In *State of the World 2007: Our Urban Future: A Worldwatch Institute Report on Progress toward a Sustainable Society*, 66–85. New York: W. W. Norton, 2007.

Norman, Jonathan, Heather L. MacLean, and Christopher A. Kennedy. "Comparing High and Low Residential Density: Life-Cycle Analysis of Energy Use and Greenhouse Gas Emissions." *Journal of Urban Planning and Development* 132 (1) (2006): 10–21.

Nowlan, David. "Jane Jacobs among the Economists." In *Ideas That Matter: The Worlds of Jane Jacobs*, ed. Max Allen, 111–113. Owen Sound, ON: The Ginger Press, 1997.

O'Flaherty, Brendan. *Urban Economics*. Cambridge, MA: Harvard University Press, 2005.

Ó Gráda, Cormac. *Famine: A Short History*. Princeton, NJ: Princeton University Press, 2009.

Ohl, Michael, Janet Tate, Mona Duggal, Melissa Skanderson, Matthew Scotch, Peter Kaboli, Mary Vaughan-Sarrazin, and Amy Justice. "Rural Residence Is Associated with Delayed Care Entry and Increased Mortality among Veterans with Human Immunodeficiency Virus Infection." *Medical Care* 48 (12) (2010): 1064–1070.

Omran, Abdel R. "The Epidemiological Transition: A Theory of the Epidemiology of Population Change." *Milbank Quarterly* 49 (4) (1971): 509–538.

Ondetti, Gabriel A. *Land, Protest, and Politics: The Landless Movement and the Struggle for Agrarian Reform in Brazil*. University Park: Pennsylvania State University Press, 2008.

Orians, Gordon H. "Habitat Selection: General Theory and Application to Human Behavior." In *The Evolution of Human Social Behavior*, ed. Joan S. Lockard, 49–66. New York: Elsevier, 1980.

Orians, Gordon H., and Judith H. Heerwagen. "Evolved Responses to Landscapes." In *The Adapted Mind: Evolutionary Psychology and the Generation of*

Culture, ed. Jerome H. Barkow, Leda Cosmides, and John Tooby, 555–579. New York: Oxford University Press, 1992.

Orr, David W. "Refugees or Homecomers? Conjectures about the Future of Rural America." In *Earth in Mind: On Education, Environment, and the Human Prospect*, ed. David W. Orr, 185–203. Washington, DC: Island Press, 1994.

Orr, David W. "Re-Ruralizing Education." In *Rooted in the Land: Essays on Community and Place*, ed. William Vitek and Wes Jackson, 226–234. New Haven, CT: Yale University Press, 1996.

Otto, Betsy, Katherine Ransel, Jason Todd, Deron Lovaas, Hannah Stutzman, and John Bailey. "Paving Our Way to Water Shortages: How Sprawl Aggravates the Effects of Drought." American Rivers/Natural Resources Defense Council/Smart Growth America, 2002.

Owen, David. *Green Metropolis: Why Living Smaller, Living Closer, and Driving Less Are the Keys to Sustainability*. New York: Riverhead Books, 2009.

The Oxford English Dictionary. 1989. 2nd ed. 20 vols. Oxford: Clarendon Press.

Ozorio de Almeida, Anna Luiza. *The Colonization of the Amazon*. Austin: University of Texas Press, 1992.

Pacione, Michael. *Urban Geography: A Global Perspective*. London: Routledge, 2001.

Paehlke, Robert C. *Environmentalism and the Future of Progressive Politics*. New Haven, CT: Yale University Press, 1989.

Page, Max. *The City's End: Two Centuries of Fantasies, Fears, and Premonitions of New York's Destruction*. New Haven, CT: Yale University Press, 2008.

Parés-Ramos, Isabel K., William A. Gould, and T. Mitchell Aide. "Agricultural Abandonment, Suburban Growth, and Forest Expansion in Puerto Rico between 1990 and 2000." [online] *Ecology & Society* 13 (2) (2008): 1.

Parmelee, Maurice. *Criminology*. New York: Macmillan, 1918.

Patel, Ronak B., and Thomas F. Burke. "Urbanization: A Humanitarian Disaster." *New England Journal of Medicine* 361 (August 20, 2009): 741–743.

Patil, Ashok Vikhe, K. V. Sonasundaram, and R. C. Goyal. "Current Health Scenario in Rural India." *Australian Journal of Rural Health* 10 (2) (2002): 129–135.

Patz, Jonathan A., Peter Daszak, Gary M. Tabor, A. Alonso Aguirre, Mary Pearl, Jon Epstein, Nathan D. Wolfe, A. Marm Kilpatrick, Johannes Foufopoulos, David Molyneux, and David J. Bradley. "Unhealthy Landscapes: Policy Recommendations on Land Use Change and Infectious Disease Emergence." *Environmental Health Perspectives* 112 (10) (2004): 1092–1098.

Pauchauri, Shonali, and Leiwen Jiang. "The Household Energy Transition in India and China." *Energy Policy* 36 (11) (2008): 4022–4035.

Paulozzi, Leonard J. "Recent Changes in Drug Poisoning Mortality in the United States by Urban-Rural Status and by Drug Type." *Pharmacoepidemiology and Drug Safety* 17 (10) (2008): 997–1005.

Paumgarten, Nick. "Up and Then Down: The Lives of Elevators." *New Yorker* (April 21, 2008): 106–115.

Peek-Asa, Connie, Craig Zwerling, and Lorann Stallones. "Acute Traumatic Injuries in Rural Populations." *American Journal of Public Health* 94 (10) (2004): 1689–1693.

Pelling, Mark. *The Vulnerability of Cities: Natural Disasters and Social Resilience.* Sterling, VA: Earthscan, 2003.

Perkins, Alan, Steve Hamnett, Stephen Pullen, Rocco Zito, and David Trebilcock. "Transport, Housing, and Urban Form: The Life-Cycle Energy Consumption and Emissions of City Centre Apartments Compared with Suburban Dwellings." *Urban Policy and Research* 27 (4) (2009): 377–396.

Pickett, Steward T. A., Mary L. Cadenasso, J. Morgan Grove, Peter M. Groffman, Lawrence E. Band, Christopher G. Boone, William R. Burch, C. Susan B. Grimmond, John Hom, Jennifer C. Jenkins, Neely L. Law, Charles H. Nilon, Richard V. Pouyat, Katalin Szlavecz, Paige S. Warren, and Matthew A. Wilson. "Beyond Urban Legends: An Emerging Framework of Urban Ecology, as Illustrated by the Baltimore Ecosystem Study." *Bioscience* 58 (2) (2008): 139–150.

Pinker, Steven. *How the Mind Works.* New York: W. W. Norton, 1997.

Pitkin, Donald. "Mediterranean Europe." *Anthropological Quarterly* 36 (3) (1963): 120–129.

Platt, Rutherford H. "The 2020 Water Supply Study for Metropolitan Boston." *Journal of the American Planning Association* 61 (2) (1995): 185–199.

Polèse, Mario. *The Wealth and Poverty of Regions: Why Cities Matter.* Chicago: University of Chicago Press, 2009.

Polsky, Colin, Sarah Assefa, Kate Del Vecchio, Troy Hill, Laura Merner, Isaac Tercero, and Robert Gilmore Pontius, Jr. "The Mounting Risk of Drought in a Humid Landscape: Structure and Agency in Suburbanizing Massachusetts." In *Sustainable Communities on a Sustainable Planet: The Human-Environment Regional Observatory Project*, ed. Brent Yarnal, Colin Polsky, and James O'Brien, 229–249. New York: Cambridge University Press, 2009.

Pong, Raymond W., Marie DesMeules, and Claudia Lagacé. "Rural-Urban Disparities in Health: How Does Canada Fare and How Does Canada Compare with Australia." *Australian Journal of Rural Health* 17 (1) (2009): 58–64.

Poumanyvong, Phetkeo, and Shinji Kaneko. "Does Urbanization Lead to Less Energy Use and CO_2 Emissions? A Cross-Country Analysis." *Ecological Economics* 70 (2) (2010): 434–444.

Price, Richard. *Observations on Reversionary Payments.* 2nd ed. London: T. Cadell, 1772.

Pyne, Stephen J. *Fire: A Brief History.* Seattle: University of Washington Press, 2001.

Pyne, Stephen J. "The New American Fire." *New York Times* (October 28, 1991): 17.

Quarantelli, E. L. "Urban Vulnerability to Disasters in Developing Countries: Managing Risks." In *Building Safer Cities: The Future of Disaster Risk*, ed. A. Kreimer, M. Arnold, and A. Carlin, 211–231. Washington, DC: The World Bank Disaster Management Facility, 2003.

Rahman, A., S. R. Mashreky, S. M. Chowdhury, M. S. Giashaddin, I. J. Uhaa, S. Shafinaz, M. Hossain, M. Linnen, and F. Rahman. "Analysis of the Childhood Fatal Drowning Situation in Bangladesh." *Injury Prevention* 15 (2009): 75–79.

Ramsden, Edmund, and Jon Adams. "Escaping the Laboratory: The Rodent Experiments of John B. Calhoun and Their Cultural Influence." *Journal of Social History* 42 (3) (2009): 761–792.

Rao, S. K. "Population Growth and Economic Development: A Counter-Argument." *Economic and Political Weekly* 11 (31/33) (1976): 1149–1158.

Redfield, Robert. "The Folk Society and Custom." *American Journal of Sociology* 45 (5) (1940): 731–742.

Rees, William E. "Global Change, Ecological Footprints, and Urban Sustainability." In *How Green Is the City? Sustainability Assessment and the Management of Urban Environments*, ed. Dimitri Devuyst with Luc Hens and Walter De Lannoy, 339–363. New York: Columbia University Press, 2001.

Register, Richard. *Eco-City Berkeley: Building Cities for a Healthy Future*. Berkeley: North Atlantic Books, 1987.

Rehfuss, E. A., N. G. Bruce, and K. R. Smith. "Solid Fuel Use: Health Effects." In *Encyclopedia of Environmental Health*, vol. 5, ed. J. O. Nriagu, 156–159. Burlington, MA: Elsevier, 2011.

Reice, Seth R. "Ecosystems, Disturbance, and the Impact of Sprawl." In *Nature in Fragments: The Legacy of Sprawl*, ed. Elizabeth Ann Johnson and Michael W. Klemens, 90–108. New York: Columbia University Press, 2005.

Ribaudo, Marc, and Robert Johansson. "Water Quality Impacts of Agriculture." In *Agricultural Resources and Environmental Indicators*, ed. Keith Wiebe and Noel Gollehon, 39–47. New York: Nova Science Publishers, 2007.

Robbins, Paul. *Lawn People: How Grasses, Weeds, and Chemicals Make Us Who We Are*. Philadelphia: Temple University Press, 2007.

Robbins, Paul, and Julie T. Sharp. "Producing and Consuming Chemicals: The Moral Economy of the American Lawn." *Economic Geography* 79 (4) (2003): 425–451.

Robert, Vincent, Kate McIntyre, Joseph Keating, Jean-François Trape, Jean-Bernard Duchemin, McWilson Warren, and John C. Beier. "Malaria Transmission in Urban Sub-Saharan Africa." *American Journal of Tropical Medicine and Hygiene* 68 (2) (2003): 169–176.

Robinson, Peter J. *North Carolina Weather & Climate*. Chapel Hill: University of North Carolina Press, 2005.

Rome, Adam. *The Bulldozer in the Countryside: Suburban Sprawl and the Rise of American Environmentalism*. New York: Cambridge University Press, 2001.

Roseland, Mark. "The Eco-City Approach to Sustainable Development in Urban Areas." In *How Green Is the City? Sustainability Assessment and the Management of Urban Environments*, ed. Dimitri Devuyst with Luc Hens and Walter De Lannoy, 85–103. New York: Columbia University Press, 2001.

Roszak, Theodore. *The Voice of the Earth*. New York: Simon and Schuster, 1992.

Roth, Dennis. "Thinking about Rural Manufacturing: A Brief History." *Rural America* 15 (1) (2000): 12–19.

Rudel, Thomas K., and Maria Perez-Lugo. "When Fields Revert to Forests: Development and Spontaneous Reforestation in Post-War Puerto Rico." *Professional Geographer* 52 (3) (2000): 286–297.

Rudel, Thomas K., Laura Schneider, and Maria Uriarte, eds. "Forest Transitions," special issue of *Land Use Policy* 27 (2) (2009): 95–179.

Rupert, Michael G. "Decadal-Scale Changes of Nitrate in Ground Water of the United States, 1988–2004." *Journal of Environmental Quality* 37 (supplement 5) (2008): S240–S248.

Sack, Robert David. *Human Territoriality: Its Theory and History*. New York: Cambridge University Press, 1986.

Sadler, Jon, Adam Bate, James Hale, and Philip James. "Bringing Cities Alive: The Importance of Urban Green Spaces for People and Biodiversity." In *Urban Ecology*, ed. Kevin J. Gaston, 230–260. Cambridge, UK: Cambridge University Press, 2010.

Sahn, David E., and David C. Stifel. "Urban-Rural Inequality in Living Standards in Africa." *Journal of African Economies* 12 (4) (2003): 564–597.

Sánchez-Rodríguez, Roberto. "Urban Sustainability and Global Environmental Change: Reflections for a Research Agenda." In *The New Global Frontier: Urbanization, Poverty and Environment in the 21st Century*, ed. George Martine, Gordon McGranahan, Mark Montgomery, and Rogelio Fernández-Castilla, 149–163. Sterling, VA: Earthscan, 2008.

Satterthwaite, David. "Cities' Contributions to Global Warming: Notes on the Allocation of Greenhouse Gas Emissions." *Environment and Urbanization* 20 (2) (2008): 539–549.

Satterthwaite, David. "How Urban Societies Can Adapt to Resource Shortage and Climate Change." *Philosophical Transactions of the Royal Society A* 369 (1942) (2011): 1762–1783.

Satterthwaite, David. "The Transition to a Predominantly Urban World and Its Underpinnings." International Institute for Environment and Development. Human Settlements Discussion Paper Series. London: IIED, 2007.

Satterthwaite, David. "Urban Myths and the Mis-Use of Data to Underpin Them." United Nations University World Institute for Development Economics Research, *Working Paper No. 2010/28*, 2010.

Saunders, Peter. *Social Theory and the Urban Question*. 2nd ed. New York: Holmes & Meier, 1986.

Schmitt, Robert C. "Implications of Density in Hong Kong." *Journal of the American Institute of Planners* 29 (3) (1963): 210–216.

Sepúlveda, Jaime, José Luis Valdespino, and Lourdes García-García. "Cholera in Mexico: The Paradoxical Benefits of the Last Pandemic." *International Journal of Infectious Diseases* 10 (1) (2006): 4–13.

Shandra, John M., Christopher Leckband, and Bruce London. "Ecologically Unequal Exchange and Deforestation: A Cross-National Analysis of Forestry Export Flows." *Organization & Environment* 22 (3) (2009): 293–310.

Shapiro, David, and Tesfayi Gebreselassie. "Fertility Transitions in Sub-Saharan Africa: Falling and Stalling." *African Population Studies* 23 (1) (2008): 3–23.

Shapiro, David, and B. O. Tambashe. "Fertility Transition in Urban and Rural Sub-Saharan Africa." *Journal of African Policy Studies* 8 (2/3) (2002): 103–127.

Sharlin, Allan. "Natural Decrease in Early Modern Cities: A Reconsideration." *Past & Present* (79) (1) (1978): 126–138.

Short, Thomas. *New Observations, Natural, Moral, Civil, Political, and Medical, on City, Town, and Country Bills of Mortality.* London: T. Longman, 1750.

Simmons, Alan B. "A Review and Evaluation of Attempts to Constrain Migration to Selected Urban Centres and Regions." In *Population Distribution Policies in Development Planning*, 87–100. New York: The United Nations, 1981.

Simmons, I. G. *Global Environmental History.* Chicago: University of Chicago Press, 2008.

Slovic, Paul, Baruch Fischoff, and Sarah Lichtenstein. "Rating the Risks." *Environment* 21 (3) (1979): 14–20, 36–39.

Small, Christopher, and Robert J. Nicholls. "A Global Analysis of Human Settlement in Coastal Zones." *Journal of Coastal Research* 19 (3) (2003): 584–599.

Smith, Karly B., John S. Humphreys, and Murray G. A. Wilson. "Addressing the Health Disadvantage of Rural Populations: How Does Epidemiological Evidence Inform Rural Health Policies and Research?" *Australian Journal of Rural Health* 16 (2) (2008): 56–66.

Smith, Kirk R. "Fuel Combustion, Air Pollution Exposure, and Health: The Situation in Developing Countries." *Annual Review of Energy and the Environment* 18 (1993): 529–566.

Smith, Kirk R. "In Praise of Petroleum?" *Science* 298 (5600) (2002): 1847.

Smolinski, Mark S., Margaret A. Hamburg, and Joshua Lederberg, eds. *Microbial Threats to Health: Emergence, Detection, and Response.* Washington, DC: National Academies Press, 2003.

Soja, Edward W. *Postmetropolis: Critical Studies of Cities and Regions.* Malden, MA: Blackwell, 2000.

Solecki, William D. "Rural Places and the Circumstances of Acute Chemical Disasters." *Journal of Rural Studies* 8 (1) (1992): 1–13.

Solecki, William D., and Robin M. Leichenko. "Urbanization and the Metropolitan Environment: Lessons from New York and Shanghai." *Environment* 48 (4) (2006): 8–23.

Solomon, Gina M. *Trouble on the Farm: Growing Up with Pesticides.* New York: National Resources Defense Council, 1998.

Somervell, Philip D., and George A. Conway. "Does the Small Farm Exemption Cost Lives?" *American Journal of Industrial Medicine* 54 (6) (2011): 461–466.

South Commission. *The Challenge to the South: Report of the South Commission.* New York: Oxford University Press, 1990.

Srinivas, Hari with Iván Villarrubia Lorenzo. "Footnote on Footprints." http://www.gdrc.org/uem/footprints/tokyo-fprint.html.

Stage, Jesper, Jørn Stage, and Gordon McGranahan. "Is Urbanization Contributing to Higher Food Prices?" IIED/UNFPA Human Settlements Working Paper Series, *Urban and Emerging Population Issues-1,* August 2009.

Steinberg, Ted. *Acts of God: The Unnatural History of Natural Disaster in America.* New York: Oxford University Press, 2000.

Steinberg, Ted. *American Green: The Obsessive Quest for the Perfect Lawn.* New York: W. W. Norton, 2006.

Stockholm Environmental Institute. *China Human Development Report 2002: Making Green Development a Priority.* Oxford: Oxford University Press, 2002.

Stone Jr., Brian, and Michael O. Rodgers. "Urban Form and Thermal Efficiency: How the Design of Cities Influences the Urban Heat Island Effect." *Journal of the American Planning Association* 67 (2) (2001): 186–198.

Stone Jr., Brian, Adam C. Mednick, Tracey Holloway, and Scott N. Spak. "Is Compact Growth Good for Air Quality?" *Journal of the American Planning Association* 73 (4) (2007): 404–418.

Stradling, David. *Making Mountains: New York City and the Catskills.* Seattle: University of Washington Press, 2007.

Stucki, Philipp. "Water Wars or Water Peace? Rethinking the Nexus between Water Scarcity and Armed Conflict." *PSIS Occasional Paper 3/2005.* Geneva: PSIS, 2005.

Sverdlik. Alice. "Ill-Health and Poverty: A Literature Review on Health in Informal Settlements." *Environment and Urbanization* 23 (1) (2011): 123–155.

Sweeney, Shannon M. "A Comparison of Resource Consumption for Rural, Suburban, and Urban Environments." Senior honors thesis, Department of Geography, Colgate University, 2007.

Swift, Jeremy. "Why Are Rural People Vulnerable to Famine?" *IDS Bulletin* 20 (2) (1989): 8–15.

Tacoli, Cecelia, Gordon McGranahan, and David Satterthwaite. "Urbanization, Poverty and Inequity: Is Rural-Urban Migration a Poverty Problem, or Part of the Solution?" In *The New Global Frontier: Urbanization, Poverty and Environment in the 21st Century,* ed. George Martine, Gordon McGranahan, Mark Montgomery, and Rogelio Fernández-Castilla, 37–53. London: Earthscan, 2008.

Tavernise, Sabrina, and Robert Gebeloff. "Once Rare in Rural America, Divorce Is Changing the Face of Its Families." *New York Times* (March 24, 2011): A18.

Tenner, Edward. *Why Things Bite Back: Technology and the Revenge of Unintended Consequences.* New York: Knopf, 1996.

Terborgh, John, Carel van Schaik, Lisa Davenport, and Madhu Rao, eds. *Making Parks Work: Strategies for Preserving Tropical Nature.* Washington, DC: Island Press, 2002.

Terrie, Philip G. *Contested Terrain: A New History of Nature and People in the Adirondacks.* 2nd ed. Syracuse, NY: Syracuse University Press, 2008.

Thacker, Maria T. F., Robin Lee, Raquel I. Sabogal, and Alden Henderson. "Overview of Deaths Associated with Natural Events, United States, 1979–2004." *Disasters* 32 (2) (2008): 303–315.

Thwing, Julie I., Jules Mihigo, Alexandra Pataca Fernandes, Francisco Saute, Carolina Ferreira, Filomeno Fortes, Alexandre Macedo de Oliveira, and Robert D. Newman. "How Much Malaria Occurs in Urban Luanda, Angola? A Health Facility-Based Assessment." *American Journal of Tropical Medicine and Hygiene* 80 (3) (2009): 487–491.

Thompson, John, et al. *Drawers of Water II: 30 Years of Changes in Domestic Water Use and Environmental Health in East Africa.* London: IIED, 2001.

Thompson, Michael J., ed. *Fleeing the City: Studies in the Culture and Politics of Antiurbanism.* New York: Palgrave Macmillan, 2009.

Tilt, Bryan. "The Political Ecology of Pollution Enforcement in China: A Case from Sichuan's Rural Industrial Sector." *China Quarterly* 192 (2007): 915–932.

Timmerman, Peter, and Rodney White. "Megahydropolis: Coastal Cities in the Context of Global Environmental Change." *Global Environmental Change* 7 (3) (1997): 205–234.

Tonooka, Yutaka, Hailin Mu, Yadong Ning, and Yasuhiko Kondo. "Energy Consumption in Residential House and Emissions Inventory of GHGs, Air Pollutants in China." *Journal of Asian Architecture and Building Engineering* 2 (1) (2003): 93–100.

Topalov, Christian, Laurent Coudroy de Lille, Jean-Charles Depaule, and Brigitte Marin. *L'aventure des mots de la ville.* Paris: Robert Laffont, 2010.

Torres-Duque, Carlos, Darío Maldonado, Rogelio Pérez-Padilla, Majid Ezzati, and Giovanni Viegi. "Biomass Fuels and Respiratory Diseases: A Review of the Evidence." *Proceedings of the American Thoracic Society* 5 (5) (2008): 577–590.

Torrey, E. Fuller, and Robert H. Yolken. *Beasts of the Earth: Animals, Humans, and Disease.* New Brunswick, NJ: Rutgers University Press, 2005.

Transnational Institute. "Debating the Global Land Grab." http://www.tni.org/article/debating-global-land-grab.

Trigger, Bruce. *Understanding Early Civilizations: A Comparative Study.* Cambridge, UK: Cambridge University Press, 2003.

Troy, Austin. *The Very Hungry City: Urban Energy Efficiency and the Economic Fate of Cities.* New Haven, CT: Yale University Press, 2012.

Tuan, Yi-Fu. *Landscapes of Fear.* New York: Pantheon Books, 1979.

Turnock, David. "The Planning of Rural Settlement in Romania." *Geographical Journal* 157 (3) (1991): 251–264.

Tversky, Amos, and Daniel Kahneman. "Judgment under Uncertainty: Heuristics and Biases." *Science* 185 (4157) (1974): 1124–1131.

United Nations. *Population Distribution Policies in Development Planning.* New York: Author, 1979.

United Nations. *World Urban Prospects: The 2005 Revision.* New York: Author, 2006.

United Nations. "World Urbanization Prospects: The 2011 Revision." http://esa .un.org/unpd/wup/index.htm.

United Nations Development Programme. *Reducing Disaster Risk: A Challenge for Development.* New York: UNDP Bureau for Crisis Prevention and Recovery, 2004.

UNDP China. *China Human Development Report 2005.* UNDP-China, 2005.

United Nations Human Settlements Program. *The Challenge of Slums: Global Report on Human Settlements, 2003.* London: Earthscan, 2003.

United Nations Human Settlements Programme. *Enhancing Urban Safety and Security: Global Report on Human Settlements 2007.* London: Earthscan, 2007.

United Nations Human Settlements Programme. *State of the World's Cities, 2006/7.* London: Earthscan, 2006.

United Nations International Decade for Natural Disaster Reduction. *Cities at Risk—Making Cities Safer . . . Before Disaster Strikes.* Author, 1996.

United Nations Population Fund. *State of World Population 2007: Unleashing the Potential of Urban Growth.* New York: Author, 2007.

United States Census Bureau. *State and Metropolitan Area Data Book 2006.* Washington, DC: Author, 2006.

United States Census Bureau. 2010 "Census Urban and Rural Classification and Urban Area Criteria." http://www.census.gov/geo/www/ua/2010urbanruralclass .html.

United States Department of Agriculture. "Measuring Rurality: Rural-Urban Continuum Codes." http://www.ers.usda.gov/briefing/rurality/ruralurbcon.

United States Department of Agriculture. "United States Farm and Farm-Related Employment, 2002." http://www.ers.usda.gov/Data/FarmandRelated Employment/ViewData.asp?GeoAreaPick=STAUS_United%20States.

United States Department of Labor. Bureau of Labor Statistics. "Number and Rate of Fatal Occupational Injuries, by Industry Sector, 2010." http://www.bls .gov/iif/oshwc/cfoi/cfch0009.pdf.

United States Environmental Protection Agency. "Rural Recycling: Bridging the Gaps." http://www.epa.gov/smm/web-academy/2010/videos/apr/apr10_trans.htm.

United States Global Change Research Program. "Natural Hazards, Human Impacts, and Disaster Reduction." http://www.usgcrp.gov/usgcrp/seminars/97514DD.html.

United States National Oceanic and Atmospheric Administration. "Tornado Myths, Facts, and Safety." http://www.ncdc.noaa.gov/oa/climate/severeweather/tornadosafety.html.

van den Berg, Agnes, Terry Hartig, and Henk Staats. "Preference for Nature in Urbanized Societies: Stress, Restoration, and the Pursuit of Sustainability." *Journal of Social Issues* 63 (1) (2007): 79–96.

van de Poel, Ellen, Owen O'Donnell, and Eddy Van Doorslaer. "Are Urban Children Really Healthier? Evidence from 47 Developing Countries." *Social Science & Medicine* 65 (10) (2007): 1986–2003.

van de Poel, Ellen, Owen O'Donnell, and Eddy Van Doorslaer. "What Explains the Rural-Urban Gap in Infant Mortality: Household or Community Characteristics?" *Demography* 46 (4) (2009): 827–850.

VandeWeghe, Jared R., and Christopher Kennedy. "A Spatial Analysis of Residential Greenhouse Gas Emissions in the Toronto Metropolitan Area." *Journal of Industrial Ecology* 11 (2) (2007): 133–144.

Veitch, Craig. "Impact of Rurality on Environmental Determinants and Hazards." *Australian Journal of Rural Health* 17 (1) (2009): 16–20.

Verwimp, Philip. "Development Ideology, the Peasantry, and Genocide: Rwanda Represented in Habyarimana's Speeches." *Journal of Genocide Research* 2 (3) (2000): 325–361.

Victor, David G. "Seeking Sustainability: Cities, Countryside, and Wilderness." *Population and Development Review* 32 (supplement) (2006): 202–221.

Vogt, Paul L. *Introduction to Rural Sociology*. New York: D. Appleton and Company, 1917.

Wackernagel, Mathis, and William Rees. *Ecological Footprint: Reducing Human Impact on the Earth*. Philadelphia: New Society Publications, 1996.

Wahl, Richard W. *Markets for Federal Water: Subsidies, Property Rights, and the Bureau of Reclamation*. Washington, DC: Resources for the Future, 1989.

Waldman, Eliseu Alves, José Leopoldo Ferreira Antunes, Lucia Yazuko Izumi, Renata Ferreira Takahashi, and Rafael Carvalho Cacavallo. "Cholera in Brazil during 1991–98: Socioeconomic Characteristics of Affected Areas." *Journal of Health, Population, and Nutrition* 20 (1) (2002): 85–92.

Warsh, David. *Knowledge and the Wealth of Nations: A Story of Economic Discovery*. New York: W. W. Norton, 2006.

Weeks, John R. "Using Remote Sensing and Geographic Information Systems to Identify the Underlying Patterns of Urban Environments." In *New Forms of Urbanization*, ed. Tony Champion and Graeme Hugo, 325–345. Aldershot, UK: Ashgate, 2004.

Weeks, John R., Dennis P. Larson, and Debbie L. Fugate. "Patterns of Urban Land Use as Assessed by Satellite Imagery: An Application to Cairo, Egypt." In

Population, Land Use, and Environment: Research Directions, ed. Barbara Entwisle and Paul C. Stern, 265–286. Washington, DC: National Academies Press, 2005.

Weeks, John R., Arthur Getis, Allan G. Hill, M. Saad Gadalla, and Tarek Rashed. "The Fertility Transition in Egypt: Intraurban Patterns in Cairo." *Annals of the Association of American Geographers* 94 (1) (2004): 74–93.

Wenke, Robert J., and Deborah I. Olszewski. *Patterns in Prehistory: Humankind's First Three Million Years*. 5th ed. New York: Oxford University Press, 2007.

Whately, Richard. *Elements of Logic*. 7th ed. London: B. Fellowes, 1831.

White, Morton, and Lucia White. *The Intellectual versus the City, from Thomas Jefferson to Frank Lloyd Wright*. Cambridge, MA: Harvard University Press, 1962.

Whitten, Anthony. "Indonesia's Transmigration Program and Its Role in the Loss of Tropical Rain Forests." *Conservation Biology* 1 (3) (1987): 239–246.

Wills, Garry. *John Wayne's America: The Politics of Celebrity*. New York: Simon and Schuster, 1997.

Wirth, Louis. "Urbanism as a Way of Life." *American Journal of Sociology* 44 (1) (1938): 1–24.

Wisner, Ben, Piers Blaikie, Terry Cannon, and Ian Davis. *At Risk: Natural Hazards, People's Vulnerability and Disasters*. 2nd ed. New York: Routledge, 2004.

Woods, Robert. "Urban-Rural Mortality Differentials: An Unresolved Debate." *Population and Development Review* 29 (1) (2003): 29–46.

World Health Organization. "Hepatitis B: Fact Sheet #204." http://www.who.int/mediacentre/factsheets/fs204/en.

World Health Organization. *World Health Statistics 2011*. Geneva: Author, 2011.

World Resources Institute. *World Resources 1996–97*. New York: Oxford University Press, 1996.

Wright, Angus. *The Death of Ramón González: The Modern Agricultural Dilemma*. Austin: University of Texas Press, 1990.

Yeager, Rodger. "Demography and Development Policy in Tanzania." *Journal of Developing Areas* 16 (4) (1982): 489–510.

Yixing, Zhou, and Laurence J. C. Ma. "China's Urbanization Levels: Reconstructing a Baseline for the Fifth Population Census." *China Quarterly* (173) (2003): 176–196.

Zelinsky, Wilbur. *The Cultural Geography of the United States*. Englewood Cliffs, NJ: Prentice-Hall, 1973.

Zlotnik, Hania. "World Urbanization: Trends and Prospects." In *New Forms of Urbanization*, ed. Tony Champion and Graeme Hugo, 43–64. Aldershot, UK: Ashgate, 2004.

Zwerling, Craig, C. Peek-Asa, P. S. Whitten, S.-W. Choi, N. L. Sprince, and M. P. Jones. "Fatal Motor Vehicle Crashes in Rural and Urban Areas: Decomposing Rates into Contributing Factors." *Injury Prevention* 11 (1) (2005): 24–28.

Index

and nature preservation, 29
and neglected tropical diseases
(NTDs), 116
noise levels, 98–99
occupational injuries, 101–102
and political action, 55
and population density, 6
populations of, 1, 7–8
poverty in, 21
recreational hazards, 103
resource consumption in, 37, 46–47,
56
rural-urban migration, 30–35, 86,
108–109, 125–127
smoke pollution, 58, 61–62
and spillover pollution, 66–67
tornadoes in, 76, 79–80
traffic accidents, 94–95
and urban growth, 13
and urban slums, 119–121,
128–130
and waste disposal, 72–73
water consumption in, 48–49
and water pollution, 69–70
Rwanda, 35

Sack, Robert, 139
Safety regulations, 102
Sahn, David, 128, 130
San Francisco, 91
Santa Catarina, 31
Satellite-based remote sensing, 9
Satterthwaite, David, 45, 88
Savanna, 142–143
Scavenging, 71–72
Schistosomiasis, 116
Secondary deurbanization, 13, 38,
134, 148
Septic tanks, 70
Settlement change, 12–13, 19.
See also Migration, rural-urban
Sharlin, Allan, 110
Sharp, Julie, 26
Simmons, I. G., 48
Slovic, Paul, 96–97
Slums, 12, 21, 119–121, 128–131
Smallpox, 117

Smith, Kirk, 58, 62
Smoke pollution, 57–62
Snow-related accidents, 104–105
Social groups, 136–137
Social sciences, 139–140
Socioeconomic classes, 42–43
and agricultural pollution, 68–69
and city spatial patterns, 134
and energy consumption, 44
and smoke pollution, 61–62
Soja, Edward, 15
South Africa, 126
Specialization, 15
Species
extinctions, 25
native/non-native, 26
Sprawl, 19, 38
and ecological disruption, 24–25
and ecological footprint (EF), 53
and infectious disease, 116
and ozone pollution, 63
Sprawl: A Compact History, 25
Squatter settlements, 12
Standards of living, 127–128
State tenure, 130
Steinberg, Ted, 142
Stifel, David, 128, 130
Stone, Brian, 63
Storm Events database, 79, 149–150
St. Petersburg, FL, 109–110
Sub-Saharan Africa, 86
fertility rates in, 34
malaria, 115–116
natural hazards, 84–85
urbanization in, 10
water and sanitation, 118–119
Suburban areas, 11, 21–22
and agricultural pollution, 68
and ecological footprint (EF), 53–54
energy consumption, 52
household emissions, 43
and monocultures, 26–27
risk of leaving home, 96
and urban warming, 27–28
water consumption, 50
and water pollution, 70
Suburban drought, 50

Urban and Industrial Environments

Series editor: Robert Gottlieb, Henry R. Luce Professor of Urban and Environmental Policy, Occidental College

Jason Corburn, *Toward the Healthy City: People, Places, and the Politics of Urban Planning*

JoAnn Carmin and Julian Agyeman, eds., *Environmental Inequalities Beyond Borders: Local Perspectives on Global Injustices*

Louise Mozingo, *Pastoral Capitalism: A History of Suburban Corporate Landscapes*

Gwen Ottinger and Benjamin Cohen, eds., *Technoscience and Environmental Justice: Expert Cultures in a Grassroots Movement*

Samantha MacBride, *Recycling Reconsidered: The Present Failure and Future Promise of Environmental Action in the United States*

Andrew Karvonen, *Politics of Urban Runoff: Nature, Technology, and the Sustainable City*

Daniel Schneider, *Hybrid Nature: Sewage Treatment and the Contradictions of the Industrial Ecosystem*

Catherine Tumber, *Small, Gritty, and Green: The Promise of America's Smaller Industrial Cities in a Low-Carbon World*

Sam Bass Warner and Andrew H. Whittemore, *American Urban Form: A Representative History*

John Pucher and Ralph Buehler, eds., *City Cycling*

Stephanie Foote and Elizabeth Mazzolini, eds., *Histories of the Dustheap: Waste, Material Cultures, Social Justice*

David J. Hess, *Good Green Jobs in a Global Economy: Making and Keeping New Industries in the United States*

Joseph F. C. DiMento and Clifford Ellis, *Changing Lanes: Visions and Histories of Urban Freeways*

Joanna Robinson, *Contested Water: The Struggle Against Water Privatization in the United States and Canada*

William B. Meyer, *The Environmental Advantages of Cities: Countering Commonsense Antiurbanism*